Hang In There…
Wherever "There" Is

Anorexia Recovery

I0099812

Nicole Roberge

chipmunkapublishing
the mental health publisher

Nicole Roberge

Published by
Chipmunkapublishing
PO Box 6872
Brentwood
Essex CM13 1ZT
United Kingdom

http://www.chipmunkapublishing.com

Copyright © Nicole Roberge 2010

Edited by Aleks Lech

Chipmunkapublishing gratefully acknowledge the support of Arts Council England.

Acknowledgements

Thank you to the following people who were integral to my recovery. Your care and support gave me strength and hope to get me to where I am today:

The Bond and Roberge Families—Meme, Popie, Grammie, Buttsie, all my aunts, uncles and cousins, for always being there for me; Boomer and Molly, for sharing food with me; Erin Cusack for caring, and for always getting turkey clubs with me; Danielle Shea Dolan, for knowing more about my health than I did, and confronting me when I needed it; Holly Finley-David, for being my nutritional guru; Grant Ducharme, for keeping me off the scales. You will always be missed; Jason Filardi, for reminding me to eat. It worked!; Comer Rudd-Gates, for listening and helping me to talk even when it was hard; Mitch Herz, for cooking for me, and getting me to eat pasta; Ann Hood, for teaching me the craft of the memoir; Dr. Mark Ligorski, because you helped me to defeat the eating demon; Carol Martin, my partner in crime; Charlotte Martin, for helping me through the struggle and sharing your beautiful life; Mom & Dad, for your love and being there through everything. I cannot thank you enough; Eric Morin, for being a friend and for your beautiful artwork for this book; Matt Nathanson, for reminding me of the little victories; Wendy Nurock, for being there when I needed someone the most; The Renfrew Center, for saving my life; Dan Roberge, for being an amazing little brother-one I look up to in many ways; Robin Axelrod Sabag, for helping me to unlock the layers; Carolyn Wason, for getting me to eat beans!; Kelly Wilson, for being the sister I needed and for my rehab blanket; and Tim Wilson, who offered to break me out of rehab. I'm glad I didn't need you but it's nice to know you'd have been there if I did! And to all who helped me while struggling or recovering (Frew Crew!)—Thank you. You were there for a reason, and I am grateful you were. I love you all!

Nicole Roberge

Dedication

For my parents, who always encouraged me in my recovery and writing, and stuck right by me through all the ups and many downs-- I love you so much and am so blessed to have you. And in loving memory of Buttsie, who always opened his snack cabinet to me. Sending you a big hershey kiss and eating plenty for you.

Nicole Roberge

About the Author

Nicole Roberge was born in 1982 and resides in Connecticut amongst her entire extended family, including her father, Larry, mother, Sue, sister, Kelly, and brother, Dan, as well as her two English bulldogs, Boomer and Molly. Her Journalistic accomplishments include The Los Angeles Times, Rolling Stone, ELLEgirl, Gotham Baseball and She Caribbean. Her career has been highlighted by music—writing about singer/songwriters to Reggae bands, being the founder and editor of the online music magazine, Tuned in Music. She writes a weekly dating/humor column as well and has also been published in the book compilations, "Hungry" and "Recovering the Soul." She holds a BA in English and Certificate in Communication from Saint Anselm College and a Certificate in Screenwriting from the University of Los Angeles.

She began the non-profit "Beautiful Lives" for the education and prevention of Eating Disorders in Connecticut. Here, she speaks with middle and high school students to tell them her story and about what eating disorders are. She also lobbied in D.C. for right of Eating Disorder patients.

Roberge struggled greatly with Anorexia, something that never seemed remotely possible for her. Grateful for her 4 years recovery today, she does struggle with Post Traumatic Stress Disorder from a life-changing event, as well as Anxiety, but knows that if she can beat Anorexia, nothing can hold her back.

She enjoys writing, reading, art, jewelry making, Yankees baseball, bulldogs, the tedious walk up the hill to her house, ice cream, yes definitely ice cream, pumpkin flavored anything, and naturally, The Michelin Man!

Roberge's battle with Anorexia put a stop on her writing and through recovery, she picked up her pen again. She found that writing helped her to recover, it brought her back to life again, and so…this is what she wrote.

www.nicoleroberge.com

Hang In There… Wherever "There" Is

Introduction

Though I had used diet pills in my teens and learned how to purge in college, it wasn't until my early twenties that the reality of an eating disorder set in for me as I developed Anorexia Nervosa and faced the harsh reality of the disease when I almost died. That's when I realized the kind of terror I had been living in and that I wanted to get out of, and how many others there were like me—trapped, isolated, stuck within their tormented minds, showing their unhappiness through their body. Begging for help, but unable to speak the words—shrinking to be noticed.

I spent a long time being unhappy with myself, not just the way I looked, but the way I felt. And I spent so much time harbouring these feelings, and pretending everything was okay, that they only harvested themselves and grew over time, until soon they became so enraged that they manifested themselves into the form of a full-blown eating disorder. It was a tortuous, devastating, and incredibly scary time for me, and the even scarier thing was that I couldn't stop it. When I started a diet and exercise programme, it soon became obsessive, and while there was much going on in my personal life, I soon diverted my attention away from those stresses and difficulties and focused on the diet and exercise, which soon became extreme. With a four-hour workout every day, and a diet of only fruit, I was devoted, and soon, addicted. I couldn't pull away, even when I wanted to. The eating disorder controlled me, and I wanted help, but couldn't ask for it. The only thing I could turn to was my best friend—my eating disorder.

Eating disorders are scary and highly misconstrued in today's society. People hear the term and think of thin celebrities or teenagers who crave attention by starving themselves, and this is a shame, because they should realize that eating disorders are not a choice, they are a disease, and they do not apply to a particular "type" of person, age group, or sex. They affect males, females and all ages. They do not discriminate.

Anorexia has the highest mortality rate of any mental illness. It is scary to hear people joke about how they wish they could be anorexic for a while, just to lose some weight. It is not a disease to joke about, and it pains me now to see anyone suffering with an eating disorder. It is something that I never thought would happen to me, and it still seems surreal that it did. Growing up, I always wanted to lose weight. I never thought I really could, and then I did, but I couldn't stop. At both extremes, I wasn't really happy, and through recovery, I have found happiness, and I know it doesn't exist within the numbers on the scales.

I wanted to write this book because, like many who have suffered from an eating disorder, the experience is overwhelming. Once you realize and accept that you have one, there is a choice; do you want to recover? I did, and I continue to strive towards that goal, as you will see throughout the book. It is a lot of hard work, but it is so worth it. Some people don't make the choice to recover, because they are stuck within the eating disorder, and I know how hard it is to get out of it. And for those of you who have not yet acknowledged that you have an eating disorder, I hope you do, because it's your health, your life. For me, I knew what I was doing wasn't right, but it took a life-threatening situation for me to admit to my disease and claim recovery for myself. If anything, I want to use my story to reach out to people, for them to see the truth of eating disorders—the devastation, the poor medical treatment, the struggles of attempting recovery on your own, accepting you need outside help, and then continuing recovery and trying to build a life, while preventing relapse. By writing about my eating disorder, through reflection and the process of recovery, I could hopefully unravel the path my life has taken and see how I could get back on track, and hopefully help others on the way. They say having an eating disorder is like a full time job, and not everyone can do it, and in a sad way, it's true. It's time consuming, it's maddening, and you have to be dedicated to your addition. The same is true for recovery, but it's harder. You have to get out of a lifestyle that your mind is still battling to keep you in. It is a constant struggle, but there is hope. There has to be, or you wouldn't here.

While this is by no means a humorous disease, I did want to look at the lighter side of some situations. I had always been known for my laugh, but found myself numb during my disease. When I was inpatient, I remember the first time I laughed, I mean a really good out-loud bellyache laugh, and it felt so great. I remember the other things that happened throughout my eating disorder that were just ironic, and when I was in recovery, that I just had to laugh at or invoke some humour with, and that is what I had to add here. We all need comedy to realize it's not hopeless. We need laughter in life's crises. The disease is depressing, but if laughter is the best medicine, then it is desperately needed during an eating disorder. It is such a struggle, and everything around you seems bleak. If you can find something to laugh at, to bring you a smile, then that will warm your heart, and for me, that was something that hadn't happened often. When I was able to find something to laugh at, I almost shocked myself. And I had been a girl whose laughter everyone had once known. The eating disorder takes that away. I want to give it back to those who are suffering, and those who are trying to help sufferers. Anorexia is hard and painful enough. There's only so much suffering a person can go through. You need to laugh a little.

And lastly, if you are reading this out of interest, thank you for opening your eyes to this disease and increasing your awareness. If you are a sufferer, or a family member or friend of a sufferer, remember that there is hope. I didn't believe so at times, but you have to. Think of all the things that you've wanted to do in life, and work through your illness to get there. Before family and friends knew I was sick, just that I was a little down, they kept telling me to "Hang in There." Then when they knew I was sick and in recovery, again they said, "Hang in There." Even as I continued my recovery, they told me that they didn't know what else to say except just, "Hang In There." Well, where is *there*? Where exactly am I supposed to be hanging out? I was frustrated at first, thinking that was all the advice they had. Then I realized no one has the golden key. They wanted me to hang in there, work through it, keep going, hang in there, and get to the other side of this disease. So "there", is wherever you want it to be. If "there" is with your family, then go there. If it is getting treatment, go for it. For me, *there* was an issue of staying in Los Angeles or going back home to Connecticut, but it had to be where I would get the best treatment. The *there* is important for you, and wherever you decide that is, just keep going. So to everyone, hang in there...wherever there is.

Nicole Roberge

Hang In There... Wherever "There" Is

Prologue
October 19, 2006

Hunched over, I wrap my arms around my jutting ribs and shiver down the hall of the Emergency Room. Careless and oblivious nurses, interns and doctors pass me like a ghost, not realizing or caring that I had been in one of their rooms. After waiting in that room for the doctor for over an hour, and on a stretcher in the hall for an hour before that, I was released with a diagnosis that had nothing to do with my symptoms or with my true illness. When she finally came in, she could barely stand to look at me, never mind listen to me when I tried to tell her what was wrong. My blood burned and my heart raced, beating so fast I thought that eventually it would have no choice but to stop. I truly thought I was having a heart attack. And while waiting, I wanted to call out to someone, but the only people who kept passing the door were nosy people chatting away, and if I cried "help," I was afraid it would be with my last breath.

I continue to walk, each slow step a reminder that there is still a little bit of life in me, but I don't want to risk anything. I have never been so conscious of the real feeling of living before, even though I don't feel so alive. Maybe because I was so close to death, I kept making the note that I was alive just in case anything weird started to happen, so I could let someone know, and maybe this time they would listen and save me.

No, I think, I need to save myself.

The cheery nurse at the desk by the door says "goodnight." I give her a weak smile and use my whole body to push the door open. Already frozen in the cool California night air, I see Sam's car pull in the ER driveway. I let my fragile body drop into the car, my bony spine aching against the backrest. I thank her, feeling like a burden—as if her first ER experience with me wasn't bad enough. As if having to live with me isn't bad enough.

"I can't believe they aren't admitting you," she says.

"I know," I tell her, and I mean it. I don't want to live like this any more. Afraid to live because I might die. "They barely looked at me and wrote it off as anxiety."

I press my hand against my heart to keep it warm from the cold. There isn't much protecting it, and it needs all the help it can get.

"I really thought I was going to die in your kitchen." I can't look at Sam. "I didn't think the ambulance would get there on time. Then all I could think was, "what if I never see my family again?"

I start to feel sick and tap my feet to get some blood pumping. Once I find my voice, I tell her, "I really don't feel well and I know something's not right."

We were already out of the hospital parking lot and at one of the many stoplights in Santa Monica. "They should have admitted you and had you on I.V. fluids and a feeding tube," she says, somewhat shakily. She pauses. This brave, funny, bold, brash, courageous woman pauses and looks to her side window, then shakes her head and says straight to me: "I know you don't want to hear this, but I think you're anorexic."

The light turned green.

Part I

In Patience

"Just when the caterpillar thought the world was about the end, it became a butterfly." -Unknown

Nicole Roberge

Hang In There... Wherever "There" Is

Chapter One
Renfrew: First Day
January 5, 2007

I never thought I would be at a treatment centre for eating disorders. Yet, here I am, meeting with a therapist, nutritionist, psychiatrist, doctor and nurse, and telling them each the same exact story about why I am here. I thought they were supposed to give me all the answers.

My sister Kelly, two years older than me, drove me down from Connecticut to New Jersey, where we picked up her boyfriend Tim, and they both took me to the Renfrew Center for Eating Disorders in Philadelphia. Not as scared as I expected to be, rather, I was shocked that it was my sister who took me to be admitted. She was the one, out of all my family, who seemed most in denial of my illness.

Something changed when she got there. Seeing me perhaps ready to enter "food school," as I call it, or maybe noticing the other "sick" girls, brought her to the reality that yes, I have an eating disorder, and I don't know how to get out of it. Her little sister, always the overweight one, had truly almost died of anorexia. Going to Renfrew was my one chance for survival.

Kelly and Tim wait around all day while I go through the admissions process. Finally, it's time for them to leave, so I walk them out. I say "bye" to Tim first and thank him, then turn to my sister.

She is crying.

I start to cry.

"Why do you have to do that?" I say through my sobs.

"Are you gonna be okay here?" she asks. With her gentle hug, my bones throb as her hands touch me.

"If not," Tim interrupts, "call me and I'll come get you."

"Thanks," I say, and laugh. "But I know I need to be here." I do. I want to get better, almost as much as I want this cruel disease.

I turn back to my sister. "Thanks for bringing me down here."

"I'll send you some comfy clothes, and a blanket. I know how cold you get. And call me later and let me know how dinner goes."

Dinner? Oh, how I dread dinner.

I give her another hug and stand there as they leave the sidewalk and make their way to the car. I squint as they drive away until I can't see their car any more. I swipe at the trace of tears on my face. Now, I'm alone. There are 40 other girls suffering inside, just like me, but I am alone. Worse to come; they are going to pull my eating disorder away from me, and it is all I have. How will I survive 28 days here? Hopefully, I will simply survive.

I turn and look back at the building—my home for the next month. It is large enough, but plain. A brick building with windows, and that is mostly it. There is a small driveway and a walkway to another building where I had gone through most of my admissions. Larger rooms spread off of it, and I could only guess that is where we have groups. "Groups," they call them. Groups will heal us.

When I first spoke with admissions, they told me about the vast acres they had. I thought I could walk, exercise in the fresh air. A few seconds later, any physically fit expectations were squashed. As it turned out, us eating disorder folks were told we're "too weak" for strenuous activity. We can only walk the stretch of the sidewalk and back. Once. If we do it twice, that is called "over-exercising." Then, we will get into trouble.

Missing my sister already, and my mom, dad, brother and even my eating disorder, I took my first step up into the building; ready to enter a world I didn't know. One of recovery. Will I truly survive here? More importantly, how did I get here?

Chapter 2
Looking Back:
Growing Up, and Out

I always knew I was overweight as a child. I sensed I was insignificant compared to others, though I always wore a smile to hide the hurt, and it was very convincing. People used to tell me I had a nice smile. They all thought I was so happy, but deep down, beneath the layers of fat, I wasn't. My weight troubled me. I was teased in the playground and on the bus. I was just a kid, a good kid. Should weight be all that others saw? No. But unfortunately, I found that it was.

In fifth grade, we were playing on the slide. I went up but the slide was really hot and dry so when I sat down, my legs stuck to it. I held on to the sides and shimmied my way down. The other girls laughed and said, "You got stuck on the slide!" They thought I was too heavy to make it down. I told them no, it was too hot to slide down. They didn't forget that, and reminded me of it years later. They couldn't let go, so neither could I.

In sixth grade, our desks were pushed together in fours, and our teacher asked us to spread them out. I pushed my desk forward and then my chair, but it got stuck on the carpet. The girl next to me said, "You're so big you can't even move." It wasn't worth explaining. Girls were my friends one minute, but when they were witty enough to sound cool in front of their friends and crack a joke, they would do it to embarrass me. Next minute, we're all friends again. As my friends grew up and came out of their shells, I grew deeper into mine, never understanding my weight and why it was the focus of everyone's attention. I was uncomfortable in my own skin. In many ways, I grew up faster than my classmates, gaining a sense of maturity about life and its cruelty. I also grew faster in the physical sense, and it was something I was never able to deal with, so I had to hide those feelings. I couldn't let anyone know how much it bothered me.

In seventh grade, our class purchased t-shirts for a school function, and one of my favourite but overweight teachers had us come up one by one to get sizes. She asked me what size I needed and I told her I didn't know. I was embarrassed to say a medium, never mind a large. All the other girls were getting smalls. She held a shirt up to me and goes, "You have broad shoulders like me." It sent a ripple through me. *Broad shoulders? What does that mean? Isn't that what boys have?* I knew what it meant. It meant I was big.

High school brought different issues. In many ways, it was a new start for me. I thought that I could finally branch out a little and there wouldn't be the pettiness that middle school had. I signed up for the tennis team—which was fun. I met new people and was hopeful I'd lose a little weight. That didn't happen. Despite the rigorous practices, running and the constant matches, my weight stayed the same. I reached my breaking point. I was tired of being the "bigger girl" in my class. At this point, I had many friends and participated on the Student Council and Yearbook committees. I wanted to do more, to be more. I wanted to "fit in." I just wanted to fit in with the other students, into normal activities, and into normal clothes.

I began skipping lunch, which had no affect on me. Even with the workouts and skipped meals, my weight wouldn't budge. I had a better idea. My body just needed a little extra help. I went to the mall one day with some friends and we split up. With babysitting money in tow, I walked past the nutrition store a few times until I was brave enough to go in. I looked back to make sure no one had seen me.

"Do you need any help?" I heard behind me.

I jumped, turned, said "no" to the kid with the name tag and ran to the vitamin section. I spotted the weight loss products. I eyed which one looked best. I knew what I needed. I picked the one that read "all natural," "weight loss supplement." This promised to speed up your metabolism and to help you shed pounds with diet and exercise. I was already exercising and dieting, so this had to work. I brought it to the counter.

"Okay, will this be all for you?"

"Yes," I urged, and checked over my shoulder to make sure I was still unspotted.

"Because we have our new vitamins on sale."

"No, thank you."

"Would you like to apply for a discount card?" he asked, eager to sell more.

"No. Just this please."

"Okay, that'll be $39.99."

A ridiculous amount, I thought, for 20 pills that needed to be taken twice a day, but I knew it was worth the money. I tucked the bag deep within my purse and ran out to meet my friends.

I was very excited about my purchase. This was the golden opportunity to lose weight. I made sure to hide them in the back of one of my dresser drawers so no one would find them, and they didn't.

I started taking my miracle pills, and waited for the pounds to shed.

After several more boxes of those pills, I wondered how long I would have to wait. Why didn't they work? I even tried other diet pills. Why couldn't I lose weight? What was I doing wrong? I was exercising, skipping meals, taking diet pills, and was still overweight. How come everyone else could eat and not gain weight? What was wrong with me?

After tennis was over, I wanted to stay active, so I joined indoor track, though it wasn't as intense as tennis. I had gym second semester, but that also brought about reminders that my weight wasn't good enough. I wasn't good enough. After all, in gym class, it's your body they judge you by.

As we all lined up in a row, one by one, the gym teacher took our weight. The boys and girls in our class would stand around to see what everyone weighed. Torture. Embarrassing. They made comments that I should try and lose a little weight. Didn't they understand that I was trying? I was usually close to last during the mile and 2-mile runs, even though I pushed myself hard. A few people just walked the whole thing, so at least I beat them.

There was the day that the gym teacher took the girls aside to do a body-fat analysis. With some weird contraption, she had us stand in a group and lift up our shirts a little so she could see how much belly fat we had, and if we were in the healthy range or not.

She did one girl, and said, "Now see, she doesn't look very thin, but she doesn't have a lot of body fat on her. It's a lot of muscle."

I couldn't believe that she was commentating on everyone.

She got to another girl, and said that she was just great.

Then she got to me. I seized up.

"Relax," she told me.

I barely lifted my shirt, and then sucked in my belly. She placed the cold contraption on my skin and then squeezed it, trapping my fat and judging me based on a number.

"Whoa," she said. "That's not good."

"I know," I whispered.

The other girls looked away.

Mortified, I wanted to cry, but wouldn't. I hated myself and I hated that they did that. I hated that everything depended on your weight or body fat, and that was all people saw. I hated that because there was another Nicole in my grade, someone once distinguished us as the fat and the skinny one. I knew which one I was. I hated living in a body I couldn't understand and didn't appreciate. I felt trapped. The more I kept these feelings in, the more isolated I became, and also, the more vulnerable.

I tried to eat less, especially with friends. If they already saw me as fat, I didn't want them to think I pigged out on food. When I went to my friend's house, I ate as little as I could. Her parents commented on that, and it became a running joke, how I "ate like a bird." I despised it, because then it was as if I couldn't eat more in front of them. If I did, they'd comment on how I was eating more, and then I would feel like the pig I was. But every time I restricted, I'd come home and eat more. I'd sneak food and bring it to my bedroom, because I didn't feel as if I was allowed to be eating. I shouldn't have been eating. It would get out of control and I'd just hate myself all the more. It was an endless cycle, and this pattern of disordered eating was one that I would not recognize until years later.

***

It was my sophomore year of high school that I grew a couple of inches, and the lengthening was good for my image. It stretched out my weight.

One day at tennis practice, an older girl said to me: "Have you lost weight, Nicole?"

"I don't know," I said. I loathed any question that regarded weight.

"You look good," she told me. "Not that you didn't before, but...you were pretty chubby last year."

I turned my head.

"But you're such a pretty girl. You look great now."

I wasn't sure if I should take it as a compliment or not. Knowing that my weight had stayed the same and my height had only gone up didn't make me much happier, but if my image had changed in the eyes of others, it must be some improvement.

The rest of high school remained the same. I gained a little more weight, but did come out of my shell a bit, and stayed active in school activities. My weight was still bothersome, and the damage it did to me mentally would prove to have a significant effect on me in the future. The seed was planted at an early age that my weight was not the "right" weight. It is hard when you hear all those voices that touch you deep within. People don't realize how what they say can haunt you so much. Weight adds so much pressure to a kid. When people see you, they see one thing first— what you look like. If you're heavier than the norm, they are not as accepting. As I got ready to go to college, I had many hopes that things would be different, and I could start a new chapter in my life. I was wrong.

Chapter 3
Renfrew—First Meal
Tray Level

Starting out here, I am on the first level of eating: Tray Level. That means myself and the other girls on "Trays" line up like animals and wait to be called in for dinner. When we enter the small dining room, our trays are all set up for us and have a menu with our names on it. We sit next to someone different each meal.

I search the room desperately trying to find my name when one of the counsellors calls me over and points to a tray. Spaghetti. Figures, doesn't it. A girl who hasn't had carbohydrates or anything other than fruit in so long is now faced with a pile of pasta and cheese. I don't know how I, or my stomach, can handle it. Will my body be able to process it?

It looms at me and looks like something that should be in a nursing home. I feel sick. Each item is covered: the plate of spaghetti has a lid, a bowl of watery peaches has plastic wrap over it, and a plate with bread has wrapping over it as well. My cup is turned over. I look at my menu. It reads: Nicole R. That's me, all right. On it are several selections. I wonder who made these menu choices for me? I guess I'm stuck with spaghetti and watery peaches, so I must eat it.

I take off the lid and one of the girls, Amy, stops me. Her hand is raised in the air.

"You have to wait for a counsellor," she tells me. "Raise your hand."

Is this middle school? Like when you had to raise your hand to be dismissed from the table. Does that mean I can leave?

I raise my hand and the counsellor went to Amy first. I watch in amazement.

Carol, the counsellor, takes the menu and looks at Amy's plate.

"You don't have your cheese," she tells her, and walks away for a second.

"Damn," Amy says. "Didn't think she'd notice."

"What's going on? Is she like, 'Inspector Gadget?'"

A couple of girls giggle, but Carol comes back, then plops a plastic cup of shredded cheese on Amy's tray. She checks her menu again, twice, like Santa Clause, then takes her lid and plastic wrap, and trudges over my way.

I am frantic, and hopeful, that I have cheese.

"Hi," I say.

"You're new, right?" Carol asks. She seems so tall. Maybe these chairs are short. They do that in some places, to make you feel insignificant, and give the other person a power trip. I already feel insignificant. You win, Carol!

"I came in this afternoon."

"Welcome. Menu?"

I pull the menu out from under my plate, and then brush off a bit of spaghetti that has stained it. "Sorry."

"You need to remove your lids and wrappers by the time I get to you, OK? I know you're new, but that's how it goes. Remove those, then check your menu, make sure you have everything, and then you can raise your hand."

So much to remember just to eat a damn meal! Maybe it isn't worth eating after all.

I hurriedly unwrap the nasty peaches and hard as rock bread, then lift the lid to the spaghetti. I lay eyes on it at last. So much spaghetti.

"Good job. I need the plastic cap to your cheese container too."

"Oh yay, I do have cheese!" It was hiding behind my plate. I take off the top and hand it to her.

"Enjoy your meal, Miss Nicole."

"Thanks."

I look at the other girls, already eating. Amy rolls her eyes at Carol.

"It's such a weird process, but once they know that you're doing well on Trays, you get to move up to 'Fix Own,' where you can pick your own menu and go through the line."

"Much more freedom," adds Jackie, another girl, who hasn't touched her food yet, but instead was reading from trivial pursuit cards. She notices that I have noticed.

"It relaxes me before I eat. Calms my anxiety."

Amy interrupts. "Yeah, sometimes we do '20 questions.' Takes our minds off the meal."

"But don't forget," Jackie continues without looking up from her cards, "we only get 45 minutes to eat, and tonight's your first night…"

"So you don't need to finish it all. But starting tomorrow, you will. Or…"

"Supplements!" The girls all ring out.

"Shhh!" Carol hushes.

I whisper across the table. "What's a supplement?"

"Ugh," Amy says, fork flailing about while spaghetti drips off of it. "That's the deal here. They make you eat everything on your plate. I mean everything. One time, this girl Margaret forgot to use her second packet of Maple Syrup with her pancakes, so she had to drink it. But trust me, that's better than taking a supplement. They are so disgusting. It's better to just eat. I guess that's how they get you to do it, but one way or another, they're gonna get calories into your body."

"Ladies!" Carol howls. "Just a reminder. No food or calorie talk while eating, or at all."

"Whatever," Amy says. "What else do any of us have to talk about?"

Hang In There... Wherever "There" Is

She was right. That was all we knew. I finally feel comfortable, knowing I am surrounded by people who understand me. I settle into my chair, ready to make my attempt at dinner.

Or maybe not.

The plate glares at me like a gun. "Eat me or die." I know I have to do it. I pick up my fork, swirl it around a little, and bring it to my mouth. Just do it, Nicole! I place the mangled spaghetti in, chew fast, and swallow. To my surprise, it doesn't taste that bad, but I can't admit that. The hard part is, after one bite, I am full.

My life has been controlled by anorexia for so long. I want to eat, but I know what the food will do to me. The thought, the feeling of food inside of me; I can't have it. It destroys me. The food crawls within and I can't have it win over me. I can't even know it's there. If I am clean of the food within, then I am pure. There is nothing better than pure. Pure is what I wanted with my eating disorder, and these monsters were trying to take that away from me. The pieces of spaghetti inside are already destroying me.

They want me to give up my eating disorder, but they don't know what asking me to give it up will do to me. It's like asking someone to give up their passion. Like asking a writer to give up their pen, or an artist to give up their paints. My eating disorder is an art form. Like an artist, I don't have any real control over it. It's a gift, in a cruel, disgusting way. It's as if the only thing I am good at is my eating disorder, and to want me to give that up...how could you ask such a thing of me? What would be left of me? What would I be without my eating disorder?

Part of me wants to eat, for several reasons. First, that's why I'm here, to eat and get my body healthy. To get my mind better. To prove I can do it and I'm not afraid of food. Second, though I've been so scared of it for so long, I do like food. I always have. Which scares me too. I may fall back into that trap of eating too much.

I struggle with the spaghetti. It is piled on the plate. Pasta, sauce and mounds of cheese. I pick my way through it, nauseous with each bite. The girl across from me, Linda, gets my attention, and gives me a bit of wisdom: "I know it's hard, but it's going to make you healthy, Nicole." The words came from another resident, but could have come from an angel. It was what I needed to hear.

She was right. I was so unhealthy. I don't like the food, yet I must eat it. I have to take a different approach. My body and mind need a different approach. The food, though hard to get down, may not be easy to accept as something I need or want, but my body needs it. If I have to treat it like medicine, so be it. Food will make my body and mind healthy. I feel disgusting, but I have to realize it is going to help me. It is going to bring me back to life. I so very much want a life again.

Not just the food, but also my inpatient time will make me healthy. The people I meet will help to make me well. Learning about myself will make me stronger. These people and this place are here to help.

Exploring the darkness and depths of my disease will make me healthy and free.

So, pasta here I come.

I picked up my fork, and ate my spaghetti. After I did what I could, the other girls at the table congratulated me. It may seem strange to be congratulated for eating a meal, but when you have gone for so long without one, it is our natural response. They knew how hard it was. I felt full, sick and guilty. I repeated the words—it is going to make me healthy. Had I been alone, I would not have done that. If I had had to eat that meal on my own, I would have been in tears. The genuine support and compassion of the other girls was something I had never experienced. They know the difficulty of that first meal in treatment. Not only that first meal, but any food when you have been scared of it for so long.

They looked at me and saw a girl who walked into this place, just as they had, not knowing what to expect, quite unsure of how she had got there, but who wants to get out of the prison she trapped herself in. We are all in this together.

I look at them and see tremendous strength and wonder how they can be so courageous to finish their meals while encouraging me at the same time. I want to be that strong. I'll be surprised if I get there, but hope I can. I know it will take time and a lot of hard work reliving every step on the path to this place.

Chapter 4
College:
First Purge

My ascent to college from high school reinforced trouble with weight more than any other time. There's that old myth about the "Freshman 15," that I didn't really believe. I knew that some people gained weight, but since I was already a bit larger than most college freshmen, I figured I was safe. Wrong again.

As I prepared to leave for Freshman Orientation, I already knew that this was not the school for me. I thought that I wanted something tiny, being from a small town and all, but I was mistaken. Rural New Hampshire did not do it for me.

My Dad suggested I look into schools in Boston or larger state schools. I was adamant about a small school, and looking back, I wish I had listened to him. I even made the attempt to transfer schools three times, but was never brave enough to do it. I'm not sure if it was the college itself, the lack of diversity, or myself that I disliked so much during those four years, but the frustration with it all accumulated and when the four years were up, I was happy to leave.

I didn't fit in right away. I tried out for the tennis team. Didn't make it. I met people, but was scared to hang out with them. I felt unwanted and undeserving of their companionship. I remember how hard those first couple weeks were. I wouldn't go to the cafeteria with anyone. If I ate, I'd get something to go and eat in my room. A recluse on the college, a recluse in my body.

My room mate, Karen, was nice, but had so many friends already. Most of the people were from Massachusetts and knew each other from high school or local high schools. She introduced me to a girl down the hall, Erin, who would turn out to be my best friend. Her roommate, Danielle, would become our fourth, and we would travel in a pack to parties or even just to each other's dorm room for pizza late at night.

Oh, how I loved late night pizza, snow day pizza, or pizza just for the hell of it.

Erin and I became close and we found ourselves basically living in the cafeteria when we didn't have class. We'd grab a soda and chips, or maybe an ice cream, then a table. The cafeteria looked like a ski lodge, and when it snowed the atmosphere was warm and soothing. It was a nice break from classes and reminded us that we were "home" in a way.

We would talk about our crushes and mostly just giggle about stupid stuff. We both laughed—that is what we became known for. The giggly girls. People said they'd be walking somewhere and hear laughing and would know it was us. She was my partner in crime.

We found ourselves in the cafeteria a lot that winter of the freshman year, so much so that our friend Tim designated us "Caf Rats."

We held that name with honour, just laughing at it. It's not as if we were eating the whole time we chatted. I had finally found a friend.

All that time in the cafeteria caught up with me. While Erin didn't mind the constant treats, it weighed on me. In my heart and on the scales.

I remember one incident when I was sick and couldn't go to dinner.

"Well, you can't just stop eating," Danielle, who was a nursing student, told me.

"I feel sick, I can't"

"It's not going to help you if you don't eat."

"I'll eat later, I have snacks."

I won. They went off to dinner. I was glad to be sick. It gave me a chance to skip a meal, which I could surely do without.

I remember a time in freshman year when I became very conscious about my weight. I was overweight and met thinner friends who went to the gym, so thought I should too. I joined the dance club, tried karate—but quit that one fast. I tried out for the official dance team, but my body was not nimble enough. Rejected.

Food became a focus. I don't remember why, but I started keeping a journal with the food I ate and calorie counts. It was minimal eating, but again that did nothing for my weight.

Days would read:
Monday
Breakfast: Nothing
Lunch: yogurt and fruit.
Dinner: a few carrot slices
Snack: some m&ms (damn that sweet tooth).

I stuck with this pattern for a few days, but it didn't last. I couldn't last. I was hungry. I wanted more out of food, out of life, than it would give to me. My diet failed, and so had I.

***

Sophomore year came, and with it, more problems. That was the year I wanted to transfer, and after looking at many schools and dragging my Dad along, ultimately I didn't have the courage to do so. I became depressed. I was a Politics major, and the classes were harder than the first year. I changed my major to English.

It was that year that I tried one of the worst things—Ipecac syrup. Mostly used in children if they swallow something poisonous, it is then given to them so they can vomit and eliminate whatever they swallowed. I saw it as a way of ridding myself of the food I ate. I ordered it online, and was thrilled when the brown box came in the mail. My saviour. I could eat dinner, take some syrup, and eliminate the food.

The first time I took it, the taste was disgusting. I chased it with root beer.

It didn't work at first. I had to manually put my hands down my throat to help it along, but then I felt it. The syrup gurgling in my tummy, making its way up my esophagus and out of my mouth.

I threw up.

Erin was outside the bathroom.

"Are you OK?" she yelled in.

"No, I feel sick."

This wasn't the last time, but I didn't use it much longer. The effect the Ipecac left on my stomach was so painful I couldn't keep up the routine. Turns out, that was a good thing. I found out later, many bulimics use it, and it can cause damage to the heart, and ultimately death. After those few excruciating times, I was done.

***

Junior year was more about drinking than weight. The depression was still there and I tried to remove it in the form of a bottle, which only increased the weight gain. I was in a single, and of all places, in the "Wellness Dorm." This meant—no drinking allowed. I broke the rules. I drank, sloppily, was ushered back to my room several times, and wow, did I gain weight. The most I've ever been. About 200 pounds. I hated myself, not that this notion was anything new, but for a moment, the drink felt good, and I couldn't stop.

The summer after Junior year, I hit the gym at home, drank less, ate better, and lost pounds. Not much, I had thought, but when I got back to school, people commented on my weight loss. Maybe it was 20 pounds or so, nothing to me, still being big, but a compliment nonetheless. Still overweight, I knew I had work to do.

Senior year is when I truly learned how to purge. I didn't necessarily know it was a learning process; it came naturally to me.

At that point, Erin and I had an apartment with two other friends, but Erin and I were alone one night hanging out. We ordered pizza, hot fudge sundaes and made margaritas—all good. But by the end of it, I was disgustingly full. We had plans to go out, so I went to take a shower. I stood in that shower, my stomach bloated, and all I felt was nausea and a need to get that food out of me. I stuck my finger down my throat and in an instant, stuff came out.

I moved out of the shower, because it was gross to leave remnants there, and instead headed for the toilet. I was amazed at this new discovery. How just sticking a few fingers down my throat could eliminate my evil deeds. I did it again, and more came out. Again, and more, and more, and more, and finally, I sat down. My stomach had settled, and so had I. There was space now in my body and I thought to myself, if I can eat this much now and get rid of it, I can do it again.

So I did. When we went to the campus coffee shop and I got a sub, I'd go back to the apartment and purge. To the cafeteria, back to the apartment, and purge. Even when I made dinner, I'd purge. No one knew. It was my secret. So simple, so easy, yet so painful. I hated the process of it, but loved the feeling afterward. Free. Pure.

It wasn't as if I was binging and purging, it was just when I felt full. It was a release. A way to feel better. After graduation, I brought that feeling home. After dinner, purge. Then, guilt. In college, it was okay, but when my parents were supplying dinner, the guilt weighed on me at disposing of the meal they had bought or made. How could I get rid of it? They had put so much work into it. Disgusting, evil, guilty, and empty. Me and my secret—it tore me apart.

Chapter 5
Renfrew: First Full Day
I'm Short and Full

I awake to the sound of my alarm, much more early than I am used to. 5:30. Isn't this supposed to be recovery? Doesn't that require sleep? Apparently not. Recovery requires us to strip down to our undies and climb into a thin gown, and then go into the hall and wait for our name to be hollered. What a wake up call.

I do the drill, put on my lightweight gown, close it tight around me, and wait on the bench with the other girls. I can't help but compare myself to them. She is skinnier than me, and so is she, but no, she isn't. It is a game here, and we all know it.

"Andrea," the nurse calls, and one girl gets up, holds her gown taut around her, ribs piercing through. The bones in her arms stick out as her loose skin hangs over it, while her elbows seem like rocks between it all. Did I look like that?

"So," I ask, to anyone who will answer. "We do this every morning?"

"Every morning," Amy, the girl from dinner, replies, "for the first week or two, until your vitals are normal. Then it goes to three times a week, then two...then hopefully, you're outta here."

"Hopefully. So what do they do in there, and why these nasty gowns? It's freezing!"

"Yeah, they're doing construction right now, it doesn't help," she informs me, as we watch carpenters walk by us, each shivering at the sight of them. No one wants to be seen practically naked in a gown, especially those with eating disorders, insecure enough. But especially not those who have been sexually abused, like several of the girls here have.

"They take your vitals," Amy continues, "and be prepared for Gatorade."

I hate Gatorade. What does she mean?

"Next?" yelled the nurse.

Shit. That's me.

I gather my gown around me and wander down the hall, looking around at the front desk and all the things I hadn't noticed so clearly before. It is still surreal where I am. I turn the corner and find myself in a small room.

"Scales," she orders. What a bedside manner.

I hop on, afraid to see the number.

134 pounds. The scales gleam at me. Up two pounds from yesterday.

Up 20 pounds from my lowest. At the height of 5'9, I figure that should be enough, but they were still pushing me to be more, in the weight of the "average" range. At least 10 more pounds. Fat. I gained so much while I was home. I want to be little again.

She takes my height and to my surprise, it's 5'8. "I'm 5'9," I tell her.

She re-checks it and says, "I'll give you 5'8 ½."

"I've always been 5'9."

She has me sit on the table. "Chances are," she tells me, "you shrunk a bit."

I laugh a little, until I realize she is serious.

"Most people with anorexia experience bone loss because of malnutrition, vitamin deficiencies, especially calcium, and lack of estrogen. When was your last period?"

Let me think. It's January... "June," I say.

"So you have Amenorrhea. That absence of a period can be dangerous, especially to your bones. We give you calcium supplements and plenty of milk here, but we recommend you go for a bone scan when you get home."

"Is it permanent?" I ask, while I pat my shrunken head.

"You won't grow, but you can prevent further damage. You could have Osteopenia, which is on the way to Osteoporosis. Osteopenia is treatable. Osteoporosis, no. That's why you need to be nourished."

"I know."

"Now, lie down." I do, but still have a hard time with this whole shrinking thing. Even though I have always wanted to be shorter, this wasn't the way to go about it. Well, there was really no way to go about it.

She checks my pulse and it turns out I'm "orthostatic." Who has ever heard of such a thing? Not me, surely. Sounds like some awful, incurable disease. Really, it was just the results of a simple test—they took my blood pressure when I was lying down, then waited a minute, then took it when I was standing. If there is a twenty-point drop in my blood pressure or pulse, it means that I have orthostasis, and could mean that I'm dehydrated or my electrolytes are off balance. Well, hell, I knew that much! Want to know their cure? Gatorade! Yep, Gatorade. I have to drink a small cup while I'm there, and then am told to bring the other cup back to my room.

Also, I must drink a giant cup at lunch and at dinner. These people think Gatorade can cure everything. You stub a toe—"hang on dear, let me get you some Gatorade." Headache? "Oh, Gatorade will cure that." Miss home? "Gatorade!"

Gatorade became the running joke, and actually made the drink go down a little smoother.

After weights and vitals, nervous of the calories, I dump the other cup in the sink back in my room. I watch the contents of my second cup of Gatorade slide down the bathroom sink. I was worried, like I might get caught, but I did it. I then had two options—I could go back to bed for some more sleep, or get ready to start the day. Breakfast was not until 8:30. The reason for early vitals is so that all the staff would be ready. Again, what about the patients?

Hang In There... Wherever "There" Is

I chose to climb back into bed. As soon as I did, Amber, my 18-year old roommate, burst out of bed and I swear leapt right into the shower. She was a go-getter. Another Anorexic who became too fond of the gym. As a college freshman, she was too high-energy for me. My other roommate was 13. They told me I was to have a double-room with someone my age, but when I got there, they couldn't find a room for me. They almost put me in a quad. Yet they found this triple and I took it. Besides, I had to be on the first floor near the nurse's station, at least for the first few days. All new admissions do.

Caitie, the 13-year-old, is quiet, but when you talk to her about something she loves, like her clarinet, she'll talk forever. She's been in hospitals for years and hates that she misses so much of her school activities. A great artist too. Even at meals, she doesn't try. She'll take the supplement. She's too young and sweet to suffer like this, and keeps herself isolated. I hope I can at least talk to her and break through a little. If anything, maybe I can be a warning sign of how she doesn't want to end up.

I can't sleep. As soon as Amber is out of the shower, I run for it. Our room is a suite. Three beds in ours, then a hall with a bathroom, and then another room with 2 beds. It's like the Brady Bunch room. However, and this completely confused me at first, but the other room has two girls who suffer from Bulimia, so the whole suite is on locked bathroom.

"What does that mean?" I had to ask the counsellor, after I had rushed to get her because our bathroom door was locked and I really needed to pee.

"We have to keep the door locked so that certain residents don't use their symptoms..."

Symptoms?

"When those residents need to use the bathroom, we open it for them, but have to leave it open a crack, just to be safe. But since you are not on locked bathroom, just come and get us and we'll open it for you. Just make sure it's locked when you're done," she explained.

I couldn't believe that the counsellors had to stand outside the bathroom, with the door cracked, while girls peed, or worse, poo'd. I found out that symptoms were all those things that us eating disordered gals did—binged, purged, restricted, over-exercised, etc. Symptoms...interesting word for our actions. It made the medical aspect so much more real though.

The counsellors come into our room at about four in the morning to unlock the bathroom so that we can get ready for weights, vitals and shower. It's nice I guess, but after that, it is locked. Sort of a pain in the ass, but I can deal with it. I know that all of us are suffering from something, and it must be worse for those dealing with a locked bathroom and who have to be supervised.

I get showered and ready for breakfast. Of course, when I get there, my tray wasn't there. Just my luck. It literally was not there. They

tell me that I can pick from the menu, which brings even more anxiety—
what would I pick? I was really having a difficult time, but then they found
my tray. A relief and terror all in one. The result was: half a raisin bagel,
peanut butter, yogurt and raisins. That's like a whole day's meal. Or, what
used to be a whole week's meal.

It was a lot to handle and I haven't had a bagel in so long.
Besides that, the toasters weren't working, so it made it even more
unappetizing. I ate the bagel, with peanut butter on it, and became insanely
full.

I sat there and ached for a while.

"Just do it or you'll have to drink a supplement," Amy tells me.
Amy, the sweet 16-year-old, became my little supporter. She knew the
ropes, and though suffered herself, wanted to help others.

I felt so full, but I did it, and then felt sick.

Whatever happened to "eat when you're hungry and stop when
you're full?" I guess those rules don't apply when you're re-feeding.

After breakfast, we have Community Meeting, where all of the
girls get together to check in and bring up any issues going on. Then we
split into smaller groups for our consultations. I express my concerns about
eating—about stopping when full, about eating just to eat, and to get it done
within the time limit. They gave me the same old spiel.

"You have to adjust to the food and your body has to become
comfortable with what you need," they tell me. Lame.

Lunch is worse. After the groups, I put my things back in my
room, and wait with the herd for our meal. I can see through the window,
and it glares back at me: a sandwich, chips, veg, fruit and cake.

I say to my roommate, Amber: "A whole sandwich?"

She replies, "You can't do a whole sandwich?"

"No, just a half, barely. And that was up from a quarter."

We go in, I find my tray, and to my surprise, and luck, I am still
on Meal Plan A, the standard—when you're first admitted—so I just have
the sandwich, veg and the cake. No chips! The cake I can do, because I
like my sweets. The lettuce and tomato that came with the meal, I put on
my sandwich—chicken curry with raisin on raisin bread. Who has ever
heard of such a thing? Gross.

Needless to say, I have a really hard time with the sandwich. It is
not something I really like and it fills me up. So much food. The girls see
me having trouble and are amazing and supportive.

The ones at my table all chime in: "Just eat it. We're all full, but
you have to do it, you don't want the supplement." Then as I ate, they say,"
Good job, Nicole, you're doing great!"

It was so nice. I did end up finishing, but felt so disgusting, guilty
and gross. One of the girls told me that I "kicked ass." Hey, I did, didn't I?

Hang In There... Wherever "There" Is

At the end of the meal, you of course have to get checked off that you ate it all, and when Carol came to check my tray, she says, "Good job. I know you were having a hard time with this one."

It was nice of her but I still don't understand the point of gorging yourself, eating things you don't like and within a time limit. It seems like it creates a negative association with food for me, which only stirs the eating disorder more. I want to be able to look at food in a positive way and learn to enjoy food again, and when it's gross and there are time limits, I don't focus on the food, I focus on finishing so I don't get in trouble.

This re-feeding process is tough. There is a reason you learn how to eat as kids and not adults, besides the fact that you need food to live. It is a difficult process, both mentally and physically. I really have to remember to eat and think how to eat again. To try to enjoy it. I don't like a lot of the foods that I used to. Nothing tastes good and I don't have an appetite. The food is taking a physical toll on me as well. I have gone from eating basically just fruit to everything now—starches, protein, fats. The starches make me physically ill, so much so that when I eat, my heart rate goes up, my pulse is off and I can feel the blood rushing through me, as if trying to catch up to the food that moves through my body.

It is scary. I spend much of my time in the nurse's station as they too are worried about my reaction (physical—everyone here has a bad mental reaction to the food). There are worries about my kidneys and blood sugar, and they did tests, which ultimately came back okay. My body is just having a hard time metabolizing the food because it hasn't seen it in so long. It's in a bit of shock. Like, "what the hell are you putting into me?" The nurse's tell me it's all part of re-feeding, but I think they are giving me too much too soon. It seems kind of dangerous. They say it will take time for my body to get used to processing food again. That is why, after all, I am here. To mentally process the eating disorder, and to physically redevelop the method of eating again and allow my body to adapt to the foods my body has missed and needs.

I hadn't realized that while I thought I was being "healthy," eating my fruit and veg and working out, not only had I been doing damage to my body, but also it would hurt to undo the damage. Eating disorder treatment is a painful process, mentally and physically, but a process that is extremely needed. That is why I can't do it on my own. Because once the pain starts, I probably would make it stop—by not eating. I have to learn to push through the pain. There has to be some relief on the other side.

People here tell me it will get better...then it will get worse...then better. I always heard it will get better, and I guess it has to when you are at your lowest point, but to have it get worse again is pretty discouraging. The worst part I guess is supposedly good. It is when you really delve into those difficult issues and it means you are working hard in your treatment to give up the eating disorder. It is hard, and involves a hell of a lot of conflicting emotions. Hopefully, in the end, it does get better. I am so looking forward to the better.

I talked with both my Mom and Dad. Mom was more concerned with my health problems, being a nurse, and Dad was more concerned with how I was feeling. He said that he understood my concerns but that the center must have a good system if they do so well. I told Dad how hard it was for me to see such skinny girls and think of how I was before and he said: "What, almost dead?"

We were talking about all I had done to myself—why I was orthostatic and dehydrated, due to the laxatives and diuretics, and he said, "It's amazing you're still alive. I might sue GNC." I know he gets kind of heated when talking about all the damage I did to myself, and he even brought up the long-term damage that I have done, but I want to be honest with him.

He told me: "I know it's gonna be hard, but it's only the second day."

Which is true, I'm still so new to this.

I talked to Kelly last night and she told me it was early and things will get better. I'll get healthy. I told her about the night with the spaghetti and how I struggled, and what that girl said to me, and it made me think about what my friend Jason said to me: that's the end goal, to get my health back, to get my life back. I want that so badly.

Kelly and I had a good talk and I'm surprised by all of the contact we've had. It has been nice to talk to someone. I've been writing in my journal non-stop. A lot of the girls here knit, or do art stuff, or socialize around the TV. During free time, I hang out in my room. It's too distracting up there, and I don't desire chit-chat. I want to do my own thing. I brought my journal up this morning and tried to do some writing but then people started talking, plus, I came here for me and to focus on myself—I want to read some books and write. That's what I'll do. For now. Dinner is soon. The battle continues.

Chapter 6
Lost Angeles:
June 28, 2005

As I crawl down busy Sunset Boulevard, through the stoplights that flicker every two feet, I am amazed at all the huge billboards everywhere. I finally see the bright orange restaurant—the landmark I was supposed to look for, which meant "my" street was across from it, and that apparently I was in West Hollywood. It was pretty bizarre seeing signs for Los Angeles and made it a bit more real that I was no longer in Connecticut.

The choice to move to Los Angeles was to explore my writing further. My mind had become tangled around the idea of screen-writing. After writing two books while I was home the year after college (books that were, well, finished, yet had no direction—much like myself), I decided to explore other forms of writing. I searched online and saw that UCLA offered a summer screen-writing course. It then so happened that I did an interview with Jason Filardi, a screenwriter who lived in LA, but was from my area in Connecticut. I saw it as a sign, and in June, I packed my car and drove cross-country.

My family was worried, but supported me in following my dreams. After all, it was only for the summer—or was it? I already had in the back of my mind that I might stay longer. Call me psychic, but I did.

The summer went well. I sublet an apartment in West Hollywood, and it was nice to have some freedom and independence. The beaches were gorgeous, the landscape was incredible, the stores were nothing like at home, and the people...well, they were all doing their own thing, just as I was. I made a couple of friends in my class who I went out with, but at the end of the summer, they all went home, and I opted to stay. I had finished my script—the only one in my class to complete it—and didn't want to give up there. Pursuing screen-writing was not about writing one script and calling it quits, so I decided to enroll in UCLA's 9-month Professional Program in Screen-writing. I loved the craft of this form of writing, and my family supported that. Did I love LA? That much, I wasn't sure of.

After my West Hollywood sublet, I sublet yet again, but this time in Hollywood. It sounded good at first, until I realized that it was two blocks up from the tourist trap of Hollywood Boulevard. I'd walk down the street and Shrek would come out of nowhere and lunge at me, to see if I wanted a picture with him. No thanks, creepy Ogre, I'll pass.

It became an isolating place—just me, my sublet, and an Ogre around the corner. I didn't like walking around too much, for fear of what crazy character would jump out at me next. So I stayed in my apartment mostly, writing. The people in my new class were all local and had their own thing going, so meeting new people wasn't really happening.

It's easy now to say that I was depressed, but at that point, I didn't know what that meant. I was lonely, disappointed in myself for not doing more, and missed my family terribly. I wanted friends but didn't know how to make them, and wouldn't go out on my own to try. Los Angeles can be an isolating place, and to someone who is best friends with isolation, it only makes it worse. It seemed as if I were stuck—trying to do what I wanted; yet not knowing how. I wasn't giving up, but I didn't know how to move ahead.

I did all the writing and my teacher liked it. I kept writing comedies because that is what I enjoyed. The classed laughed when we read it out loud and I saw that as a good sign. However, I had that constant reminder of our first lecture when they told us, "It takes an average of seven years to sell a screenplay, and that's if you're one of the lucky few." Seven years in LA? Yikes!

I reconnected with Jason, the screenwriter I had interviewed who was local to me in Connecticut but who lived in LA. He read my script, gave me feedback, and even a referral to a doctor. He seemed like my only ally in a world I did not know. But I was glad to have him there if I needed anything. We kept in touch, bantering over email about how my Yankees were so much better than his Red Sox. I still believe I'm right.

Fall came, and surprised me. 80 degrees in the fall? I hit the beach just a week before I went home for the holidays. It seemed so surreal. I figured I should go home with a tan, to at least prove I had been out there. But as I prepared to go home, I thought of all the things I would tell them about: the beach, the Yankees games I had gone to in Anaheim, Beverly Hills, how Hollywood Boulevard is really just a scummy sidewalk, how I didn't see a cloud in the sky for 3 months, that I saw the sets of "General Hospital" and "Grey's Anatomy," that Santa Barbara is probably my favorite place in California, how I had written one and a half scripts already and what the whole lifestyle was like.

As I packed my bags, tan and all, I prepared for my trip home, 6 months after I had left. I was excited to see my family, and they sounded excited to see me. It would be a nice break from my isolation, and I needed family time.

When I got home, I did not get what I was expecting.

It was 80 degrees when I left California and 40 degrees when I reached Connecticut. I didn't care. I was home.

My parents picked me up at the airport and it was good to see them—they weren't just a voice on the other end of the phone. They both said how good it was to have me home. *Home*.

Mom, Dad and I went to dinner and we had grinders—a real grinder.
They don't have them in LA. I had a beer with Dad. It's those little things you miss. When I got home, Boomer, our bulldog, and Molly, our new

bulldog, greeted me at the door. Then I caught up with my brother, Dan, and sister, Kelly, and everyone went off to bed.

That's when I realized...it's weird to be home.

6 months earlier, I packed my car and headed west. Way west. I couldn't decide if it seemed so long ago, or if it was like yesterday. It was strange, but nice to be back.

I went to see my grandparents, Meme and Popie, and Meme kept commenting on how much weight I had lost, which completely struck me. Me? Lose Weight?

"How much have you lost?" she asked.

I was stunned.

"I don't know," was all I said.

Then we went home and I saw my cousin Katie. She gave me a hug and said, "You look fantastic!"

"Thanks, so do you." Awkward. I had no idea what was going on.

She stood back and took another look at me. "You look fantastic! Oh my gosh!"

I had no idea what she saw that looked fantastic.

That night, I went to Dan's football game. It was cold. I used to consider myself a bit of champ when it came to the cold—wearing my flip-flops in the snow. I must really be a California girl now, as Kelly told me, especially since I had to sit in the car during half time with the heat on.

When I was in bed that night, a drunk Katie called me. "You have to come out with us on Friday. To Margaritas in Mystic," she slurred.

"Maybe," I responded, groggy myself. "Why?" I hated going out.

"You look so great! How did you do it?"

"Do what?"

"Lose all that weight?"

Hmm...I didn't know I had. I sunk down in my bed, uncomfortable, even in all that cushioning. "I haven't really noticed," I told her.

"Oh come on," she pressed. "What are you, a size 6?"

I got quieter. I had always been a 14, but I noticed my pants had been much looser lately and I couldn't wear most. I did buy a smaller size than that recently. I just hadn't realized. "In some things...maybe," I told her, trying to appease her. In dresses, because they are loose. I think I'm a 10. Why did I tell her, "in some things?" I'm an idiot.

"Well you look great," she insisted.

"You're full of it." Tell me more.

"Are you kidding? You're a bombshell!"

No one had ever told me I looked great, never mind called me a bombshell. She must have been really drunk. She kept going.

"I'm so happy for you. I've been telling everyone I know how amazing you look. They can't wait to see you!"

Oh great, false expectations.

"Everything…just looks…great!" she trailed off.

Oh, the effects of alcohol.

I did not understand these comments. I was still fat! People don't realize that I lost a couple pounds before I left for LA and then maybe a few more out there. So, combined, yes, they may see a difference. But my weight and stomach are still over the top. People keep making comments to me about my weight and while on one side it's nice to hear that I've made some progress, on the other side, it's so frustrating that my weight is all they can focus on—just like always. I've been in LA for six months now working on scripts and all they want to know is what the scales say. Will they ever give up? Will I?

It is odd to realize that I have lost some weight without even noticing it. I guess I was so busy, and cannot make real meals on my own, that some of the pounds slipped away. I weighed a lot before and am still heavy. My family and friends back home are just used to seeing me really heavy, so any weight loss will seem like a huge difference to them. After all, I've been gaining weight my whole life. I've never lost it. It's been a constant upward motion. It's a bizarre realization that this is the first time in my life that my weight has taken a downward slant. Not that I'm happy with my body at all, but it's still better than gaining the amount I lost. It is bothersome that people comment on that—on me. Why is it such an issue for them? Why do I have to focus on it all the time? I think that's worse.

It's also discouraging that I know the truth. I know what number the scales say. I know what my body looks like beneath the clothes, and it's not a pretty sight. Worst of all, I know that no matter how much dieting and workout videos I do, I can't seem to lose any more weight. I will always be big. This is the Nicole I am destined to be. I hate it.

Chapter 7
Renfrew: Supplement
First, and Last

Dinner was hard. Worse than usual. I got to my tray and it says, "Chili Mac." What the hell is "Chili Mac?" I open the cover and it's disgusting. It's noodles and beans and chili and there's this sauce. Geez. I can't eat this shit. Who does? Then there's broccoli and apple sauce on the side. It makes no sense because I don't think any other human on earth would eat crap like this.

I turn to Vanessa, the girl next to me, also new, but who has been here before. Three times, actually. She tells me that it is because I am new and haven't been able to pick out my own menu yet.

"Do what you can and tell your nutritionist later," she tells me.

I eat the applesauce, broccoli and pick out the macaroni, and some of the tomato chunks, but can't do the other stuff. Vanessa says, "You're going to have to do some of the Ensure."

I drink my milk and I know I can't do the rest. I hate beans and chili and am already full. Vanessa reiterated, "They're gonna give you the supplement."

Oh no, the dreaded supplement! Well, I had been warned. Can it really be that bad?

The bitchy counsellor comes over to look at my tray.

"Did you get a butter?" she asks me.

"Where?" I had literally not seen a stupid butter.

She points it out.

"What's that for?"

"Broccoli" she says. Clearly, the broccoli!

"But I don't use butter on broccoli."

Vanessa shrugs. "They just put it there, they don't know why."

I try to hide my giggle. I can't.

The counsellor looks at her and I, we laugh, then look at the counsellor and say "sorry" and she gives us a snotty look. The girl next to us says, "They aren't supposed to look so disappointed in you." It was true, and I felt guilty but I shouldn't have. They gave me crap for dinner that I didn't want to eat, and I shouldn't have because I didn't choose it, but I ate some stuff and had an afternoon snack that day. Screw them.

So sure enough, the counsellor comes over with a huge cup of Ensure for Vanessa and me. Vanessa had found a hair in her food so she wouldn't finish it. Hell, I wouldn't have either. I start to drink it and Vanessa tries to comfort me by saying it wasn't so bad at first—it tastes like a milkshake. She actually likes them. So at first, I was OK, but then it was never-ending, and finally, I just had to gulp it down and I felt so full and sick afterwards, but it really hit me a few minutes later—like a rock in my stomach. I felt pregnant. I went back to my room, my stomach bulging with my Ensure baby. Vanessa was in the room across the suite. I ask her if I was supposed to feel this gross and she says, "oh yeah, but it will pass." Everyone says you don't want Ensure. The taste wasn't bad but it's the feeling afterward. I wasn't disappointed in myself because it wasn't fair that I got that meal and how the counsellor treated me. What I was disappointed in was the feeling that came next.

I stand in the hall between our rooms, and say, "I haven't done this in a long time, but I just want to get rid of it." I wanted to purge so badly just to get rid of the food and the crappy fake milkshake in my stomach. The mix of macaroni and applesauce and the supplement swirled around, taking up too much room and making me feel sick. My body, and I, could not handle it. I haven't purged since April of last year, and here I am at an eating disorder center to get better and it triggers me to purge.

Vanessa tells me that she thought about it too. "If you do it, it'll just be a quick release. It might feel good now, but then it will start up that same old pattern and you'll want to do it all the time."

She was right. If I did it and realized how easy it was, I'd be back on the same path of fear, and I do want to recover. I need to just "sit with it" as they say. Vanessa invited me to hang out with them, but I said I was going to make some phone calls to take my mind off of it.

I call Kelly and she says the same thing: "Your stomach isn't used to having so much in it, and Ensure will give you nutrients." Yeah, and calories.

I talk to Dad and he was frustrated, not sure what to believe about dinner, or the other girls' issues with food. He still sees the disease, and not the efforts I've made or that I do want to get better. It's when things get in the way to hinder my progress that I get upset.

I had a chat with my Aunt Jeanette who calls to check in every so often. She fills me in on the family and tells me that my grandfather, Buttsie, wants to get my car back from LA, but she told him to hold off. Thank goodness! She has been so helpful and checks in to see how I am and really wants to know how things are going. She sent flowers too, which is a nice addition to my desolate room.

After the calls, I was still upset from the Ensure baby I was carrying, so I took some Ativan and went to bed. While I was at the Nurse's station, I got to sign up for a new "weights and vitals" time slot, and I got 6 a.m. A bit better. As I trudged my way down the hall to bed, I made a promise to myself: Eat all my meals, and no more supplements!

Talking to my family did help. After I explained how upset I was, they weren't sure whether to be sympathetic or to tell me that this is what I need. They know it is tough and don't like to hear me cry or be upset, but they know I need treatment. So do I. Eventually, the gross, sick feeling passes, but it is the anger that sticks with me. First, anger at not being able to pick my meal, second, at being force-fed a supplement, and third, at the trigger to use my symptoms. I am mad because they gave it to me and mad at myself for feeling this way. I guess this was part of treatment though—to explore these areas of anger, symptoms and feelings.

Hang In There... Wherever "There" Is

My issues with food, my feelings of fullness, and my need to feel "empty." My emotional feeling of empty versus the physical feeling of empty. It is a hard lesson that I learned tonight, but I know that there are many more ahead. I am happy I didn't give in to my symptoms and that I found a friend across the room that understood me. I am glad to be in a place where many people understand me. I have felt misunderstood for so long.

Today I was okay. I already had an aftercare meeting to talk about what I will do when I return home to Connecticut. They recommend a 2-week day programme. Maybe they'll reconsider.

I got to do my meal plan for the next 2 days—a lot of chicken, which is good. I meet with my psychiatrist, Ann, and tell her about my experience the night before and how now I was nervous about tonight's dinner. What if I can't handle it? What if I have to take the supplement again? I can't take the supplement again!

"There's no need to be worried and thinking about food the whole time," she tells me.

"That's what I always do though. The past year I thought about food every second, dreamt about food. It's torture."

"You should take 1mg of Ativan before the meal to help with the anxiety of eating. That way if you don't like it and need the Ensure, you won't be so nervous about it."

We also spoke about how I want to be completely open with my parents, but I think it's hard for them to understand the prison that is my mind. They don't understand the real torture a meal can be for me. I don't want them to think I'm whining all the time, I am truly being honest and want them to know where I'm coming from and where I want to get to. Ann supported me in the idea of supplying them with some literature on the disease, and maybe highlight the parts that applied to me most.

Then it was off to Family Therapy—what timing. My therapist, Robin, is helpful and the first therapist I have ever had. I never thought I'd have a shrink, never mind be able to open up to someone. I was sceptical at first. After all, how can she understand me? She doesn't have an eating disorder. To my surprise, she really listened, and it was nice to be able to unlock the layers inside my head and throw away a lot of the nonsense.

We spoke about my issues before the call to my parents: about how I want to keep communication open with them, because I still don't understand my eating disorder myself, so I don't expect them to. It'll just take time.

We called, and Mom and Dad began by saying they were glad I was there and working towards getting better, and that they wanted to support me in any way. Then the spotlight was on me.

Nicole's History of her Eating Disorder: 101.

I was scared. They knew of the recent anorexia, but not how bad I felt in elementary, middle and high school, and college, and about being overweight. How insecure I was, and my self-hatred.

"I had no idea," Dad says. "You always seemed happy and I thought that was just your personality. If I had known anything was wrong, I would have done anything to help you."

Of course I am bawling at this point. I don't want to hurt them. I just want them to know that this wasn't an L.A. thing. My problems with eating and body image and depression started long ago.

"Why didn't you say anything?" Robin asks.

"Because I didn't want to bother them."

They say of course I was never a bother.

I know I have amazing parents. I never want to worry or hurt them, and the next thing I told them was hard.

I told them about how I purged in college, and then when I was home for a year, I continued purging. Robin asks if they knew.

"No," my Dad says. "We had no idea. She hid it very well."

I was afraid to tell them that part, but at least they know now that I have always had eating issues. We then spoke about the supplement issue and how I thought tonight's meal would be hard, but I will work through it.

Then my Dad says something to bring on the water works.

"I think you're perfect," he says. "And I'm not saying this just to say it, but I admire all that you've done. You went away to pursue your own dreams, and have had articles in The LA Times, and maybe monetarily it's not where you'd like to be, but if you keep working hard, you'll get there."

I am lucky to have them. I know a lot of girls here who have strained relationships with their families, and I am so grateful for mine.

It was a good talk and they were quite supportive. Dad did say that he wants the "old Nicole" back. I want the happiness back and my family, but I want a new and improved Nicole to work on. There are a lot of demons that come with that old Nicole.

I conclude with a big thanks and tell them that I'd like to keep an open line of communication. "I love you and I appreciate your support…and I'll try not to be so negative. I do want to get through this, but there are going to be times when I have a bad day, and I might call up and be negative, but just know that it's part of the process. I don't understand this either, but we'll learn together."

I know how fortunate I am to have my parents and such a supportive family. I would be a skeleton on the streets without them.

I was happy with how it went, and it was nice to be so openly honest. It was nice just to hear them and talk, and Robin is "proud" of how I did, and that I said what I wanted. She tells me I need to speak up for myself more. Go figure. My eating disorder has made me numb to any emotion. I am just starting to feel again. No, not happiness yet, mostly anger and frustration, and that all points to myself and the eating disorder within.

Hang In There... Wherever "There" Is

I return to my room and before I enter, I hear my name called down the hall.

"Nicole R.! Delivery."

I walk back and there is a beautiful bouquet of flowers, but from whom? I glide back to my room—can't run, that would be exercise—and open the card. It's from Grammie, Buttsie, Aunt Jeanette, Uncle Lou and all my family. Beautiful.

I call Aunt Jeanette to thank her, yet she was more interested in how I was.

"Just work towards a healthier self and it'll all be worth it in the end. I know it's hard but it's very courageous for you to be there and that's a big step. Just hang in there," she assures me.

Dinner time again. It's so bizarre that these meals keep popping up and surprising me. I'm not used to eating so much and so often. Yet, here I go again, and as I survey my menu, this time I was prepared.

"Okay, I can do stuffed peppers," I say as I sit behind my tray to ready myself for the meal. "As long as I get meat and not beans. I hate beans."

I peel up the lid off of the plate and there they are, glaring back at me. Beans. Everywhere. In the pepper. On the plate. It was like the Green Pepper threw up beans. Then I guess that would make him bulimic and I should tell a counsellor. Or I should stop focusing on the food and figure out what to do.

"You don't like beans?" asks Jamie, the sweet redheaded girl across from me. She was only fifteen years old, yet so mature for her age, and I can't believe that she had only entered treatment a few days before me. She was so poised and courageous, and beyond that, supportive of others. I hope that one day I can be as strong as she is.

"Why did you pick that out on your menu?" she asks then, as she clears the lids and plastic wrap off of her tray and got checked off by a counsellor, then dug into her beans. She loved her beans.

"I didn't," I tell her. "I'm still on their menu plan. Since I just got here, they pretty much gave me the vegetarian option each night just in case, which means..."

"Beans," she nods knowingly, and went on with her conquest of the food in front of her. The other girls slowly swirl the food on their plates around, and eventually plop it into their mouths, not quite sure what to do with it.

I had a plan, though I did not completely like it.

"I'm just going to eat the pepper part. That'll be at least half, so then they will only make me supplement for the beans, right?" I ask Jamie, as if she was my nutritionist.

"Yeah, that sounds about right," she replies.

So I eat my pepper, and though it's not the best meal I've ever had, I know I have to do it—not just to get checked off for the night, but for

45

my own health and benefit. I do not want to supplement again. After doing it already, I cannot handle downing two bottles of Ensure again. It makes me even more mad to know that I probably could have finished this meal if had I been able to pick what I wanted.

I slog through the green pepper, and as much sauce as I can get down, and soon all that was left on my plate were the beans. A sloppy pile of tasteless, mushy beans.

"You did good," Jamie tells me, and it's nice to hear that encouragement, although, where else does someone praise you for eating?

"So you really don't like beans?" she adds.

I shake my head, averting my gaze from the nasty little things.

"What if you just tried one, and then chased it with your Gatorade?"

I give it some thought, and decide that one bean can't really hurt. I put it on my fork, take a deep breathe, cringe for effect, then put it in my mouth, chew quickly, swallow, and then take a huge gulp of Gatorade.

Jamie smiles.

"That was disgusting!" I say. More like, seemingly tasteless and a, "what's the point?" kind of food.

I look down the table. Everyone else ate, or didn't eat, with such tension, fear—afraid of the unknown of what a piece of food might do once inside their mouths. One girl swirls her food on the plate, one just pushes it away, ready for her supplement, and one talks so much that she has no time to eat, and interrupts the other girls' eating time. I don't want that. I want to do this.

I turn my attention back to Jamie. "Yeah, it's pretty gross, but…"

"But you did it!" she tells me. "Now, try putting a few beans on your fork, and then drinking Gatorade."

Okay, I think, *she's on to something*. I put a few beans on, do the cringe and chew method, and drink my Gatorade.

"I did do it!" I tell her, amazed at myself for just eating beans.

"Now, if you do that a few more times, you'll be all done, and you won't have to have the supplement!" she says, overly excited for my bean-eating. Must've been something in the beans, I guess.

Jamie ate so gracefully, as if she had been doing it all her life. Well, she had been, mostly. Until recently. Relearning how to eat is easier for her I guess.

I want to. I want to get better. And I know that. But there is that part of me that says no. It yells at me in voices I can't bear to hear any more— "You are nothing without your eating disorder."

For so long, I believed those voices.

But now, bean by bean, I was defeating those voices. All that power, within a bean. The disease that controlled me for so long, I was now able to control for just a few minutes, and despite the pain of it, I knew these were the first steps to defeating that voice for good.

Hang In There… Wherever "There" Is

Though I do not like it, I figure if I had already done it a couple times, I could do it a few more, and it would be stupid to end up taking a supplement for a meal that I was almost finished with. So, forkful by forkful, I eat my beans with Gatorade, and soon enough, I finish. I ate a meal, first of all, that I never would have liked. But more importantly, I ate a meal.

Jamie was ecstatic. "You ate all your beans!" she cries.

"I did!" I say, and laugh. The Counsellor comes over to check me off as having completed my meal, and I could then settle in with the thought of being full, and the guilt weighing in of what I had just eaten.

For the first time, there was the sense of accomplishment next to that guilt. I may not like what I ate, and to me it seems pointless to eat it, but I know that my body needed nourishment and I was able to give it that.

After the meal, the group got together for MST (Meal Support Therapy), where we talk a little about how we feel about the meal and how we were doing emotionally and physically. It's a tedious process, because everyone always says, "I'm full," and the counsellor wants to know, "but how do you feel?" We can't talk about those bad things called calories or even about the food really, we just have to talk, and most of the time, we all feel shitty, and they say, "just sit with it, the feeling will pass." You sit with it.

When it came time for Jamie to talk, she said that she really liked this meal, even though she's uncomfortable with the fullness, but wanted to point out how great I did with mine. She knew it was hard for me but I really pushed through it. I couldn't believe this girl, she was amazing. I told her that when it came my time to talk. I could not have got through it without her encouragement.

I don't think I'll ever eat beans again, but I also don't think that I'll ever look at them the same way. I still think they're gross, but I have a little more respect for them and those who eat them. I now know that if I have to eat them, I could. As long as I had some Gatorade handy.

To think that someone else, a stranger really, helped me and was proud of me gave me hope that I can do these meals, even though painful. She was proud of me. Someone was proud of me. That was nice.

I'll call my parents after dinner, I thought. I know they'll be really proud too.

Nicole Roberge

Chapter 8
First Gym Membership:
Losing to Win
February 6, 2006

When I returned to LA, my mind was still swollen with the voices of others who were fixated on my weight.

I know they think they are compliments, but ten pounds is not much when you are my size. All they see if a difference from really-big-Nicole to a little-less-big-Nicole. In addition, they hadn't seen me in a while, so there is going to be a noticeable change. More importantly, are looks all that people can keep mentioning? No one really asked me how my screen-writing was going. It makes it seem as if I'll never amount to anything in writing, because a fat girl will never accomplish anything. A fat girl who writes is still a fat girl. But a fat girl who lost weight and writes is still a fat girl who lost some weight. So much for my writing.

I started taking this diet pill. It's supposed to especially help women. I lost a couple of pounds, but it was mostly weight I gained when I was home. I can't seem to break that barrier and get lower than this certain point. It fluctuates in this 3-pound range. I'd like to lose 20 pounds. I'd be comfortable at that weight, and it's the average for my height, 5'9. I've been working pretty hard at it, with no luck—doing stupid workout videos every day, and I eat pretty sensibly. So why the hell can't I lose weight? I guess I'll have to do more.

Going to Los Angeles when I was 22, now 23, was supposed to be a fresh start in my life. A new adventure. I was fascinated with all the different forms of writing and wanted to wrap myself up in screen-writing. Know everything there is to know about it. Now I had a new mission, a new adventure: weight loss. Without realizing it, I had lost about 15 pounds or so, and that was without really trying. I got so many comments and compliments from family, and while it was nice, it was a bit discouraging that my weight was all they could focus on. I had ambitions out in LA, and no one seemed to care. So maybe, my ambitions should change.

I always had issues with my weight. Most people do, but having been overweight for so long, I was sick of it. When I went to LA, it was no different. I would purge if I ate too much, but apparently, I wasn't even eating as much as I used to. I'm not that great of a cook, so meals weren't too extravagant.

I decided to be proactive in my weight loss. If I could lose weight without trying, what would happen if I did try? I joined a gym in February, and remember the application process with Eduardo.

"So, how much weight do you want to lose?" he asked me.

Twenty pounds.

"Fifteen," I told him.

"No, no. Ten. You don't want to be a stick."

48

Yes, I do.

"Okay, sure. Ten."

I started my workout that day, doing cardiovascular and weights. I wanted to be lean, something I had never been. I tried to go every day, and then slowly increased my workout. But for some reason, I couldn't lose weight. Only five pounds, initially. Something was holding me back.

Luckily, I had a doctor's appointment coming up for a numb foot I had. Yes, the occasional numb foot. That's normal, right? I asked him about a medication I was on and if I still needed it. I had researched it and though it didn't cause weight gain, it did inhibit weight loss. He took me off of it, and put me on a new med for my foot, which had the side effect of slight weight loss. The combination was perfect, and the pounds started to drop.

Weight, and not screen-writing, became the emphasis of my stay in LA. I still went to classes and wrote, but I had more motivation for the gym. It was, after all, what was providing more results. I was still eating, but minimally, and just didn't have an appetite—probably from the new medication. It was the first time in my life where I could start to fit into clothes I liked, without feeling uncomfortable, or holding my arms in front of my stomach. Finally, liberated.

I made a chart of my weight loss. Every week, I would weigh myself, measure my waist, stomach, arms and thighs, and see how far I had come. Some weeks it would be a pound, some weeks it would be two. If it stayed stagnant, I knew I had to work out more.

Losing weight was the one thing I always wanted—I never thought it would happen. Publishing a big piece of writing was also something I always wanted, and somewhere along the line, I completely forgot that that dream existed.

I did, however, accomplish a dream that I never thought would come to fruition. I bought a bikini! I was nowhere near ready to wear it yet, but it was motivation. Not only had I never bought one before, but also I had never even worn one. I don't know what insane moment I was having that prompted me to buy this cute peach bikini, with little ruffles on the bottom, but I did, so I must be certifiably insane. Who is going to want to look at me in one? I don't even want to look at myself in one. When I put it on and looked in the mirror, I was completely disgusted with myself. I am so out of proportion. There is lots of work to be done on this body if I even plan on stepping foot outside my apartment in this thing, never mind take off my sun dress to expose myself in it.

I truly don't know why I got one. I think it's the desire to go to the beach and get colour in places that have never seen it. Like my stomach. You haven't seen pale until you've seen this rotund thing. Maybe a light tan will make it look more toned.

On the other hand, I was actually able to put the damn little thing on. When has that ever happened before? Never. So it fits, just not…well. But that's encouragement for me to do more work. When I was young, my sister always got the bikini, and I got the one-piece, and the one-piece barely fit. I was bulging out of it. So screw that. I have lost some weight. I may have chub, but I am wearing a bikini. Not yet, but soon.

For a girl who has never had a real boyfriend, I was hoping the scene would be a bit better here, but so far, the guy situation is not too promising. I do get quite a few interesting comments, however. On the walk to the gym the other day, I heard, "Excuse me, ma'am, could you spare some change?" Without any time for me to respond, he immediately added, "do you have a boyfriend?"

Awesome. I'm worth about 2 quarters and a penny.

I get propositioned a lot on the street, but then again, it is Hollywood Boulevard, and a little sleazy. Last time I checked, I didn't look or act like a whore.

I was asked out at the gym by a 73-year-old man named "Maurice." While working out on a machine, he rudely interrupted: "Are you done yet?"

I kept my cool and explained that I almost was, and then he switched gears and told me I was, "Sweet, like a chocolate or cherry."

Interesting, Maurice. Interesting.

I moved and gave him the machine, yet he went right on talking to me.

"My name is Maurice. I'm from Israel originally. Are you from California?"

"No, Connecticut," I told him as I hovered between two weight machines, anxious to finish my workout.

"That explains why you are so sweet and not snotty with your nose in the air like the girls out here."

Oh Maurice, you crack me up.

I smiled and said, "Thank you," and that he was sweet too, and that seemed to be the end of our exchange. Until...

"Listen," he said, as he intruded on my silent count of bicep curls. I stopped.

"I'm 73. But I'd like to take you out for coffee sometime. You think about it. I'll be around..."

With that, he went off to his machine and I hurried through the rest of my set, skipping the end of my arm workout to get the hell out of there.

This is why I shouldn't talk to people.

I went to do crunches and he showed up in the "Abs" area—of the gym, not the area of body.

"Good, you're still here!" he shouted. Very loudly. "I thought you forgot about me."

I was trying, but then you showed up again.

I fast-tracked my workout even more and was towards the end when I saw him yet again.

Hang In There... Wherever "There" Is

"I love youuuuu..." he sang with a little wave. It went from flattering to embarrassing to full-on stalker. Seriously. I can't believe that I can only attract old and creepy men. Not sure what that says about me...and I probably don't want to know.

2.5 pounds lost in a week! I'm finally under that mark on the scale that always scares me when nurses have to move it up one notch. Like it's too heavy for them to move and they're annoyed. Yup, I am under 150. Better than that, I also noticed that I have collar bones! It's insane. Who would've thought? I never knew before that you were actually supposed to be able to see them, but you are. And I can. I used to think their boniness was gross, but now, I like it. A lot.

There is still a lot of work to do on myself. Weight must be lost if I am to gain something for myself—confidence in myself and my body, freedom to be in public and not be embarrassed, not hide, and find happiness. I am continuing to go to the gym every day. I have been losing about 2 pounds a week, but I know it will slow down soon, so I will need to work harder. I've been losing more inches around my waist, arms and thighs too. I'm losing, but I'm winning.

My friend Kristy is in L.A. We went to high school together and now she is living out here. We made plans to go out to dinner and her first comments to me were: "You look so good. You're so skinny. Almost too skinny."

I try to hide my smile, but it made me feel as if my hard work has paid off.

Then she hits me with, "You look like you lost 800 pounds!"

Wow.

I laugh. "Thanks. So you thought I weighed 800 pounds. Awesome."

"No!" she yells. "You just look skinny. Are you eating?"

"Yes, I'm eating. I'm just working out." I don't look so skinny, and plus, as usual, I was sucking it in. I am eating right and working out for once. The fasting and purging didn't even help in weight loss and made me feel worse, so I'm done with that.

March already. Crazy. So many months out here, and though I'm doing different things, I don't feel as if I've established a "real" life for myself. I'm still in limbo, hovering above LA almost, not quite sure where my place is. I'll find it soon. I'll know where I belong. I know there is a reason I am here. For now, I am still attracting weird old men. Gotta love it.

I was on a machine at the gym the other day and a cute old man said, "You look so serious."

"I'm working out," I told him, with a smile of course. "And I'm just ready to go home."

"You should smile more," he told me. "You have a beautiful smile."

He was sweet and did really make me smile. He told me to keep smiling, but I was determined. I needed to get that workout in. There's no smiling when there's a goal in mind.

It's funny because people used to know me for my smile. "There's Nicole, always smiling," they would say. "Do you ever stop smiling?" or "Every time I see you, you're laughing!"

If only they knew the Nicole on the inside who was hurting. I used to be able to smile through that hurt, but I find it harder now. At the gym, I'm focused. Maybe there's just no one, or nothing, to smile for. Maybe this has been the real me all along. Frozen, numb. No smile to be found. The smile fades when the real me shines…or rather, disappears.

**Chapter 9
Renfew:
Moving on Up**

I am no longer a newbie! I now have a room upstairs with double beds, and a cool roommate named Erica. A little more freedom, it seems, away from the nursing station. The living room with the TV is right there, so I won't avoid socializing and may even come out of my room. Those stairs were just so daunting.

Though I have moved up a floor, I still have not moved up on Meal Level or General Level. I am still a level three and would like to be a four because then I can go out on pass.

Blankets are a hot item in treatment. Every girl has one and keeps it with them at all times. We are not Lemmings, we are the Eating Disordered versions of Linus from Peanuts. Kelly sent me mine—a very soft green one, my favourite colour, and I too take it everywhere. I wrap myself in it to keep warm and cover up during weights and vitals, take it to groups and have it with me even just hanging out in the living room. Each girl has a different colour and different type. We are all distinguished by our blankets.

One of the groups here is Art Therapy, so I choose to go even though I am a terrible artist. Maria, the art therapist, gives us a prompt: pick what you think recovery is like and draw it, then draw another picture of where you are now.

While most people say that they view recovery as "utopia," I can't. Recovery is not in my view yet. I'm scared of it. I can't see any life other than where I'm at now. Maria comes over to talk about my blank page.

I explain to her my problem. She tells me it's not a problem at all, and to do what I feel and that I don't need to follow the prompt exactly.

I think about it, and at the risk of sounding geeky, tell her, "Maybe it's a heart. I want to follow my heart but right now I'm in the prison of my mind—a self contained prison."

"Do that," she says.

So I draw a heart with prison bars over it, and a lock on the bar. The key is on the floor. For some reason she likes it.

She comes over to analyze it. "I love how at some parts, the heart bleeds through, and at other parts, the heart is behind the bar."

That wasn't done purposely.

She tells me I did a great job and asks for the name of my therapist.

I had a session with Robin later and she tells me Maria called and would love to do an individual session with me.

Surprised, I tell Robin, "I can't draw."

"That doesn't matter. She was impressed. She said you're very expressive. Without talking much, you really get your emotions down on the paper and communicate that way."

"It was fun, I didn't think I'd be able to do it. I guess I'd be up for my own session."

She asks me how things are going and I tell her I can't believe it's been a week.

"The meals are getting better and I think I've made progress. At lunch today, I sat with two new admissions. They ate their salad and fruit, but not the entrée, which was turkey chili. Yeah, gross. But I ate it. It was nasty. A week ago, I was just like them, and even when I did eat things, I had a hard time with it. Now I feel full, I still don't like it, yet I know it is better for me to do it."

We also talk about my past issues—how I liked seeing my bones, how my 4-hour workouts were torture, and some of the things I did were just awful. I look at the things I did as if it were another person. Even though I'm nowhere near recovered, it's hard to think of where I've been.

I then met with my nutritionist, and we talk about how the meals were better, but of course my weight came up.

"It's been stable since you got here," Nancy tells me. "We'll see where it goes, maybe it will stay here, but it's hard to tell because you don't really know what your 'normal weight' is." Which is true, because it was overweight to Anorexic.

"For your height, the number is still at the lower end," she tells me. "Listen to your hunger cues, like the grumbling stomach you had the other day." I hated to admit that to her. "If you're feeling hungry, your body needs more, so go to snack."

She wants to move me off Trays to Independent Eating, but knows that I am still anxious at meals. She says we'll wait until after the weekend. She also read me off some "food rituals" that the counsellors noted. These are things people do with their food to either avoid eating it, or to help them eat it.

Mine were:

1) Pushed beans out of stuffed peppers.
2) Cut broccoli into little pieces.

Moron counsellors. I tell her about my annoyance and explain each one. First, that I don't like beans, but that I ate the pepper first and prevailed in eating the beans after. She understood. Second, I tell her that the broccoli was huge, and I cut large pieces of food so I don't choke. She says it's fine, they just write what they see, and she isn't worried.

Not being allowed to talk about food here, this is really my only time. I tell her how I spoke with my Dad about my issues and wanting to get better, and how I couldn't do it at home even though I tried. It's safe here. I am eating now because I have to clear my plate and because they tell me I have to eat. They make me, so I do it. Otherwise, I wouldn't. But it's OK, because when the trays are out, I know I have to put food in my belly. Here, they are in control. On my own, the eating disorder is in control. I want Nicole to be in control.

Ten days here! Ten days without using my symptoms. Ten days without using my addictions—to laxatives, diet pills, diuretics, the gym, and restricting. In one way, it feels good, in another, it scares me.

I talk to Melissa about it. She was admitted with me, so we automatically became buddies. We understand each other, even though she is here to deal with her issues with bulimia.

"I can't wait to go back," I tell her.

She's appalled. "I can't believe you just said that."

I can't either, but it's true. I just want to lose this fat. I weighed in at 135.5. Gross. I've also been doing crunches secretly in my room, whenever I can sneak them in. Shhh...they're just a couple of crunches. I want to keep some tone at least. I hate having another secret though. "Secrets make you sick," they say here, and I have kept so many damn secrets for so long. If I told one of the counsellors, they would put me on contract. I'd have to read it in a community meeting, say what I have done wrong, and ask for the community's help. Then they'd watch me like a hawk. No, I won't. It's just a couple of crunches.

Melissa and I talk longer. I tell her that the food dreams are back. Those food dreams that I had all during the depths of the disorder, when all I thought about was food. I thought they would go away, and they had, but they are back. Maybe it's part of recovery.

"It was a carrot cake muffin," I tell her. "I scouted everywhere for one, because I needed a low-fat birthday cake. It was horrible. Searching and searching for the right kind of food that wouldn't corrupt me."

"I love carrot cake," she says.

I laugh. "Yeah, so do I! I haven't had it in so long. I didn't even have a birthday cake on my birthday in November, because it was the week I got home from L.A., and I was too scared. Pathetic. We're gonna have it one day when I get home."

"That's good. I'm proud of you."

"Maybe when we both bust out of here, or go on pass, we can have some carrot cake. That would be a risk, as they say."

"Deal. Now I want some."

I spoke to Dad later and told him about the food dream and how hard it was, but again, it's something people don't understand. It's worse because I haven't had them in a while. Just like the picture I made of the heart, no one really understands this prison I'm in. There's a huge lock, but the key is out of reach, and somehow, I have to find a different way out.

One of the girls here, Andrea, got caught purging. Actually, she fully admitted to it. She got dropped back to level one, which means she can't do anything. I feel bad, because she was honest about it at least, but now they watch her constantly.

To make matters worse, last night there was a thrown-up piece of bread on the sidewalk. Disgusting, yes, but they blame her. She's devastated, claims it wasn't her, and I believe her. She's very sweet. She says if she was honest the first time, why would she lie now? And why would she do it on the sidewalk? This place is a madhouse. It truly is.

I don't think that I've realized that I'm here yet. I guess that it hasn't hit me. I know events have happened to get me here and I am supposed to be working through them, but it is all so mechanical. I'm going through the motions and do what I am told. I know that if I do all the right things then eventually I'll get out, then I can go back to my healthy "diet."

I remember the girl—the bony one, who would plan her whole day around going to the gym, cry on the way there, suffer for four hours, then eat a peach or an apple perhaps, some vegetables and cottage cheese. If I had seen that girl pass me on the street then, I would have felt pity for her, been scared for her. She probably would have snapped back at me, glared at me as if to say, "What are you looking at? You're just mad because you're not as thin as I am." That girl was me.

Now I am here at Renfrew. I was not so nervous when I came. I was upset that I had got fat, but not scared to be here. The meals were hard at first and pissed me off, but eventually I started to eat because those are the rules. I had a couple of good days, then bad. I go to groups and therapy, talk about why I think I have this, but don't get anything really out. It's all stuff I've talked about before. I have hidden emotions that I think I need to address, yet I can't seem to dig them out. There's so much more in me that I need to discover to really knock this disorder out of me. To kill the disease before it kills me.

The thing I am afraid of is to talk about those things within, because I don't know what my therapist would think of me, or if we would then talk about it in family therapy. It is better to suppress things and go on like a robot, like I always have. Better to hurt myself than others.

I should be struggling more. Maybe that means I'm not trying hard enough. I'm doing the program, but not recovering. I only have 28 days here, now less, and I want to take advantage of it. This is just the beginning of recovery, of a lifelong process, of a new life. I know that I am here, but I don't feel as if I am truly here yet.

Chapter 10
Spring, 2006
Scaling the Days

Walking down Hollywood Blvd. is always interesting. Coming back from the gym one night, I passed a group of five young black girls. One of them smacked my bum and yelled, "Nice ass." I was shocked, but all I could think of to do was be polite, so I turned around and said, "Thanks." After all, I have been working on it at the gym, so maybe it is paying off.

That was not the comment they were expecting, and they erupted into laughter, and so did I. They kept walking their way, and I mine, a little happier about my bum and that I made someone laugh, even though some weirdo had their hand on my tush.

My second screen-writing course has ended and a new one has begun. I have written two scripts now, and have another idea for my third—yes, another comedy. This time, a college comedy, so I should be able to infuse some of my own experiences into it. That could be good, or frightening.

I went to a Yankees game in Anaheim, alone, which is totally fine by me. I got to see my favourite, Mike Mussina pitch, and they won, so it was a good day. I talked to Dad before, during and after the game. I wish he could have come with me—he would have loved it. I guess there is a bit of a distance to travel between Connecticut and California though. I got back to my apartment and went out to get an ice cream. I ate too much that day.

I had been eating too much lately, it seemed. The scales had been moving up and down. Sometimes more upward than I'd like. I looked online for some dieting ideas, and found a fruit fast. If I just ate fruit during the day, I could lose weight. Some fruit has negative calories in it, they say, meaning that it takes more energy for your body to digest it than is in the fruit, so you actually burn calories by eating it. I started a pattern of doing a fruit fast, then fasting, then weighing myself, and I saw the scale go down a bit. It's a hard diet to keep up with, but I could get in the habit. Occasionally, I'd bite off the corner of a piece bread, or have a bite of soup or a cracker, just to sustain myself. Eventually, I think the hunger pains will go away. My pain, on the other hand, I am not so sure of.

I heard from my friend Jason, the screenwriter from Connecticut who lives out here in LA now, who I had interviewed. He wanted to know if I could get together for lunch. Food? With a person? Shit! I said "yes," and we made arrangements, but there was work to be done. He told me the place and time, and I looked up the menu online. Salad, it is.

I decided to fast for two days before we met up, just so I might look a little less fat. I'm sure being in Hollywood, he was used to much thinner women.

The day we met, it was raining, so I was a bit covered up anyway. Probably made me look bigger.

This would be our first time meeting in person, and I already knew he was nice, so I wasn't nervous about meeting him—it was the meal. Why does everything revolve around food?

When I got there, I saw him instantly—we were pretty much wearing the same outfit. Jeans and a black shirt. That broke the ice. I felt uncomfortable with my weight because he was slender, but his smile and joking lessened that feeling. He held the door for me into the brooding restaurant, and then the chair for me as I sat down. What a gentleman. That was something I was not used to.

I was instantly at ease with him, until he handed me the menu.

"Everything is good," he told me.

I turn my eyes to the salad portion of the menu. He rattles off some other items. I focus on the salads. I order a Caesar with Grilled Chicken.

"Are you sure that's all you want?"

"Yeah, that'll be plenty."

He gets some weird tuna thing, nothing I'm brave enough to try, and neither one of us touches the bread.

We talk and talk and he takes the stress away, until, that damn food arrives.

As we ate, he continued talking, and since I can't talk and eat, I was a slowpoke. He was done and I still had a full plate. It was a big salad. The waiter came over and took his plate as I tried to pick away at my salad.

"Do you want some?" I asked him.

"No," he laughed, and continued asking questions about how L.A. was, work, and our commonalities back home.

I stopped eating. The waiter came. "I'm all set."

"Are you sure you're done," Jason asked.

"Yeah, I'm full."

The waiter asked if we wanted dessert and before Jason could answer, I said "no, thank you." We chatted for a bit longer, and then fought over the check. He won.

When it was time to leave, he asked where my car was. Since I couldn't find the restaurant right away, I'd parked a few streets down, whereas he was right in the parking lot. He offered to drive me.

"No, I can walk." I needed the exercise.

He said he'd drive me, and even opened the car door for me, restoring my faith that there were kind humans in this city; I just had to venture outdoors.

When we got to my car, he commented on how nice it was to see a Connecticut license plate. I realized how nice it was to have someone in this city to relate to.

"I have a movie to go work on out of town for a month or so, but when I get back we'll have to go out again."

I told him "sure," and we went our separate ways.

It was a nice way to spend the afternoon, even if it did involve food. And if I was going to see him in a month, then that gave me time to lose more weight. He'll see a different me when he comes back. Ten pounds, I thought.

A month passed and we didn't get together. He works a lot and travels, but we still wrote emails. Lucky for me, I had my own distractions. The gym. The ten pounds I hoped to lose did not slip off, though I did ditch about six. I am sure that it was water weight since I'm hadn't really been eating meals—just light snacks, but not very often. Still, that's about forty pounds I've dropped since last March and thirty since I've moved out here. The move to LA has done me good. Well...sort of.

My younger cousin Angela was visiting some friends in Santa Barbara and they were coming down to Hollywood for the day so I was meeting up with them. I hadn't seen her since Thanksgiving, and being April now, it had just been too long. We always have so much fun together. It was a hot, hot day, especially in Hollywood, and I had a new dress. A "Marc Jacobs" one that I treated myself to for selling a bunch of articles. One I probably couldn't afford, but now that I was fitting into things more easily, it was hard to resist.

I met up with cousin Angie and her friends in the lobby of the Roosevelt Hotel, where they were staying. She ran up to me, gave me a hug, and whispers, "You look great! You've lost so much weight." I am sure any weight difference will look huge for her to see. She's used to having me be "Big Nicole," besides being her big cousin, for as long as she's known me. I do think that some of it is my new medication and loss of appetite. And a low caloric intake, plus working out a lot. It's not like I am purposely restricting. I would eat, I just don't feel like it.

We went out to the pool area and Angie jumped in while I hung out with her friends by the side. One friend said to me, "So, I remember you from High School. You look thinner." That was an awkward comment. Good to know, though.

Later in the hotel, Angie and I went to get ice and then as we walked back to the room she told me, "You look so good. You lost a lot of weight. You look great."

It's nice and surprising to hear, but uncomfortable. What am I supposed to say to that?

I opted to joke about it and said, "You look great too, we should go out sometime," with a wink. Then we giggled our way back to the room.

I don't feel great though. I still look and feel fat. I can't be too confident because the people who are telling me I look good and have lost weight are the ones who have seen me at my heaviest. So someone new, just seeing me for the first time, would probably think that I could stand to lose a few pounds, and then some. I am one of those people.

I tried on a dress at a store and it was too big. I tried a size down. Still too big. One lower and it fit. I'm down two dress sizes! Maybe that's because I lost another six pounds. Things are really moving now, but I still need a little extra help to keep the weight loss going.

I went to GNC and got these weight training/fat-burning pills to take along with my workout. They highly recommend them, so we'll see. There was a little Chinese man working there, and of course he asked about my routine and what I was doing. Then he had me turn around for him.

"Yeah, you really need to lose weight in the middle," he told me.

As if I didn't know. "Yeah," I agreed, embarrassed. "I know." I'm such a failure.

It was discouraging. I wanted to explain that I had a loose dress on, but knew the ugly truth. I was fat. Fat Nicole. Everyone else knew it too. Even GNC man.

"Some women find that this pill you have works better with another pill to release water," he said, showing me a bottle of blue pills. "A lot of women have water retention." He asked about my urine and if I could empty my bladder all the way. Gross. Weirdo. I'm so not talking about my pee with you.

I got the pills I already had and left.

But I went back the next day.

I wanted to do everything I could to lose weight, so I asked him about the whole water retention thing.

"Can I feel your arm?" he asked. Better than looking at a urine sample, I suppose.

He jiggled the underside.

"That's not all fat. You've got some water there," he informed me.

I guess that was good, knowing I'm not all fat. I had noticed since I'd been working out and doing weights that my arms are definitely not as jiggly as they used to be. So I got the pills for that, too. Diuretics, they called them.

"Hopefully, that combo will work good for you," the smiling man said. "Come back and see me. Let me know."

I thanked him, knowing I would be seeing much more of him.

I turned in my script. My final one. Hard to believe it's May already and I've been out here for almost a year. Harder to believe that I've made the decision to stay longer to work on rewriting my scripts and get them out there. I mean, why write them if I'm not going to do anything with them? My parents understand. My family misses me and I miss them, but they know this is what I want right now, even though things have been hard lately.

I feel really depressed. I'm trying to do things, but it's all on my own. Like the other day, I went to the gym, to a bad movie, the store, then came back to my apartment and just sunk into this weird depression. I don't know what's the matter with me. Maybe it's not having any friends, or real work, or that the class is over. Could be my boring life, or the fact that it seems I have no real "purpose" out here now. Or a combination. I feel lost and foolish for all the stupid things I do. I'm a mess. I have been here for about a year and really, what have I done? What have I accomplished? No real job. I have been out of college for 2 years now and I haven't worked at a real job. I'm "freelance," baby. Then I look at people out here, trying to be writers or actors, or who have realized their dreams, and they were waiters or working in stores, and they succeeded. It takes time, I know. I can't just sit around and wait for it to happen. Not that it's going to happen. I need to be getting more work. I can't be an out-of-work freelance journalist! What a joke. I need to be more proactive. That was pretty much my hysterical, crying, nervous breakdown. I'm just devastated and I don't know what about. I am lonely. But...I am visiting my family soon, and maybe this trip home will do me some good.

Do you want to know what's worse? How shallow I am? I'm afraid that going home will screw up my weight-loss regimen. Awfully vain, isn't it? I'm down to my lowest weight I can ever remember, which is pretty amazing, but I know that even though I have no appetite, I will have to eat a little bit and we will all go out to dinner at points. I'm afraid I will gain all my weight back in those weeks.

I am down five more pounds and have lost inches on my stomach, arms, thighs and waist. It's good, so this is what I want to keep up at home. I hate being so worried about it. Having worked so hard at it makes me think about how bummed I would be if I gain it back. I can't. I won't.

I am excited to go home. I've missed my family. Dan is graduating high school. Time really does fly. I still feel like he's twelve. I know these two weeks will fly by too, just like this year has. I wonder if I have changed much in this past year. Maybe I haven't, but I have a different version of who I want to be. Knowing that I really like screen-writing, whereas before I looked at LA living in baby steps—three months, nine months, a year—now I can definitely see it as long term and not need anyone's permission to do it. I feel comfortable with my decisions, and I'm a terrible decision-maker. I just hope they are the right ones. After all, what could go wrong?

So, here's to a year in LA. Did I ever think I'd actually come out here? Or write scripts? Lose weight? Nope. So one year completed...possibilities ahead.

**Chapter 11
Renfrew:
My Inner Child**

More puke on the grounds. This time, it was in bags. As in, someone puked in a bag and threw it out of their window. Then, someone puked right on the front steps, as if they were sending a message to the counsellors and administration. This place is really going downhill, and naturally, everyone is gossiping.

I listen, but try and stay out of it. Makes me somewhat relieved I'm Anorexic, so I can't be blamed. The bulimics are all nervous though.

The Summer Camp feeling has passed—that going-through-the-motions routine of waking up, eating, groups, eating, more groups, therapy, eating, groups, bed, and repeat. Like I'm just here eating food for a while to pass the time, not really understanding what I'm doing, just doing it to do it.

I have my first real freak out—I realize I am here. Shit. Now what? Have I been wasting time? What am I doing? What have I done? How does this work?

I sit in a group, a boring one, and stare out of the window. It is warm for January, I notice. Why am I in this room, I think?

I look at all the girls around me, and then listen to what they are saying.

I look outside again. At the long driveway, the large building next to us, and then inside the room we are in—large bouncy balls everywhere, mats, a mirror, chairs, and a therapist. Group therapy. For eating disorders. I'm in treatment for an eating disorder. I had an eating disorder? Whoa! Time out, when did this happen?

Freak out.

All day I want to cry, but there is no safe place to cry here.

Luckily, I have therapy, so I sneak into Robin's office and just burst into tears.

She looks at me stunned, as I had never done that before. It was my first moment of reality when I tell her, "I don't know what I'm doing."

"Okay," she says, and turns her chair toward me.

"I think that maybe the thing is I never thought I would be here, so I can't believe that I'm here. I've just been going through the motions of eating and going to groups, but not feeling it or experiencing it."

"You have been compliant and it's a good thing that you realize now you are here, because sometimes it takes that realizing you're truly in treatment for you to hit rock bottom, to really search for recovery."

I explain to her how I keep having visions of my Anorexic self at my worst—the bones, the gym, the daunting grocery store, searching for fruit, and then about how I would feel sorry for myself if I had passed me on the street. I think of the people who used to stare at me and what they must have thought. I was pitiful.

Hang In There… Wherever "There" Is

She asks me how I feel about the girl now.

"I feel bad for her too, because she's a mess. But she's trying, so that's a good thing. Those two girls are heading in totally opposite directions. I am heading in a more positive one, while she is headed nowhere…or to the gym," I joke.

At my last meeting with Nancy, my nutritionist, we talked about moving me up to Independent Eating. She is away on vacation, so there is her "understudy" taking over for the week. I run into her in the hall and ask if I can move up. She says, "no."

"I know you're ready to move up," Molly tells me, "but you've been consistently losing weight."

Today I was 134.2, which I was happy about, because it has been going down about .2 a day. But really, .2 pounds a day? Losing weight?

"Why don't we try you on optional snack tonight and see where you're at tomorrow? Sound good?"

No.

I give her the rundown about how I had been using laxatives before, and since I had been here, I couldn't have a bowel movement. Yes, I spoke about my bowel movements. That was the norm here. We all talked poop, especially on raisin day when we had raisin bagels for breakfast and a box of raisins, and a sandwich on raisin bread for lunch. They knew what they were doing to us.

"They just put me on medicine to get things moving," I tell her. "So that could be why my weight is fluctuating."

It didn't change her mind, but it raised my anger. I wish Nancy were here, even though I hate going to see her and have her tell me why I need to eat.

Perhaps my metabolism is kicking in. When your body is in starvation mode, it slows down so much to keep you alive. Now that I'm eating, it could be picking up and actually causing me to lose weight. I feel so knowledgeable about food, nutrition and weight now, I could almost work here.

She knew I was angry.

"Don't think this is holding you back. Let's just try it out, see how you feel and then we'll talk." Then she scurried away.

It does seem as if it's holding me back. Everyone else I was on Trays with has moved up. I'm at a normal weight. I can show them my fat. At least they have apples at snack, which has negative calories. See, now I'm back into my negative way of thinking. Thanks, Molly.

Back at Robin's office, we delved again into my mind.

"Yesterday seemed tough for you, with the realization of being here. How is today?"

"Better. Yesterday was strange because I hit that moment where I'm aware that everything happened, but it still feels dreamlike. I never imagined I'd be here. Back in high school, college, or even in L.A., did I ever think I'd be in an eating disorder facility? Never."

"Again, it's good that you realize you're here and you do need to work on recovery. It takes time to accept that."

"Okay. Now what?"

"What do you want to do here? Do you think you haven't been working on recovery?"

"I have, but I guess in the general way. I have my own story—that I had issues with weight and eating, so I dieted and exercised, then I restricted, then there was the point of uncertainty in my life and the eating disorder took over. Almost destroyed me. Now I'm here. That's the same story I've had to tell all the doctors and everyone here. It's the truth. But it's all on the surface. These are the current issues that made me hit rock bottom," I tell her.

I think for a minute, because I know my eating disorder was so much more than that. "There is something festering inside of me that has been building up all of these years that I think is at the real root of this eating disorder, and that is what I want to pull out and get rid of. I can walk away and say, 'OK, I acknowledge that things were tough, I was in a rut, I lost control, and I'll get better'—but I won't. Maybe for a little bit, but if that thing is still inside of me, then I will go right back to where I was, and I don't want to be that scared again. Something is eating away at me, literally, and I want to find out what it is."

I sit back in the chair. Wow. I have some serious demons to work with, and so does Robin.

She listens the whole time. I'm not used to that. I am usually the one to listen. It's nice to have someone to talk to, even if I sound crazy.

"It's good that you can acknowledge all of that. It's quite an accomplishment, and it gives us a lot to work with."

We begin with childhood, how I never quite fitted in, and she wants me to write a letter to myself as a child and talk to "her" about what I saw or what I could do to help her. It's actually an interesting assignment and she knows I like to write, so it'll be something different to do here.

One of the things she asks is, "if you had a picture of yourself, or just imagine yourself at the age of eight, what do you think?

"Overweight."

"There was so much more to you than that. You were just a kid. And if an eating disorder were a person, and went after your eight-year old self, what would you do?"

"I would protect her."

"You're still that girl, you're just older. Why should you let the eating disorder in now? It is hurting you just like it would her."

She suggested I get a picture of myself when I was younger to look at and remind myself that I would never want an eating disorder to harm that little girl, or anyone else for that matter. Why do I suffer then? Why can't I let go? Do I feel I deserve this torture? No. I just can't stop.

Hang In There... Wherever "There" Is

I wasn't going to have another session with Robin for a couple days, but my assignment had me thinking, so I wanted to sit down and write it. I went through the living room and said "hi" to some of the girls first. Amy, whom I met the first night, was always there, bubbly as ever. She is 16 and so sweet, but keeps herself wrapped in a blanket, afraid of her body, which is so tiny, though she doesn't realize it. Many of the girls knit, some colour, some watch T.V. It is still hard to believe this is my home right now.

I go to my room and Erica isn't there, so I get cozy on the bed and pull out some paper. How do I even begin? What do I say to this girl, myself? It's not like I had a bad childhood. I have wonderful parents and siblings and we always had fun. I just wasn't content with myself and kids said hurtful things. It was those hurtful things that made me ashamed of myself, but I shouldn't have been. I was, after all, just a kid. Kids should have fun, not be worried all the time. I guess that's a start. I pull out my pen and just write:

Dear Nicole, the child—

I'm sorry that you were often sad as a child. When you're a kid, you should be happy and carefree, and not have to worry so much. But not you—you didn't always let yourself have fun. Not only were you uncomfortable about your weight, the way you looked, but also school, friends, pleasing others, and your family and taking care of them. You were always scared that they would get hurt. You never wanted to be too far from them. Instead of spending time with your friends, you stayed home. You worried you might hurt your parents' feelings if you went out with friends instead, or what might happen if you were away. You worried a lot for a little girl. But of course, you soon realized that you weren't so little. In 5th grade, you were going down the slide. It was hot and your legs stuck to it. People laughed and for years said, "Remember that time you got stuck on the slide?" You tried to explain the real reason, so they'd know it wasn't because you were fat, but their laughter was too loud for your quiet voice.

There was the other time, in 6th grade, when your teacher asked you to move your desks. So you all pushed them forward and you then went to slide your chairs up, but the legs of yours got caught on the carpet. The girl next to you said, "Can't you move?" A couple kids laughed because they thought you were too heavy to move your chair.

It didn't help much that you had low self-esteem and lack of confidence due to your issues with weight. It caused you to not want to eat a lot in front of people at school or at friends' houses, because then they would think you were a pig. They'd think, "There's Nicole, look at all she eats." So you'd "eat like a bird," as one friend's Dad said, but when you went home, you'd sneak snacks when no one was looking, or bring them up to your room, and then you'd hate yourself for it. But you hated yourself a lot, didn't you?

Then there was your sister, tall and skinny, and you felt a bit in her shadow, because though you often had achievements in school, she was always skinny and everyone commented on that and how she could eat anything and wouldn't gain any weight. You wondered what that would be like. In her presence, you had to eat as little as you could. For her to eat a lot and stay so skinny, everyone thought that it was an accomplishment. If you had done it, people would have known why you were overweight. Maybe if you didn't eat as much in front of them, they wouldn't really notice you were bigger.

As you got older, you realized how you grew up fast. You were always the shy and quiet one, partly because you felt awkward, because you didn't like the way you looked and also because that was just your nature. It was always easy for everyone to overpower you. You became accustomed to being in the background so you also became accustomed to staying in the background. But this made you a powerful observer. You matured quickly, not getting into trouble and being a good student in school. You weren't just a student to teachers, you were also able to chat with them after class. Other students were running down the halls having fun. You felt a little left out from your peers, but didn't want to hurt your teachers' feelings, so you always stayed behind to help them clean up after class, or just talk with them.

If I could help you now I would tell you to be a kid, have fun, and know that your family loves you and they know you love them so it's okay to go play with friends. Their feelings won't be hurt. I know you were never really happy with yourself. You always wanted to make others happy, which was fine, but maybe you should have done it for yourself once in a while too. I also think that you should have stood up for yourself more. You listened to what other people thought of you too much and you shouldn't have. If you truly believed in things, or yourself, you should have said it. I know it's hard, but sometimes, it's worth it. Usually, it is. You were worth it.

You never took a chance with relationships—both friendships and romantically. Regarding friends, you had a lack of trust because you didn't know what other people would do with your feelings. You never felt that close with anyone. You held your emotions inside, and dating just never seemed like an option for you. A lot of that had to do with your weight and body image issues, but you were also scared to open up to people—afraid that they might get to know the real you and that they might not like her. But did anyone know the real you growing up? Did you?

Nicole—you grew up too soon. Maybe because you felt bigger than you were. You didn't always let yourself have fun. I wish you had. You came out of your shell eventually, but missed out on a lot and used your smile to mask a lot of things. It should have always been real. Now I see that little child, you, is still inside of me, seeing she missed out on some things because she was scared, vulnerable, unhappy, or thought she was too tough to recognize any of that. Maybe by losing weight now, I just wanted to shed all the insecurities I once had. I felt tiny and insignificant then, so I made myself look tiny and insignificant now. But really, I just wanted to be the little girl I never was.

Love,

    Nicole, the adult

That took a lot out of me. I know about my past, but not a lot of the feelings that went with it. Especially what I wrote at the end, about wanting to be the little girl I never was. I remember being in L.A. and crying in front of the mirror, looking at bones, first admiring them, then being scared of what I was doing, and saying, "I just want to be tiny. I want to be a little girl again." I was never a little girl. I was always a big girl, even when I was little. Being that tiny made me feel small, fragile, and like I needed protection. When I was younger, I always said I was tough. I never needed anyone's help, and as I stared into that mirror, I knew I needed help. I couldn't go back in time and be a little girl again, but I could make myself look like one.

Chapter 12
June, 2006
Commencement of Many Things

Home.

I'm visiting for two weeks, and it's very strange to be the "daughter visiting from L.A." It's nice to be back, and I jumped right into things, with visiting family, my brother's baseball game and even a dentist's appointment.

I went to a local gym and signed up for a week's trial so I can still work out. I need to stay in shape, though have been trying to eat okay here. It is nice to have some normal meals and snacks compared with what I'm used to.

I went to Dan's game, and immediately was hit with comments. "You've lost so much weight," one mother shouted as I walked by.

When I got around to the other side of the field, my Mom started chatting with my brother's friend's Mom, Mrs. Charles. She caught a glimpse of me and stood to give me a hug.

"Oh my gosh!" she said, and stepped back. "You're so tiny! You look like a model. You're so beautiful."

Uncomfortable pause.

"You were beautiful before, but, oh! You're just stunning now."

Her husband even told me I looked great when I passed him.

These comments are all relative to when they saw me a year ago. I know I've come a long way, but I know I still have a little way to go. Besides, most of the weight that I lost has been in the past month. So it's new to me too.

They weren't the only ones with comments. My grandmother, Meme, wanted to make sure that I was eating. When I made a comment about how I was cold, Mom said it was because I didn't have any meat on my bones, but I said, "Yeah, right. I can show you my belly." I still can't seem to lose any weight there.

I stopped by to see my other grandparents, Grammie and Buttsie, but they weren't there. I saw my Uncle Lou and he told me I looked great. Aunt Jeanette emailed me later and said she heard I looked great. Gee, I wonder how. Aunt Liz also emailed me to say she heard the same thing. My gosh, it's like I'm engaged or having a baby! Big ol' Nicole loses some weight and it's world news. Weight has always been the most uncomfortable subject for me and always gone mostly unspoken, but now that I've lost some, let's sing and shout about it and make me even more uncomfortable. They probably think I'm happy about it, which I am, and want to acknowledge it. But dwelling on it and focusing on me too much just makes me itchy.

Dan's graduation was supposed to be about him, but people turned their attention to me. The compliments got to be really awkward then. I ran into my old boss and she wanted to know where the other half of me was. Translation—you were so fat before.

I saw one of my aunts: "You go off to California and come back a toothpick!"

We sat near Mrs. Charles during the ceremony and she had to tell me "Nicole, I was doing my shopping after the baseball game and Mr. Charles called me to say, 'I just saw Nicole and she looks great!' I go, 'Is that the only reason you called me?' He goes, 'Yeah. She looks great.' Can you believe that?" She chuckled and brushed my arm. My non-toothpick arm.

I saw her after the ceremony, and she said, "Nicole, you really look stunning. I was just looking at the back of you and really, you look like a model."

A model. Can you believe that?

She's such a sweet lady and it's nice, but...over-the-top.

I am no model. I am still Nicole.

Let me lose another 20 pounds or so, then we'll see.

The compliments are nice, but I know that they are only based on what I was and not what I am.

Aside from my weight, the graduation was nice. I can't believe my baby brother is done with high school and going to college. On top of that, it's his 18th birthday. All at once, it's too much to handle. I feel like a Mom. It seems as if I was just visiting him in the hospital when he was born. He went from baby blanket to cap and gown, in a matter of seconds.

Watching him there on the field, laughing with his friends, and probably not paying attention, I was suddenly hit with guilt. We had been so close, and then I went to California and I missed his whole senior year. Not that he probably noticed, he had other things to keep him busy, but I would have liked to have been there for his senior events, his prom, and all his baseball games. They were State Champions this year—I would have liked to see that. I was so proud of him.

I'm glad to be home for his graduation and his grad party next weekend, which he made sure to plan for when I was home, because he said he wanted me to be there.

I saw the infamous Mrs. Charles at Dan's game again and she asked me the big question: "How did you lose all that weight?"

No more questions, please! And hold the comments, too. Maybe she didn't get that memo. Guess not, because she continued, and told me that I looked a very "elegant" slim, which was actually a different comment for a change, and flattering. Though, slim is not what I would call myself.

My free week at the gym is over and now I fear I may put on a few pounds. Oh well. I'm surprised that I surrendered to that, but at least I am getting some good meals in. I probably need it. Besides, I can lose the weight I gain when I get back to L.A.

I tried on a pair of Kelly's jeans when she wasn't home—just to see how I measured up. They fit. A little loose actually. I checked the tag—a size 7. It's the first time I've ever fitted into anything of Kelly's. Ever. She's the skinny one, that's how it's always been. I went to the store and got a pair like them because I needed jeans since it's supposed to rain for the rest of the time I'm home.

Today was supposed to be Dan's graduation party, but Mom and Dad had to cancel because of rain. They actually called it off yesterday when they heard the forecast. I was devastated, not because I wanted a party, but because I wanted to be there for my brother. I guess he sort of felt the same way.

Dad talked to Dan yesterday and he was of course bummed that his party was cancelled, but more upset because he said now I won't be home for it when they do have it. He wanted me to be there. Now I feel worse, but it's better for him to have a nice day for it. We went out to dinner tonight instead, at my favourite restaurant which he got to pick, but he did so because he knew I liked it. I do have an amazing brother. I was surprised when I ordered the same thing I always do, yet could only eat about a quarter of it. I used to be able to demolish it.

I've been thinking about home versus L.A. a lot. I know what I need to do script-wise when I get back there. I can leave my stay in L.A. open-ended. If things are looking tough by the end of the year, I can always come home for good at Christmas. If things are going well, then I'll just visit. It is tough coming home and then having to go back to such a shitty place and missing my family so much. I guess maybe this is what growing up is.

My last couple days home were nice. Mom was working on Sunday, so Dad and I went out to breakfast. I ate. I was full.

We went to the store afterwards and saw my uncle, who told me…guess what? "You look great." I'm waiting for someone to tell me I look awful. I'm sure that will come.

We went home, did some chores, and Dad and I had ice cream cake and watched a movie. It was so nice to just hang out. Home. It's great. Kelly made dinner and surprise—it wasn't disgusting!

On Monday, Mom and I spent the afternoon in Mystic and went to all the little shops. Mom bought me a silver bracelet called, "The Mystic Wave," but I told her that I'd call it "The Montville Wave" to remind me of home, and I'd wear it every day. We went for a sundae at Mystic Drawbridge Ice Cream and yes, it was very good. I do have a sweet tooth.

Monday night, we went out to dinner. I forgot how much eating was a part of life. I also forgot that I was going back to LA soon. That's when I started to get sad again.

Hang In There... Wherever "There" Is

The night before I left, Mom made my favourite dinner, and I gave Dad his birthday present early. Part of it was a gift certificate to the best ice cream place nearby, Salem Valley Farms, so we decided to go there before Dan's game. It was the perfect way to end the trip home. Nothing beats ice cream with the family in the summer and then a little baseball.

When I got home I packed, so I could be ready to leave bright and early in the morning. I can't believe that it has been two weeks already. It went by so fast. Mr. Charles wished me well at the game and said he can't wait to see my name in lights, and he has a feeling it'll be soon. I hope so.

I'm still shocked I have to go back already. I will miss home so much. I'm not sure what's in store for me when I return to L.A.

Chapter 13
Renfrew:
The Gatorade Blues

I weighed 133.8 today, down .4 pounds. It's not like I am doing anything to change my weight. I eat all the meals. It's my body. I can't tell it what to do. I wish I could. I can't deny either that I'm happy that the numbers on the scales are going down.

I am still orthostatic. So much Gatorade. I do like it now. I don't even dump the second cup in the morning. I hated it when I came in, but now I get cravings for it. I've got to know the Gatorade system very well. Here, we can judge what type of day it will be by the colours of the Gatorade. If they give us red, it means it will be a good day. Yellow? Crappy day. And if we're lucky enough to get the occasional purple, well, something exciting will happen. When they are running low and it's yellow in the morning, at lunch and dinner, then it's all over.

The counsellor told me the other day: "you're going to put Gatorade out of business." She may be right. Most people are only orthostatic for a few days, but it has been two weeks for me. Which sucks, because after a week, you can be cleared for exercise—mind you, light exercise, like walking, or yoga. But—not if you're ortho. I should ask for extra Gatorade. Or just get an I.V. of it.

Aside from my dehydration, there are bigger issues to deal with here. They have found more bags of puke on the grounds, and someone puked right on the front steps of the building. That's a big FU to Renfrew. We go into the Community Meeting as usual, but surprise, it's all about puke. Who is puking? No one fesses up. It turns into people either trying to cover up or get the person to confess, so we all don't get in trouble. Purger, come forward! Some girls say they are mad, scared, triggered, and some offer support. Some don't feel safe here in a facility where we work to stop these symptoms, and people openly use them and want others to know. I think maybe they are suffering and need help, but can't ask for it. I know us girls are all familiar with that feeling. No conclusions are made and we leave, all eyes on one another. Who could it be? Let the gossip begin.

After the meeting, I meet with Ann, my psychiatrist, and good news—I am Level four! Finally! I can go out on pass now, for four hours at a time. Part of me is not sure if I want to go out on pass, if I am ready. Because a pass includes a meal and 'meal' means a restaurant, and that means a hell of a lot of anxiety. But at least if Mom and Dad come down, then I can go out. Apparently, Ann made the decision days ago, but no one told me. Nice. She tells me she also heard I have some anxiety at meals, and I tell her yes. Such as people watching me, or if I'm eating at the wrong pace, and today I realized that I didn't have to choose mayo to go on my sandwich but I did, and it pained me to put it on. So she is putting me on some medication to stop anxiety before it starts, which I will take before lunch and dinner. They sure are med happy here.

That might explain the crowds at the window during med-time. There are three different windows for each team—blue, purple and red. It figures that I am on the blue team and that is the longest line. As soon as the clock strikes 9, 12, 5 and 8, the building shakes as girls run to get their medication. Well, as much as it can for a stampede of eating disordered gals. I'm not sure if it's because no one wants to wait in line, or because those nurses are giving away good stuff. I hope I get some good stuff.

I was having weird twitches and circulation issues in my sleep last night, so I went to the nurse. My glucose level is fine, but she said that since my weight is dropping and I am still ortho, my body is probably hanging on to some fluids. My body doesn't trust me yet, and why should it? After all I've done to it. There's swelling in my ankles, which is an oedema, and she is going to tell the nutritionist that, so hopefully that medical reason for my weight loss will help move me up from Trays. Oh, and I should ask for more Gatorade during the day when I feel dehydrated. "Just come to the nurse's station," she tells me. After all, it is medicine, isn't it?

I talked to Dad for an hour. He was so excited about Level four. So was I.

I meet a sweet lady here named Gertrude. She is in her 60's and has anorexia, and boy is she a firecracker. We have bonded quite a bit. Though I swore when I came in that I would not start knitting, I never said anything about crocheting, so Gertrude is going to teach me to crochet. She is a master. She makes like an afghan a day, and they are beautiful. She is beautiful. I hope she does well here. She has so much to give—to others and herself.

I meet with Robin and the first thing she tells me is how proud both she and the treatment team are of me for fighting to be on I.E. (Independent Eating). They think my assertiveness is a really good thing, and she's not sure if that's something I've been trying to work on, but people have taken notice and think it's a great step for me and admire how I really fought my case. Wow, I was just pissed off because I was still on trays. Maybe this will get them in gear to move me up.

I read her my letter to myself as a child and she thought I got a lot out, and that obviously a lot of things still stick with me. She wants to do one about my 16-21 year old self now. Oh boy, that'll be interesting.

I realize that I am holding on to a lot of stuff still, but I don't know if by putting it on paper I am necessarily fully releasing it. It still sticks with me. Parts of it work. I told her about being tiny and that helped. I don't think that's the root issue though. I think there are layers that I need to peel back until I find the core of my problem. Maybe I just need to find something that will make me happy, instead of constantly focusing on what makes me unhappy.

I put in for two passes for the weekend. One is with fellow residents to go to Chestnut Hill, this cute area with restaurants and shops. It's a meal pass, so I have to get something to eat and the menu could be scary, which is why it will be good to go with other people. The Sunday one is a big deal for me. I used to be able to go to coffee shops and sit all day to work on scripts and I would get a sandwich and cookies and coffee and be fine. Once I got tangled in the eating disorder, that stopped. I'd walk by sandwich shops, look at menus, see stuff I liked, think of how good it would be, and then leave. Or I'd go into Starbucks, think of how nice a yummy latte would be, then think, no, I don't need the calories, and leave. I'd wonder why everyone else could get something but not me?

So my pass on Sunday is to try going out alone, maybe grab a drink at Starbucks, do some shopping, then go into a little coffee shop or café, grab a sandwich, and bring some writing to do or a book to read. It's a huge deal for me. I don't want to be afraid to do this any more. I'm tired of being afraid. I know that if I go out and try this on my own later, I won't do it. Since I'm here, I *have* to do it, and it's a meal pass so I have to get food (and it can't be just a salad, then I'll get into trouble). So I must, and then I won't feel guilty. It's safe here. Like a requirement, whereas if I'm on my own, I don't have to, but I also want to do it for me. It's a challenge, but better to challenge myself here than when I'm on my own. Practice. This is all just practice, all of it, for when I get home.

I meet with Molly, the stand-in nutritionist. I had a snack the night before and so my weight had gone up a little. We sit down.

"First of all," she says, "Your weight has maintained beautifully."

Huh? Didn't she just complain about it?

"It went up a little today," I tell her.

"Not by much."

"It had been going down though."

"I know that you really want to get up to I.E. but - "

"It's not just because I want to move off of trays and up a level. Tray Level is so easy for me now and I have a hard time making meal decisions. I.E. would be a struggle, so I want that challenge."

"I admire that, Nicole, but people have noticed that there's still some anxiety around the food. That you fixate on certain foods, like the mayonnaise, or which foods have more nutritional value."

"Of course I think about the food. I have an eating disorder," I tell her. "I'm sure I will do that for a while. I do worry about other people watching me or what they think of me eating, my pace and the foods."

"Try to be more comfortable. I'll have one of the counsellors watch you, and then maybe we can move you up to I.E. tomorrow."

So I left her and found a counsellor to talk to, Eric, the only male one.

Hang In There... Wherever "There" Is

"You seem to be doing well," he tells me. "I haven't noticed any food rituals. Molly did talk to me, so I'll get back to her after lunch and hopefully we can get you up to I.E. tomorrow."

We also had a chat about eating disorders and why he worked at Renfrew.

"I don't think you're crazy," he tells me.

I wasn't expecting that, but I laugh. "Thanks."

"I think it's like any addiction, and it's a hard thing to get out of."

I hadn't talked to him before, but it was nice to talk to a cool counsellor who wasn't hovering over me all the time and actually supported me.

Lunch went well and I had a note in my mailbox later that day: "You'll be on I.E. tomorrow!" Dad was so proud of me and excited about all the progress I have made. "That's really good for being there just two weeks, and it shows that you've made a lot of improvement," he told me. I even surprised myself.

First day on I.E. and I'm scared as hell. But just like my first day on Trays, Amy was there to help me. Basically, it is like a cafeteria line. Before you go in, you get a menu and check off what you want, but you have to meet your "exchanges" for the day—all your starches, proteins, fats, veg/fruit, etc. So I make my menu and she shows me how to choose. Decisions...not my thing. No more service, you have to get your own tray, plate and silverware, and then step in line. Most of the stuff is already dished out, except cereal and salads, so you have to do your own portions, which is part of learning how to eat again. They have measuring cups, which still bothers me. I know when I go home I won't measure food. It's seems like taking a step back.

Still, it is more freedom and all the girls were so helpful and nice. We eat upstairs in the living room because they are doing construction on the old dining room. It actually creates a more relaxed environment, so I feel more comfortable eating the meal. It's even nicer because a lot of the girls I started with on trays with are on I.E., so I don't feel so alone. We have a great time at meals now—no counsellors staring at us, no lids to take off. They check us off at the beginning and end, but that's it. I'm almost a normal person, a normal eater. Nah, scratch that last part.

I find it strange that I was held off I.E. when the girls up here are still thinner than me and have some food rituals. But we are all struggling through this, and it is just another step in recovery. We all take whatever we can to get us through a meal—messages of encouragement, knowing a visitor is coming, games like trivial pursuit or 20 questions. Whatever we can do so as not to focus on the meal. Part of it is good so that we learn to engage in mealtime conversations again, though in a way, I think it helps some people to avoid the food completely. I never like playing the games, because I am not quick enough to come up with an object or questions, and I actually need to focus on the food in order to finish. I'm also far from home, so have not had visitors yet to look forward too. I'm often quiet, but I know it'll change. I do come out of my shell.

They note often how anxious I am during meals, and I suppose that it's true. I want to make sure that I finish on time, but I am very nervous about eating in front of other people—worried about what they will think of me eating. If I eat too fast, they'll think I'm a pig. If I have something different than them, they'll think I picked a weird choice. I am not comfortable eating with other people, and afraid that I will never be. For this reason, I think I was kept on trays for so long, while everyone else moved up rather quickly, even though I finished all my meals. It was frustrating, because they were moving up and I was on trays with a lot of the newcomers. I tried to be encouraging to them, like others had been to me, but there seemed to be a shift in the community recently. People were leaving and new admissions came in, and they were not as receptive to treatment or encouragement. Whereas the people I met when I came in wanted recovery and were extremely helpful. It was a true community of support then, but something was changing.

I then had to go to a discharge meeting, and they give me my discharge date of February 2, 2007, and tell me that by January 26, I can only be orthostatic 3 times a week. I'm still orthostatic every day and have an oedema. That gives me 6 days to somehow un-ortho myself. The discharge date scares me. I only just moved to I.E., and want to be on "Fix Own" before I leave. "Will I be ready by then?" I ask her.

"You can always extend," she tells me. "Talk to your therapist."

I go to my room and call Dad and quietly mention the thought of extending my stay, perhaps by a week, and that I might talk to Robin about it. "I don't know how ready I will be to leave in two weeks, especially because I know that the last week here will be just anticipating leaving."

"That's fine, Nicole. You need to do whatever you think is best for you. While you're there, you might as well stay longer and get the help you need."

"Better to do that than leave and have to come back. I know I have a lot more issues to work on that I haven't delved deep enough into. I don't want to leave here not fully on track."

We talk about aftercare at the Renfrew in Connecticut, and it's kind of far from home so it would depend on transportation. Then Dad drops the doozy—getting my car back from L.A. to Connecticut. It is kind of devastating. He said maybe he'd get in touch with Sam and coordinate it so she could leave the keys in the car and he could get a truck to come and pick it up.

I get upset, not mad, just sad, thinking of that as another loss. L.A.

"Eventually, I have to ship all of my stuff, because it's her house and she needs it out of there."

"Don't worry about it now. You'll stress yourself. We can take care of things when you get home."

I am worried. Once I go and get all of my stuff and bring it home, it means that my belongings are no longer in L.A., so I am no longer in L.A. At least now, my things are there. Sam let me leave them there. So a part of me is in L.A. Once they're gone, I'm gone, and my dreams are gone. That phase of my life is over. I went out there to accomplish something, to really pursue screen-writing, and I didn't. I'm such a failure. What am I going to do now back home, stuck in Montville? I hate what I've done to my life. Why couldn't I have just stayed on track?

Dad tells me I can always go back to L.A., yet still, here's this little blip in the radar. I've disappointed myself, and everyone else, yet again. He also says I have a lot going for me if I do my writing at home. I hate the realization that L.A. might be over for me. I hate it so much. Now I'll be back home. Forever. Never date or be married. Never have kids. Or a real job. I look to the future and see nothing. I feel hopeless.

It is strange to feel this way on the inside and try to project something else on the outside. The girls at lunch think I am so funny, they told me today I was on a roll. One girl thinks I'm "the sweetest." No guy has ever thought that, except for the creepy ones I met in L.A. I do feel alone, which is why I bonded so well with my eating disorder. It filled that void in me, and as it's taken away, that void will be back. What will I fill it with?

The purging saga continues. It's like a soap opera. Vanessa, the girl who helped me out after the Ensure episode, was accused of purging. I knew she didn't. This is her third time here and she truly wants help now. She was accused in community and I raised my hand.

"Listen, I am not here for purging, but there was a time I did it and after a supplement one night, I felt so sick and wanted to use my symptoms. Vanessa was the one who talked me out of it. She got me through that. You can't judge people by what they did. We are all here to get help and some need it more than others. But don't point fingers at Vanessa just because you think it's an easy thing do."

Afterwards, she thanks me for speaking up for her. I say I meant it and I trust her, and I am thankful she was there that night. She is so frustrated with the accusations though, she's not sure she wants to stay.

Opposite of that feeling, I have been getting a lot of support. Kelly text messages me every morning to see how breakfast was, and then calls at night. What a change from when I first came home and she didn't want to acknowledge my problem. Now, she cares so much and it means a lot to me. She has got me through many things here and I am thankful for my big sister. I only heard from Dan once, and it was because he was driving with Dad. He told me he felt bad for not calling. I'm not sure if the realization that I was in an eating disorder treatment centre scared him. He wanted me to come here and get help, and was supportive when I first told him. I think it is hard on him, knowing I'm sick. I want to get better so we can go out for meals again.

Jason sends me text messages to check up on me, which are nice. After all, he was one of the first people I told, and I was surprised that a guy understood. He had told me before I left that he would keep me informed of all Yankees news and trades as long as I promised to get better. That's pretty decent for a Sox fan. He often sends text messages to see how I am. Of course, at first I told him it was tough. He responded: "I'm sure it's insanely hard but you will come out of it so much happier. No longer a slave to an illness and able to live your life. Stay strong!" He often sent encouraging messages like that, and though they were probably simple words to him, they meant so much to me, and truly helped me keep going.

I got a card from Charlotte Martin, my friend and fabulous singer-songwriter from L.A. She was the first person to really see me and noticed that a/I was tiny, as she said, and b/things were not okay with me. She was the first one I confided in, because I trust her and she had been through this herself.

It read:

Nicole,

Just a note to say I'm praying for you and you have my support. I pray God will make you whole on every level. He's got great big plans for you. I know it. You keep on keeping on. Light is following you through this process and you are not alone. Love you and look forward to seeing you again soon.

XOXO

Charlotte

I carry all that support with me as I leave for my pass. Unfortunately, no one else was going to Chestnut Hill, so what was to be my group pass turned into a party of one. Others seemed shocked, but it is not daunting to me. I am used to being alone.

I take a cab to Chestnut Hill—a cute little area with cobblestone walks, little shops and of course, those damn restaurants. I shop for a bit, get a few things, and stupidly try on a pair of jeans. A size 0, what I wear now, but they are too tight. I am devastated. I absolutely will not try on a size 2 because that means I am bigger and I am not ready for that.

I leave the damn store and go off in search of a restaurant, though I don't feel like eating after that situation. I find the "Chestnut Hill Grill," which was recommended to me. When I go in, the waitress tells me there is a wait, except there is a table in the corner that would seat one. I'll take it.

I had my journal with me, since I knew I'd be alone, so I write in my journal for a bit before I order. I don't get a salad. I get a turkey BLT on multi-grain toast with a side order of fruit (instead of fries). And a Diet Pepsi! So good. The Pepsi, that is. Can't have that at Renfrew. No Caffeine. You aren't even supposed to on a pass. Oops.

Hang In There... Wherever "There" Is

The dinner experience...is different. I am OK on my own. I write while I wait, and mostly don't care what people think of the girl who dines alone. Hey, I'm eating. Back off. The meal arrives and comes with mayo on the side, which I do not use. The fruit is really good and the sandwich is fine, but I get full fast. I pick out some of the bacon and then eat part of the sandwich. I mostly eat it all. I eat. I ate. Food. Alone. I can be trusted. I feel insanely full and guilty.

I hate that I was able to eat. That I could eat with no problem. It pains me. I didn't even panic that much. I knew I had to do it, so I did, but I ate a meal. It sickens me that I could eat. I want to have a tough time with it. Before, I would want food, but feel guilty about it, so I wouldn't get it. Now, I don't want food, but get it, then feel guilty about it. I feel guilt either way. It makes no sense. I make no sense.

I leave the restaurant, go to Borders, and get a couple things there. At least I get to do some walking. I call the cab and they are so busy, so they say call back in 20. I do, and they say call in 30. I call Renfrew to tell them I'll be late. When the cab arrives, he doesn't know where to go, and even though I do, we still get lost. I was late, but they were happy I called and relieved to have me back. I was glad to be back too.

Chapter 14
Back in the Habit
June 28, 2006

Back in Los Angeles—exactly a year ago since I arrived. Everyone said to give it a year here. It takes a while to get used to this city; to get used to the people, the driving, and the overall feel of L.A. Just to make friends. It's been a year and I can't say that I like it any better. I'm still trying.

I am sad to be away from my family again. It's as if that depression has come back. We always have fun hanging out, and I'm beating myself up now for taking that one-week gym pass and obsessing over my weight and food. I had two weeks to spend with my family, and I spent most of it at the gym and trying to avoid meals. What was I thinking?

I know I need more money now to stay here, so I apply for a bunch of jobs, mostly writing. I probably don't have a chance, but I'll keep applying.

I went to the gym to try and work off a little weight I knew I gained. I knew I did, because when I was sitting at the airport I could feel that my jeans were tighter.

The thing about the gym is that I hate when anyone talks to me. It is not social hour (or in my case, marathon hour), but rather, alone time. My time to be there and get the job done, and to know that what I was doing was right for me, what was needed. I was absorbed in my self-inflicted torture—it made me feel good. I got to block the world out. I did not want to be disturbed.

"You're looking pretty good," I hear next to me, as I beat myself up, climbing flight after flight on the Stairmaster. I lean forward to rest my arms on the bar a little because I would not stop my workout to talk to someone.

I turn my head. "What?"

"You're looking pretty good."

I didn't need to look down at myself to know what a mess I was. I had on tight gray sweatpants that were starting to get loose, and a purple cotton halter outlined in peach.

Sweaty. Sweaty and smelly.

My hair was sopping wet and bunched on top of my head, and my face was bright red. This all meant that this guy was crazy.

"I'm a mess," I tell him.

"Nah. I saw you here a few months back, and you were pretty chubby," he tells me.

I clench my fists around the bar.

"You're looking good now, girl. It's working."

What's working? Torturing myself? Feeling so sad that I don't even know how to function? Barely eating? Barely "being?"

I give him some form of a smile or cringe, then stop my machine and walk off.

Bastard.

How dare he say that: *Chubby*?

And to a stranger—at the gym!

I can't possibly look that much different. I guess "you look good" can be a compliment, but to hear that I was "chubby" before destroyed me.

I was fat. Everyone there had noticed. I was embarrassed and disgusted with myself and wasn't sure if I should grab my things and run home crying, or work off some more chubbiness. The only logical thing to do was avoid creepy dude and increase my workout. Then I made sure not to eat for the rest of the night.

I was once again on my best friend, the Stairmaster, at a different location in the gym, and was early into my workout. I was just getting into the routine when in the mirror in front of me, I could see creepy dude approaching. I put my head down, pretended I was completely absorbed in my workout, and hoped that he did not see me.

"Hey," I hear.

I ignore him.

He moved closer.

I could *feel* him next to me. I hated him being in my space.

"Hellooooo," he said and started waving in the mirror, trying to get my attention.

I finally turn my head to see the moron there, hoping I could quickly get rid of him.

"Remember me?" he said.

"Yup."

"Yup? Okay, well, I was just wondering…you got a boyfriend?"

"Yes," I reply, or rather, lie. I needed him away from me.

"That's too bad because I was gonna see if I could take you out one night on a date."

"He probably wouldn't like that."

"So you been together a while? No chance you'll be breaking up soon?"

"Probably not. But if we do, I'll be sure to look around for you."

"You do that," he said slyly, slithering off, and then yelling for all to hear, "You know where to find me." With that, he walked off, allowing me to breathe again.

I sure do know where to find you—harassing innocent gym-goers and commenting on their body fat. Asshole.

What made me even madder was that now he was asking me out on a date. This guy knew nothing about me, but suddenly he noticed that I lost some weight, so I was good enough to be seen in public with him. Before, I was a little too chubby to be considered datable. At each point, he didn't now what I was really like, though apparently, he had been watching me. Stalker. It just proved to me yet again that everything is based on looks, and even more so, weight. I was finally the right weight to be asked on a date and turned it down. I don't want to be judged by my weight no matter what it is.

I hated that experience, and avoided that man every time at the gym. We never spoke again. I also changed my workout clothes to a t-shirt and loose sweatpants.

I did weigh in at 136.5, which is pretty unbelievable for a girl who used to weigh 200 pounds. My goal had been 135, but I'm gonna see where this takes me. My new goal weight is 125, but as I keep track on paper, I do it in increments of 5 pound goals. But to get under that 130 mark would be incredible!

I start going to these pro-eating disorder websites where they give tips on how to lose weight, what exercises to do, foods to eat, and even have competitions. I'm sort of addicted to them because they are so helpful and all the girls and boys on them are so nice. They are like friends, people I can turn to for tips, advice, and understand when I feel desperate and lonely. They congratulate me when I lose weight and encourage me when I am trying to. I know it's an "eating disorder" site, and I am merely on a weight-loss programme, but it is still helpful. I do feel bad for the people on there. They seem tortured, yet embrace their disease at the same time.

I went out to the movies and dinner with Sam and Brian, who had been in my summer screen-writing course. Sam asked me if I lost weight and said I looked thinner. I just told her I had been working out. Later, when I was cold, she told me she wasn't but she had body fat—not that I had to worry about that. Yeah right.

I had another emotional meltdown on the day of Dan's graduation party. I was sad I couldn't go, and to know everyone was over at the house, family and friends, and I was on my couch being sad in L.A., just kind of tore at me. I called home, so I could somewhat be a part of it, and Kelly answered. She was grumpy. It was 10 p.m. their time, and she wanted to go to bed, but there were still stragglers. She said it was good. As a funny surprise for Dan, she and I had ordered a cake with a goofy picture of him on it from when he was 5. He was dancing and looked like a geek. But he's a good sport and laughed at it with everyone else.

I talked to Mom and Dad the next day and they said how I was missed, which of course only made me feel worse. I missed being there too.

I'm still applying for jobs, and though I haven't found anything permanent, I am writing biographies for some singers. Also, I'm doing an interview with my musician friend Charlotte Martin. I went to her house and we hung out, did the interview and chatted. Her new album is amazing, and it was good to see a familiar face.

She asks how L.A. is and I tell her I am kind of lonely.

"After 2 years, you'll want to stay," she says. "The first year, year and a half, I had those moments of thinking that I should just go home. Then I'd say, 'I'll just give it 3 more months.' Then those moments were shorter and of course I stayed and now I can't imagine myself being anywhere else."

She's from Illinois, and also in the creative field, so I know she understands.

"You've just gotta give it time," she continues. "You'll be okay. It's really tough to meet people, especially when you're freelance and immersed in your work, because I was the same way."

I guess I do need to give it time. She's right. And everything has worked out well for her. I shouldn't give up so easily because I think that I'm trying to find reasons to give up. I know that I'm just in a rut and a little bout of depression and missing my family and out of work and all that. I have to keep that positive attitude and realize that everything will be OK. I will keep plugging away at the screen-writing, because I do enjoy it. But if that's not what is meant to be for me then I know I can always go back home.

I'm still keeping in touch with Jason via email, with much banter about Yankees/Red Sox, but he suggested Sports writing, which is a great idea. I made some contacts and lucky me, got an interview with Moose Skowron, one of the Yankees great old-timers. I'm not sure who was more excited, my Dad or me.

***

New weight...134! Even more exciting is that I went to Express to try on dress pants for an interview. I tried on a 6. Too big. 4—a little roomy. I now wear a size 2! I had a perma-smile in the dressing room. I used to be a 14, and those were tight on me. I never thought this would happen to me, all this weight loss. It's crazy and wonderful all at once.

My friend Kristy, from high school, is living in Redondo Beach. We chatted on the phone about getting together, but then I changed my mind. I email her and tell her I was kind of in a rut. She replies that it's not good to be alone if I'm feeling that way and to come spend the weekend at her place—to get out of my apartment, out of Hollywood, and just be in a new environment. So off I went.

I park my car and she comes out to meet me. She yells, "You're so tiny!" She comments a few times on my weight, how I must be a size 2, and I probably weigh less than her. She's only 5'4.

Aside from that, it was nice to get out of the hellhole that is Hollywood and hang out. We went out to dinner, watched a movie, and the next day went to the shops around Redondo and then up to Venice Beach where I got a really cool jazz painting. Then we went for a pizza and it was back home for me.

I didn't want to go back to my apartment. I have been really, really depressed. There's the shitty apartment (some scary guy followed me the other day, some homeless people have set up camp by the front door, and two people were like trying to kill each other one day), I just want out of here. Plus, now that class is over and me not having a steady job, I feel like I have no real purpose here. No friends, family or life. I really am miserable.

I wish that I hadn't extended my sublet. It seemed easier at the time, and I was doing the owner a favour. Now I just want out. I've been a constant ball of worry and anxiety lately. The only exciting thing is that I have lost some weight, but I hate myself. I have no direction. I feel so lost. And this job thing is really weighing on me.

I talked to Dad about it and he said, "It's not for lack of trying." He told me again how I'm at a good point in my life right now where I'm young and can do this.

I'm so unhappy here. It would be nice if things could come together and I could find a job I like, an apartment I like and could afford…or if someone bought my script. Ah, wishful thinking. I do a lot of that.

I really should just give up, but I know I have to stick with it. Something's got to come along soon—that's what Mom and Dad keep telling me.

The only good thing going down in my life is my weight. 132 pounds. I saw Kristy again and she thinks I am too skinny. She told me if I lose any more weight she will be mad. Oh boy. It's only because I'm taller. Back when I was 153, the nurse thought I weighed 125, so I look like I weigh less than I do. She asked me how much I weighed, which I would not tell her, only that I had a little more to lose. She got mad. Oh well. 125 is the goal. 7 more pounds.

Chapter 15
Renfrew:
All I Have Lost

Residents come and go, change, and it is hard to get to know people but you want to. Them, and their eating disorder, because that's their real story, just like it is mine. People will not know the real me if they do not know me with my eating disorder. Unfortunately, that is who I am right now, and that is a lot of my past, and I'm afraid, for a while, it will be my future. Even as recovery calls, it will be from an eating disorder, and I hope I will be able to find other supportive people I can share my story with...my life with.

These girls here understand me, and I have never felt connected with people like I do with them. Perhaps because we are all suffering the same, but I can talk them, be open with them, and it's a relief. I had a good talk with Melissa and will be so bummed when she leaves. We have really connected, even though we have different eating issues, and I hope we stay in touch. We are going on pass together this week.

I am coming out of my shell. The nurses and counsellors think I am funny for some reason, and this girl Jane thinks I'm just a riot. Who would have known? Gertrude is still teaching me to crochet. The women here are 13-60's and I can hang with all of them. It's a nice thing.

I had a talk with Kelly about trying on the jeans and how upset I was about the size 0 not fitting. I knew I couldn't talk about it with the girls here, and if I told a counsellor, they would tell my therapist, and that would be such an issue.

"Well, that's not a normal size anyway," she tells me. "And especially not the 00 you were wearing." I love my 00 jeans.

"I wear an 8," she went on. But she looks good. I have chub now. "Your legs look weird, Nicole."

Weird? They are thin and toned. She just doesn't understand a *pure* body.

I start crying and just ramble: "Well you have a fiancé."

"You want to take him for a bit?" she says with a laugh. I know she was trying to cheer me up.

"No, that's weird. I'm never going to find anyone."

"Not looking unhealthy, you won't. And being afraid to go out to dinner. We'll go out to some bars when you get back."

"I don't want to meet someone in a bar. I'm hopeless."

I hate the ups and downs. One moment I feel okay, and the next I'm filled with dread about my future, or lack thereof.

I go meet with Ann and tell her how I had been writing and got a spark of creativity back, which had been lacking for so long.

"Nutrition can play a vital role in that," she informs me. "When you're malnourished, your brain shuts down a little and only provides for

85

what is needed most—your heart and vital organs. Creativity is not needed."

So I have to think—which is better, to be a little thinner with constant anxiety and thoughts of food and calories and no desire for a life? Or a zest for life and a creative side that will inspire me, but require a few extra pounds?

"If writing is your passion, that is what you need to pursue."

It is really eye-opening. She is so good to talk to and says the guilt with the food will pass and to keep looking at it as something my body needs.

I go out on pass with Melissa and her roommate Gwen and dine at the magnificent Chestnut Hill Grill, where I ate before. I had a peek at the menu before I left, because they keep them at the Nurse's Station, so I was all set. I get a mixed green salad with salmon, which is great. I never had salmon until I got to Renfrew. It's introducing me to all sorts of new foods. Since I get a salad, I decide I should get dessert. I do have such a sweet tooth. Even in the depths of my disorder, I couldn't resist sweets.

I get bread pudding with chocolate and bananas and vanilla ice cream. It was good, and I made Melissa and Gwen have a bite so I didn't feel so guilty. It was nice to go out with other people and have a "normal" meal. We had fun and I wasn't totally freaked out this time. I like my decision to use one pass with friends and one alone. It's a nice balance. I still need some "me" time.

After a good session with Robin, where I decide to extend not one but two weeks (because I know I need it), I call Dad.

It's a nice, positive conversation about therapy and the extension, which he thinks is good. I tell him how I think I'm getting my personality back, whereas before I was a zombie, and it's nice to be able to interact with people again.

"Everybody always asks how you're doing, and not just to ask, but because they really care. People think you're great, and I wish that you'd realize that. I don't know why you can't see it," he says.

"Sometimes I don't know if it's me just doing it to do it or if I really want to be personable."

"I don't know, but I always thought you were engaging and everyone I know always likes talking to you."

"I do notice a difference; whereas before I felt like a zombie, now I definitely feel more revived." Part of me wants to spill out how I hate the fact that everyone who thinks I'm "great" are older or girls, and I've never had a boyfriend. But I can't do that.

I tell him how I never thought I had a strong relationship with Kelly when we were young and always felt in her shadow.

"Maybe that was just the way you saw it."

"No, she literally would ignore me in school," I say, half laughing, half crying.

I guess mine and Kelly's relationship is different, since we are getting closer now, but it took a while. When she went to college, I would send her things and visit, but when I went to college, she never came to see me. Now that Dan is in college, she sends him care packages all the time.

"And she was just really weird when I first came home from L.A."

"I don't think she realized how serious the eating disorder was."

"I guess not. But since she brought me down here, she has stayed in touch every day, and that's meant a lot to me."

"I think that made her understand how severe it was."

I start crying more.

"It was hard when we were younger because she was always the skinny one."

"I wish you had said something. There wasn't anything I wouldn't have done for you. You know that. It hurts me to know you were hurting."

I tell him, "I didn't want to hurt you. It was my own fault for not saying anything. I kept everything inside. That's what I've always done and it literally ate away at me."

"Even though it would have hurt me to know how upset you were, I wish I knew because you were my little buddy. There was never a time I wouldn't run errands and you'd be by my side."

We both laughed at that. I was always tagging along with my Dad, and still do. He's not just my Dad, he's my friend, and I don't know where I would be without him. And I'd do anything for him too, and one of those things is to recover.

***

I lost weight with my eating disorder, but I never realized how much else I lost because of it. In one of the groups, we talked about the things you lose with an eating disorder—energy, friends, health, relationships, a "life," and most of all, your sense of self. The therapist told us to write a letter of apology for our losses. I had a lot.
Dear Nicole,

I am so sorry for your losses. First, to lose the ability to eat seems so tragic, but that it could not be solved by simply saying "Just eat something" is devastating. And then there are all of those things this lack of eating, this "eating disorder," did to you. You lost so much because of it.

First, was your energy. You grew tired, but never too tired to go to the gym. Then you lost your focus, your concentration. It became harder for you to work, write and pursue other job opportunities. You lost all sense of the world around you and where you belonged in it. You saw the

87

gym, you saw the apple, and the many tears that would follow at the end of the day.

You lost trust—from family and friends. Friends that you once knew so well, you felt so far from. And while you now tell your family you are working to get better, they don't completely believe you truly mean it. How could they? You can't even trust yourself because of the eating disorder.

You have lost the parts of you that you used to like. And though you have lost your focus, energy and communication with others, it is even sadder that you have lost your desire to have them back.

More importantly, you've lost that bright smile and radiant laugh that people used to tell you you had. You lost it to an eating disorder, and for that, I am sorry.

I want it back.

Love,

Nicole, the fighter

Yes, I have lost a lot besides weight, but as I see what I wrote and think about it, I realize that maybe these things are not lost. Maybe I am not lost. These things have just been frozen, like I have. Frozen in the midst of an eating disorder, waiting, like me, to be brought back to life. I have been in a frozen state for so long, will I know how to get out? Can I defrost myself?

Chapter 16
Summer of '06:
Desperate Times

My grandfather, Popie, had a stroke. They caught it early, so that was good, but there are after-effects and I'm so worried. It's hard on everyone back home and I feel terrible not being there. It's times like this when I feel that I should be home. Not that I could do anything, but if only to be there for my family, for support. I feel stupid and selfish for being here. It's his birthday soon—75—and I have to miss that too. I'm missing out on so much.

I have the gym. When I can't deal with the stress or sadness, I go to the gym. I am doing 4 hours a day now and that takes up a chunk of my day, of my loneliness. There is a Farmer's Market on the way there, and I've found that all I eat is fruit now. A plum in the morning, an apple after my workout, and then some strawberries or a peach for dinner. It makes me feel better. This is what my life has become—the gym and fruit. And the occasional yoga video when I am bored at night.

I was at the gym the other day doing the crunch machine where you put weights on it. This lady comes up to me and goes, "I gotta see that again."

"Why?" I asked.

"I've never seen a girl do 50 pounds."

I didn't even know what was on there. It was weird because I felt I was putting on a show and I had to work harder. I was so exhausted.

I've been getting sick of going to the gym lately, but I force myself. I have to go every day. There's no choice. I must go. There other day I woke up and I just ached and was sad about everything and didn't want to go, but I did. I started that mile walk to the gym, and suddenly, tears burst through my eyes. I cried the whole way there, and couldn't stop. I got to the gym, went on a machine in the corner and cried, cried and cried. I settled a bit after all my cardiovascular, and then did this arm machine, but I was so tired and moving so slow. This trainer came up and yells, "Come on, faster, faster!"

Can't you see I'm tired and have been here for three hours already?

"I'm gonna stay here until you work harder!" he says.

So I push myself. I hate being watched. I hold the tears in. He waits until I'm working hard enough and walks off, so I slow down again. Minutes later, he catches me slacking off and yells again and tries to tell me about the machine.

Leave me alone and let me suffer through my workout the way I want to!

I can't do this any more. It's torture.

I talked to Meme and she wanted to thank me for the card I sent her that told her I was thinking of her and hoping Popie was doing well. I didn't know what else to do, but she said she appreciated it. She said things were okay and he was on the rehab floor. She asked if I still went to the gym every day and I said "yes."

"Don't lose too much weight, or I won't recognize you," she said.

I told her I wouldn't. I didn't tell her that I barely recognized myself any more.

I think I have hit a weight loss plateau. I am at 131, so I need to do something to lose more.

My apartment sublet is up on September 1st, and I don't know what to do. I have been looking at apartments, but they are all so expensive and unfurnished. Also, it is a one-year lease and I don't know if I want to stay out here that long. I've been doing some freelance work, but no permanent job, and I haven't done anything with my scripts. I hate feeling so worried, anxious and depressed. I really am a mess. I'm crying all the time, just randomly on the street. It's awful and I have no one to talk to. I go to the gym, eat my fruit, and lie on the couch and cry. What is wrong with me? I'm broke, depressed, afraid to eat real meals, lonely, sad and miss my family so much, but I want to do well for them. I want to make them proud.

Everyone keeps telling me they can't wait to see my name in the movies, or they know something is gonna work out for me. But is it? I wish it would. I know it takes time and it won't happen overnight. I need to tough it out. I am tough. It's only time. I can always go home when it gets really bad.

I had a nervous breakdown on the phone with Dad. Crying and everything, which I'm sure he loved. I finally let it all come out that I was worried about not finding a place, about this potential job I might have at a museum, even though they aren't getting back to me with the details, and just not liking L.A.

"Why don't you come home?" he asked. "You can always go back."

"But I have my script submitted in this contest and it's easier to stay here now. It would be a pain to sell my car and ship everything home and move back in a few months if I win the fellowship. Plus, I came out here for a reason and I don't want to give up just yet on the screen-writing. I'm not happy here though."

"If you're that unhappy, come home."

"I think it's just a rough patch with everything going on. I've been so worried about everything, I can't even sleep."

"Don't get stressed, it's the worse thing you can do for your health."

Oh Dad, you have no idea. My health probably has all sorts of issues right now.

"Even the articles I'm writing are coming out bad, and my editors are asking for rewrites. Big rewrites. That never happens."

"Probably because you're stressed and you can't concentrate. Stop crying, you're gonna force me to drive out there in a minute."

We both laughed.

"You know you can always talk to me, right?" he said.

"Yeah," I said through tears. I'm so glad I did. I've been so worried about things and try to bring it up, but I know things have been tough for him too with Popie in the hospital and him running the business for him. I miss my family and it would be such a relief to go home, but I can't throw in the towel yet.

I told my Dad about Sam, from screen-writing class. That she is a nice lady who has a daughter around my age, and a while ago, she offered to let me live at her house. Maybe it would be a good idea to get in touch with her and see if we could set up a temporary thing while I figure things out. While I get back on my feet and decide what I want to do out here.

I emailed her and she was amazing.

"You don't need to pay rent," she said, but I told her I would.

"You are welcome to stay here, I'll just fix up the room a little. It will be good because I just got a new job where I'll be away most of the day and have some travelling, so will need someone at home to take care of the pets." That sounded fair.

"Why don't you come by this weekend and see how you like it? You seem kind of depressed anyway. It'll be good to hang out."

The plans were made and I was a bit relieved, though it wasn't part of my L.A. dream. She lives in West L.A., so I'll be further from things, but I do know that the gym is right around the corner from her house. If she's gone a lot, she won't make me eat with her.

I talked to Dad and explained the situation. Sometimes, you do what you've got to do. This is just a little stumbling block I've got to get over. I've been a little down lately and I think that Mom and Dad will feel better to know that I'm staying with someone. Dad seemed to like the idea. I know they've been worried too. It probably won't be too bad. I am very grateful and appreciate her offer. It is so kind of her. I don't deserve it and I hope it works out, that I make it over this little hump okay. I don't want Mom and Dad to worry and I hate being this worried. I wish things weren't so hard, but I know they are never easy.

I went to Sam's for the weekend. She showed me the room, which is cute, and I will have a bathroom right across the hall. The area is nice, and right near Santa Monica and the beach. On Saturday, we went to Santa Monica, to the Promenade, and split a sandwich at Starbucks before catching a movie. On Sunday, we went to one of her relative's houses for an Ice Cream Social. And this wasn't any "make your own sundae" party, this was extreme. She told me to pace myself, but I had no idea. This woman makes homemade ice cream and there were 14 different flavours. I totally binged, which was nice though, since I hadn't really eaten anything in a week. I went to town. There were flavors like Apple Crisp, Lemon, Butter Pecan, and of course chocolate. So we try all of them, then go up again, try some more, then go up again and get the ones we really liked. I was so full, but I guess it was good for me to get some calories into my body, though I don't think it knew how to handle all the sugar and food. It did a number on me.

I have been trying to eat a little these past couple days though, for a couple of reasons. 1/I haven't been eating much lately. My caloric intake is pretty low and I am still working out a lot, but I barely have the energy to do that. So I've been worried about my health a little. 2/My body is getting a little screwed up. I'm down to 130 lbs. Which is okay, but I'd like to get to 125. My weight loss has slowed down which I read is due to my body being in starvation mode. Starvation mode? I read that if I eat more for a couple of days, it will kick start my metabolism again, and then if I cut down, I can lose more weight; we'll see. I haven't had a real meal in so long.

Sam said to me, "I hadn't really pegged you for a non-eater."

"What does that mean?" I asked. Do I look big? Whatever. I've worked hard to get where I'm at.

She made a couple of other comments. One was in reference to some lady she knows and how she stays thin because, "she's like you, she takes one bite and she's full. She's not hungry any more."

So I think I'll be able to get by without eating much at her house, since she's already noticed my eating habits and that I'm picky.

The other comment was how she hadn't really seen me eat. She goes, "Well, I don't think you'll starve to death."

Which sort of struck me, and I didn't answer.

She paused, looked at me, and then said, "Right?"

"I hope not," I said. To tell you the truth, I had been a little bit worried about my health lately, but I was so depressed and with the medicine I'm on, the main side effect is loss of appetite. Also, I'm pretty on track with the gym. So it is what it is. I know that I need to be aware and healthy about it. I'm by no means too skinny. Still totally normal and have fat, but going without a real meal is not good. Fruit is good for you, crackers okay, but you need substance and meat. I know that I need to take better care of myself. Maybe now that I'm moving, I will hopefully get out of my rut and back on track.

I went back to my apartment and had an email from Jason, who had just visited home in Connecticut. He loved it. I told him I didn't know how he's been able to stay out here so long. I'm ready to pack up.

He emailed back: "Oh no…hang in there…you're doing great."

If he only knew. I didn't feel great.

Hang In There... Wherever "There" Is

I tried to make myself a frozen dinner, but picked out some broccoli and chicken and left the pasta and sauce. I went and changed into a tank top and shorts and started crying. Everything ached. As I put on my top, I could feel my ribs and my stomach sunk in. I went into the bathroom and looked at myself. It wasn't me.

My face was so much smaller and pointy. Through the tears, I could see what I hadn't before. I looked at my arms and how tiny they were. Bones stuck through where they shouldn't. I could see them in my chest, and for a moment, I was proud. No more fat, just beautiful bones. My collar bones, my toned shoulders, and my sunken chest. I hadn't accomplished much out here, but I lost weight, and my bones were proof of that. Bones were beautiful, they were the core of the body. They were pure. I wanted to be pure.

I wanted to be tiny. I wanted to be a little girl. I wrapped my arms around me and rocked and cried more. "I just want to be a little girl again," I said out loud. "I want to be little. The little girl I never was." Suddenly, the bones scared me. I realized that the changes in my body were not normal. My habits were not normal, but I could not stop them. "I want to go home," I cried. "I need help."

Chapter 17
Renfrew:
The Bond of Family

Melissa has left. My first friend here is gone, and it wasn't even on her terms. Her insurance cut out on her because they said she was a normal weight. The therapists argued that she was bulimic and at first got her a couple of extra days, but then she had to leave. It's not fair the way insurance treats mental illness. If she had a physical ailment, they wouldn't kick her out of the hospital.

It was sad to see her go, but we are going to keep in touch, and I know she will do well. She is so positive and made such an impact here. I am so glad I met her.

We go into the Community Meeting this morning and there is a big surprise for us, and not a good one. They announce that there will be room searches. They do these periodically for the safety of the community. Counsellors come in and get room mates sporadically to search their rooms together. They get Erica and I, and we basically stand there as they go through all of our stuff. Erica had gum, which is a big no-no. Then they pull out my suitcase and search the pockets. To my surprise, I had a little packet of almonds and some mints. Double no-no. They confiscated them. All I can think is that I had them in there on the way down to Renfrew, and never took them out. But when I got here, they searched my bags so it should have been their job to remove them then.

Nervous, Erica and I went back to the meeting. Then I was pissed off, super anxious, and went out for a cigarette. Next, I went to a group about being in your 20's and everyone said they feel like a failure in their 20's which made me feel even worse. Then I try and get medication to calm me down but they haven't changed the write-up yet so I start crying. All these emotions I didn't feel with my eating disorder because I was numb are now coming back. Maybe it's better to be numb and not feel.

Then it's off to therapy and hopefully some relief. Nope, not quite. I tell her about the room search and she goes, "You didn't hear? You got dropped to a level 3, but only for 3 days."

I burst into tears.

The level would not have bothered me normally, but Dad had called this morning to tell me they could come down this weekend for a visit and we'd go out on pass. They would stay the night and we would go to the Multi-Family Group together the next day. Now they can't because I'm on level 3.

I cried and cried and cried because there is no exception to the rule and I wanted to see them so badly.

Robin told me she would look into a lunch pass for Sunday and will let me know, but I doubt it. I'm so upset and hate myself for the stupid almonds and mints. I will never eat them again.

Hang In There... Wherever "There" Is

I leave therapy and call Dad, hysterically crying. I feel like I've let them down. I tell him the situation and he's mad. He thinks it's ridiculous and unfair. He's at work, but tells me to call Mom and maybe she can call Robin to see if a change can be made.

I call Mom, still in tears. She tells me not to worry and that it will all be sorted out. She calls Robin, who explains what she is trying to do with another pass, but Mom tells her that she thinks there is a break in trust. Robin says that isn't it at all. It is a procedure that had to be done. Mom tells her how I had been having a difficult past couple of days and was really looking forward to seeing them. Robin will let me know the verdict soon.

I am so devastated. It's my fault and I've lost respect for this place, not to mention now I have a negative perspective on recovery. Amazing how fast things change. I was so excited this morning when Dad called, and now I'm pissed off. The girls here are so sweet and supportive. They know I'm upset and keep checking to make sure I'm okay.

My pass was not approved. I cried on the spot. My gosh, all this crying, I'm not used to it. I was so numb during my eating disorder that I had no emotions. Now, I have every emotion in overload. I tell Robin it's not fair and is interfering with treatment. She says they can come down and visit for 2 hours, which is ridiculous seeing as it's a 6-hour drive.

I call Dad, still upset, and he's mad. He tells me he'll come and get me right now if I want. "How is this supposed to help with your recovery if they won't even let you see your family? It sounds like a lock-up place."

Being the wonderful parents they are, he made the offer to come down for visiting hours, but I said no. It's too far for such a short visit. He was still upset and I was still crying, but there was really nothing we could do but move on. He said maybe February 10 they could come, but my new discharge date is the 16th, so I'll be home soon. He said we'd talk about it. I told Robin I didn't know if I wanted to stay now. I was pretty feisty. She knows I have trust issues, and I really had built up a sense of trust with her, and that's hard for me. I feel as if it has been broken. How can I be comfortable with her or the staff now?

I went to an exercise consultation after our chat. I know I over-exercised, and I tell the woman how much, and she tells me it's dangerous to my health. Well, hey, I'm here! It is still frustrating because I have not been able to exercise yet since I am still orthostatic. Maybe I am having too much Gatorade. It is also hard because some girls are now allowed to go out to a gym, supervised, since they have been here a long, long time. When I hear them talk about it, it is triggering the fact that I miss the gym.

I get back to my room and I have a text message from Dad. It read: "I love you and we'll get together soon." It was sweet and yes, more tears.

Mom called and I was a sobbing fool. We briefly went over the big event, as it now was, and how she spoke with Robin, the trust issues, and how Mom didn't want this to set me back in my recovery. I didn't either. Mom said they could come for visiting hours, but I tell her all they do is play around here, it's not worth it. She mentions February 10th again, and I tell her we'll talk about it.

Then the waterworks. I can't believe a person can contain this many tears. I tell her I ruined everything. She tells me I didn't.

"I did. I always do."

"I wish I knew how you felt before or that you told me that you were unhappy when you were younger."

I said, "I did, or I tried, or I thought maybe it was obvious."

"I'm sorry. I wish I had known."

"It's not your fault. I kept everything in. Still do. And this is what it's done to me."

It was time for lunch so I had to go, but I didn't feel like eating lunch. I'm using that as a coping mechanism again.

"Just take it one step at a time. Go eat your lunch. It'll be okay."

I went and I ate. I rushed. I was not hungry. I was pissed off. Then we have Meal Support Therapy and I did an update and everyone was like, "I can understand why you're upset, but how can you work through this? What can we do to support you?"

Nothing. It's lame. I told them, "You can keep saying all this stuff about support, but right now, that means nothing to me. That doesn't do anything. Seeing my family would have been the best support for me right now."

I go to the Multi-Family Group at night, which I usually dread, but this one is different. It's a group where parents and families come, and the residents and families ask questions about the eating disorder and the residents answer. It's to give them a better idea of what is going on with the illness and open their eyes a little. We learn a lot from their side too.

Tonight, there was a couple who had just found out that their daughter had an eating disorder for the last ten years. She was 26 and lived out of state. They were about to fly out to see her, and were not sure how to deal with things. So, for the first time at a meeting, I raise my hand.

I tell them, "I was 23 and lived across the country from my parents. I called them up and told them I had an eating disorder, and after a month, decided to go home. My Mom told my Dad not to look too shocked when he picked me up at the airport, and though he was, he didn't show it. I think it's important to treat your daughter as she always was—treat her as your daughter, not an eating disorder. My parents were, and still are, amazingly supportive. So that's all I can offer; show that support to your child."

I get a lot of nods from parents in the crowd. I can't believe that I had finally spoken. Three weeks here must have given me some sort of wisdom, or maybe it was with me all along, just hiding behind the eating disorder.

I sat next to two women and after the meeting was over, and had a chat with them. Both of them feared their daughters were have eating disorders, so were asking me for advice. Me, of all people. One woman was afraid of her daughter's isolation and that when she goes to college she'll get worse—since she has recently lost a lot of weight. I told her I was on my own, but completely isolated. I was "taking care" of myself, and it wasn't good care. She'll have a room mate, friends, teachers, and classmates—people around to notice and care. She'll be okay. This woman started crying and I realized then the pain parents feel for their children, or perhaps not pain, but love.

The other woman consoles her and says that she worries about her daughter as she herself has had issues with eating. She checks in with her daughter and keeps an eye on her, and just hopes things will be OK. And if not, she will get help.

They are very interested in my story—how it happened, when I knew I had an eating disorder, how I sought help and what role my parents played. I surprised myself at being so open, honest and relaxed about it. I do think I have grown from this, and though I am still scared, I have gained some insight into my disease and am willing to help others. I want to help others. I don't want anyone to go through the hell that I went through. I tell them how supportive my parents have been and the women say how proud they must be to have me as a daughter. It was quite sweet.

We talk for about thirty minutes. I tell them that it's good that they already know what signs to look for, that it's hard when you're in it to admit it to yourself and recognize it—that sometimes, it takes something serious to wake you up. But then you realize how many more important things there are in life than an eating disorder. I explain that I didn't want it to happen, it just started out as a diet and exercise programme, but then it takes a hold of you. They understood that. I spend a lot of time reassuring them about their daughters, and say that they're doing a good job looking out for them and being concerned. It was a very different experience for me speaking with them. Uplifting. It put a positive spin on my otherwise crappy day. They were so sweet and kind and caring. They were parents, and concerned ones at that. They were at this meeting because they wanted to know more about eating disorders so they could protect their children. The bond between parents and children is great, and I learned that in many ways today.

Chapter 18
September Falls

"Hang in there." That's all everyone is saying to me lately. "Hang in there."

Jason sent me another email and said, "Hang in there."

Aunt Jeanette knew I was having a tough time and she said, "Hang in there." "Where is there?" I want to ask. I'm tired of hanging around. I want to get somewhere.

I went to Express today to get new jeans because mine are falling off me. A nice guy that worked there helped me. I tried on a four and stepped out.

"Are these too loose?" I asked.

"Definitely, what size are they?" he asked.

"Four."

"I'll get you a two."

I went back into the dressing room grinning like an idiot. A two. They'd better fit or I'll be embarrassed.

He came back and hung them over the door. I pulled them up and buttoned them with no problem. Again, I stepped out.

"Better?"

Now he and a girl who worked there were examining me.

"Still looks too loose. Honey, I think you need a zero. Let me grab that for you."

I went back into the fitting room and almost couldn't breathe. Zero. Not possible. He hung them over the door and I was afraid to try them on. If they didn't fit, then not only would I have failed myself, but him also.

I slid one leg on at a time and so far, so good. As I pulled them across my waist to button them, the sensation was magical. I zipped them and looked at myself in the mirror. No flab hanging over. A perfect fit. I was a size zero. The purest of sizes.

I bought two pairs and began the walk back to my apartment, still smiling to myself. A size zero, I couldn't believe it. I practically don't exist. Sometimes, I actually feel that way. From a 14 to 0. Just incredible. I'm as small as you can go. Who would have ever thought that Nicole Roberge would be a size zero? I'll admit, it's been exhausting to go to the gym every day and to constantly think about food and weight. It's August, and I'm worried about when I go home for the holidays and what I will do about the gym and how much weight I could gain. It's scary. Especially because I've come so far. All the way down to zero.

I'm still depressed, and I go from happy to confused with the changes in my body. Sometimes it's as if an alien has taken over. Perhaps living with Sam will be a really good thing.

I'm also kind of down because Dan is leaving for college in a couple weeks. My baby brother, I can't believe it. I feel guilty because I won't be there to help move him in, when he helped me all those years, when he was just a little guy. It's hard. I really feel bad about missing out on all of this. I sent him a card so that he'll get it in his mailbox when he moves in. With lots of girlie stickers and stuff, just to irk him. That's always fun.

I can't believe he will be in college. Time flies. We're all getting older. Things are changing and I don't like it. He's moving on and I don't know what I'm doing with my life. I don't have a set career path and I'm not qualified to do anything. I'll never be successful at anything.

I don't think Mom and Dad realize what a mess I am. I know they know I was in a rough patch, but it was because I had anxieties over what to do. But I can still be happy-go-lucky Nicole on the phone, and they have no idea how hopeless I really feel. I don't know what the point is sometimes. I seem like a waste. Once I move in with Sam, maybe things will be better. I got a job with an Indian Tribe at their Museum where I will lead groups and be their Education Director, so that might distract me. I'll be more productive. I hope my caloric intake doesn't sky-rocket though.

Kelly is engaged. I mean, she and Tim have been dating for five years, it was expected, but not at this moment. I guess he had the ring for 6 months, just ready to pounce. His pouncing happened by the clothesline at our house. Boomer was there and started humping Kelly's leg. I am sure it was a scene.

Another thing I missed. I would have loved to be home for my sister at that moment. Her engagement. To say congratulations, and not over the phone. They were all going out to dinner, the whole family, minus me.

Everyone is doing something with their lives except for me. Dan's going to college. Kelly is getting married. And I am just schlepping around L.A.

I am doing something though, such as...weighing in at 129. I am below the 130 mark! I am in the 120's. I was probably last in the 120's when I was five. I don't remember when. I feel so liberated. Mom sent me a card though with an ice cream cone picture on it and $20 inside. "Ice cream money," she said. I had to obey, and I hadn't eaten something real in so long, so I went to the ice cream shop around the corner. I got fat free/sugar free ice cream, but got brownie and health bar mixed in. It was a nice treat, and since Mom said so, it brought me a moment of happiness.

I had a couple of gift cards so I went to the store and was looking for a skirt in my size. The salesperson asked what size I was looking for and I said, naturally, "zero."

"You're a zero?" he asked.

"Yeah."

"Wow, you're skinny."

Not true, but it made me smile.

I've got into this mentality now that since I have hit a size zero, I will not wear anything above it. That means I have gained weight and I cannot admit to that. So zero it is for now. I am zero. I am nothing.

Tomorrow is the big move. I cried on the phone to Dad again. Something is stressing me out, and I don't think it's this move. It's this anxiety. I can't help it.

"You're really stressing me out now. If you are that miserable, you should just come home," he said.

"I'm really not. It's the moving thing. Besides, I have stuff I need to do out here."

"But you're not happy doing it."

"I am, but I haven't been able to do it because I've been so worried about other things."

"Maybe try a different kind of writing."

"I like screen-writing."

"But you have no way to get your foot in the door."

Maybe a door will just open on its own.

I have to say that I'm not looking forward to this living situation, not because of Sam, but because of me. I've been so used to living on my own for a year and a half. I don't want her hovering over me, especially given my eating habits. I do have the start of a pretty, bony chest. I will weigh myself tomorrow. I haven't in two weeks. I hope that I lost a couple pounds, though I know I won't be at 125. I don't want her to make me eat meals, because I like to graze. I know she has a lot of fruit, so that is good, and then I will stick to negative calories.

I'm so useless. I'm not sure this is the right thing. I know it will help me sort things out, but I don't feel right about it. How and when did things get so bad?

Chapter 19
Renfrew:
It's a Serious Issue

I go into my room and it smells like gas. Not human, my room mate would have admitted to that, and she wasn't there anyway. Dangerous gas. I go outside my room and it smells like gas in the hallway too. Some other girls in the living room also notice this. Down the side stairwell it also reeks. It just so happens that it is next to my room that they are doing construction during the day. They have a tarp over the room at night, but I suspect something is leaking. I go to the nurse's station where another resident is already complaining.

The nurse tries to reassure her: "We know there is a smell. It is propane. Maintenance said they are using it to keep the pipes from freezing and that it's fine. Don't worry."

Propane. Smell. Don't worry?

The other girl is extremely scared because she has OCD.

I jump in.

"I'm afraid to go to sleep smelling gas," I tell them.

They get bitchy with us. "We'll call maintenance again, but really, it's fine."

No it's not.

I go back to my room and no sooner do I enter but the fire alarms go off and the counsellors yell at girls who are grabbing their things to just save themselves.

This is definitely not fine.

They usher us over to the Manor House, where the groups are held, and eventually, after much waiting, they allow us to go back in.

Apparently, it was a propane leak. What a shock! They fixed it and aired out the building. Besides being scared, I was upset at how we were treated when we had a real concern. This battle was not over.

At Community, we talk about the propane leak and our concerns. I bring up how I got the shaft. One of the counsellors, Carrie, says, "Maybe you should try approaching them and tell them how it made you feel. Could you do that?"

"No." That got a few laughs at least. She told me to try.

That was all the time they wanted to spend on the issue. No surprise there. Then it was time for goodbyes. My room mate, Erica, and Vanessa, who I was admitted with and who helped me through my supplement issue, were leaving. It's hard to have two people you have bonded with leave on the same day, especially when you all help each other through things. I wished them the best and truly hope they do well. They deserve it.

I go to a group later on the Politics of Women's Bodies and the topic is Barbie and how at 5'9 she would have weighed 110 pounds, but should have weighed 145. I am 5'9. I want to be 110. The leader of the group asked, "Is this triggering for anyone?" I raise my hand.

I had a pass alone, and I just needed to get out of there, so I went to the mall that had a movie theatre. I got a Starbucks Latte and a muffin, and then saw a Dairy Queen, so got a kid-sized cup of ice cream. I brought the muffin to the movie, but I couldn't do it. I chewed it and then spat it out. How pathetic is that? So much for progress. I knew I'd have to make up some meal that I "supposedly" ate on my pass form.

On the cab ride back, the driver is quite chatty.

"I can't believe someone as cute as you would go to a movie alone."

"Thanks, but I actually like to."

"So do you have friends?"

"Not really," I acknowledge, sadly.

I tell him where we are going, to the Renfrew Center, an Eating Disorder facility.

"Yup," I say. "Here for a month."

There was a moment of silence, and then he goes, "So, what, you don't eat?"

"I didn't really eat for a while and I was exercising too much."

"You gotta eat."

"I know that now."

"I eat at least once a day, otherwise I'll get fat on the job," he says with a laugh. "At least have some popcorn at the movies. If I had a girl with me, I'd make her have popcorn."

I tell him next time, I will.

We reach Renfrew and as I get out, he tells me I am cute and then says, "Remember, a guy likes a girl with some meat on her."

Wow. I thank him and say I'll remember that. He was actually very sweet and it kind of made my night.

I go inside and it's snack time, which I go to after my muffin episode. I sit with Brittany, who is a singer-songwriter and I have kind of connected with. We chat about things and how we each like to take passes alone just to get a break from here. We relate on a lot of things, how with the eating disorder, you can't do your work, but sometimes it's your work that causes this. But your work makes you happy too. It's just draining.

I tell her about my struggles with the move from L.A. back to Connecticut and how I feel like a failure because I went out there to pursue screen-writing. It's as if I didn't take advantage of everything.

She is so sweet. She puts her arm around me and says, "Listen, I probably know more than anyone here how you feel, more than the therapist, because I'm in this creative business too—we're both artistic. I know what it's like to be pursuing something. I feel like we have parallel lives because I was your age when I was getting my music going.

Don't feel like a failure. You can't do anything if you're six feet under. You're talented and you'll get led back there if it's meant to be. I know it's hard to see now, but if it's in God's plans, it'll happen. Maybe it wasn't the right time. The screen-writing industry is hard and maybe you weren't ready to handle it. But you have somewhere to go, a home to go to, and you're blessed because some girls here don't."

She was right. The most important thing is my family and getting healthy. Then I can get back to the things I want. I can't do anything if I starve myself to death.

I tell her that maybe screen-writing wasn't even the right option for me, and maybe I'll work on some books I had started.

"Whatever avenue you're supposed to take, you'll get there," she tells me. "L.A. is tough, but you're obviously a talented writer. Something else I notice about you, and I know a lot of the other girls here do too, is that you have this brightness about you in the way you project yourself. This positive energy people like to be around. It's really nice."

That was very touching. The whole conversation meant a lot to me. That last part—maybe I am getting some personality back. The first part—someone truly understands me. I go back to my room and write her a card, because what she said really hit me. At one point, she told me, "I'm 34, I've got 10 years on you and I know it seems like people always want to give you advice. People did it for me and I didn't always take it. Sometimes people like to think that they know more than you."

"No," I told her. "That really made an impact on me, because no one else understands on your level. They just tell me 'You can always go back.' So thank you."

We hugged. I wrote her the card, then put it in her mailbox.

At our team meeting, a lot of the girls leaving mention how they think they will return to their eating disorder when they leave here and we were offering ways to prevent that. I raise my hand, which is something I do more now, to offer some advice.

"I think of myself at my worst point, when I really thought it was the end for me. When I had to have my friend call 911 and the only thought I had was, 'What if I never see my family again?' When I don't want to eat, I think of those moments and what happened when I didn't eat, so that I will eat."

People seemed to like that idea and said they would try it.

I tell them, "I feel like I hit rock bottom and now I'm trying to climb my way back to the top. I don't want to be down there again."

***

I have a new room mate, Diane, and she is 18, sweet, but chatty, whereas I like my quiet time. She surprised me though when I walked into the room and said, "Nicole, we would all die without you."

That is in regards to the propane, which has not got any better. We are living in a propane tank. What a whirlwind it has been. Awful. Yesterday, people's eyes were burning. Some felt nauseous and had headaches. No matter how much we complain, they don't do anything. Dad put in a call to administration, left a message, and got no return call. He told me to call the Philadelphia Department of Health. "You shouldn't be breathing any fumes," he said. "They can kill you." As if us gals aren't sick enough.

So we took charge. We called, they came and inspected. They found that propane was leaking in. Surprise. We knew that. Then we get this bogus letter from administration that says they are doing everything they can to get it fixed, that they will be shutting down the propane and using other methods to heat the construction and blow the fumes away from the building. But no fumes are good fumes.

At breakfast, we see construction workers rolling in more propane tanks, so I write a four-page letter and get residents to sign it. I send it to the medical director, the head therapist, the owner of Renfrew, the nurse manager, and the plant director of the construction project. There is now to be an open community meeting about this issue.

I am pissed off at this point. They said no more propane, but my room stinks and doesn't feel safe. April, one of the counsellors, went into Meg's room, who is in our suite, and thought it stunk. Meg tells her to go into mine, and she says it's worse.

"This is awful," April says. "My eyes are stinging. You can't stay in here!"

Meg and I end up sleeping on the couches in the living room. This is a place of recovery, so why should we be dealing with this? Shouldn't their number one priority be the patients, not construction? It's unhealthy, and I'm worried about some of the girls.

It also makes me feel so negative about treatment. My whole motivation has changed. Maybe it's because I'm being weaned off my anti-depressants, but I have been down lately, thinking again that my whole life is worthless, that I will never make it anywhere, and that life is pointless. I am pointless. I broke down and spoke with Dad.

He is always good to talk to. "I don't think you know how much you mean to me," he said. "Everyone goes through a tough time, and yeah, this is really hard, but you have so much to offer, even if it's hard to see right now."

It has been hard and I've felt so hopeless lately. I have never seen much of a future for myself, and I definitely don't see one now.

Sleeping on the couch is not such fun. Though Meg and I had a good time staying up and exploring. We tried to figure how to turn off all the lights. The weird thing was that I had a dream about needing an oxygen mask and then woke up choking and coughing like crazy. The propane is spreading, and I don't think it's part of our treatment.

On to the community meeting. It included Dr. Snow, the medical director, Lily Weeks, the construction manager, and someone from nursing. They tell us that regarding the propane tanks, they will be outside and used through two vents, so everything should be resolved. They realize that everyone has a lot of concerns, but things will settle down.

Meg and I took the couches directly across from the head honchos, and were ready to pounce.

Meg says, "I couldn't even get an order for Excedrin for the headache I had from the propane, and I had to sleep on the couch because the fumes were so bad."

"Are you room B11?"

"B9."

"I'm B11," I say.

"Are you Nicole?"

"Yes."

"We did inspect your room, and smelled no fumes. I got your voicemail this morning and checked your room and it was fine. Though, we did open a window to ventilate it."

"Actually, we ventilated it yesterday and today, so it's probably not as bad. I slept on the couch as well. April, the counsellor, came in and said the fumes were so bad her eyes started burning automatically and that we shouldn't sleep in there, so off it was to the living room," I tell them.

"We're sorry about that," Lily said. "But it's going to be resolved now."

That didn't cut it for me. It had been too long. I went off. "We came to you with these complaints two weeks ago and it was just as bad then. You kept saying that you were going to be doing something and you did nothing. This is where we came to get healthy, not sick, and that is what is happening. All of us are sick to begin with. Now, girls have headaches, burning eyes, sore throats and nausea, and who knows what else is affecting us. This is a serious issue!"

Meg popped in about how propane turns into carbon monoxide and Lily was like, "I don't think so, I've never heard that."

We told her it does, and that it kills.

Dr. Snow wanted to talk about the benefits of the construction but no one cared. It wasn't benefiting us, after all. We won't be here to see the results.

"You should be caring about your current residents," I tell her. "We are the ones who are here to get healthy. We should be your priority, not construction. You neglected us."

Other people spoke about how bad this facility had become— filthy, poor quality of living, and especially the fact that we don't have a real dining room to eat in. Everyone agreed that no one knew that there was to be construction going on here. If so, we would have gone to another facility. The administration insisted that we should have been told. That was not the case.

Since some girls were afraid to speak up, I raised my hand again.

"Well," Dr. Snow said, "let's hear from the other girls." The other girls insisted I speak. "First, what should be done about the residents who are having symptoms from the propane?"

"They should go to the nurse's station."

"They have been, and were turned away."

"Go back and they'll be taken care of."

"Another serious issue, since we were not informed of the construction, is that of men in the building. This is a women's facility and it is quite uncomfortable when we are pretty much naked in a gown and men are walking by us as we sit in the hall for weights and vitals. Not only is it uncomfortable for people who have issues with men, but some men have been making comments to the women here."

"Oh," Lily said. "That is important, and will be addressed. It is a concern."

How stupid are you people? I came here, along with the rest of the girls and women, to get better. I don't feel like it is a safe and comfortable environment. It's ridiculous, and if I didn't care so much about my recovery, I'd sign a 72-hour notice to leave this shit-hole.

After the meeting, a lot of girls came up to me and thanked me, which was a surprise. One girl said, "You were amazing, you really spoke up for all of us. I really admire you. It was so inspiring. You're everything I want to be again. I could hear the passion in your voice, you had such valid points, and you never got too emotional. You just really spoke up for all of us and did it in such an amazing way. I'd love to be able to do that one day."

I was shocked. I didn't realize I had done anything special or it would impact on anyone.

"I feel like I used to be like that," she tells me.

"Wow, thanks," I say. "You know, I feel like I used to be like that too, fighting for causes and such. Then it stopped of course with the eating disorder and I was a zombie. I had no emotion at all. I feel like maybe I just got it back."

In a weird way, maybe I needed this propane issue to come up so I could get my inspiring fighter side back. I was always about fighting about issues for others and myself.

Another girl tells me that my "one liners" were great. "When you said, 'you neglected us,' it was perfect, because it was true." I didn't think about what I was saying, I just said what I felt. The best was that people thought I could back up what I said, whereas administration had no answers. I wanted to speak up for myself and the girls, because we needed it. The administration wasn't taking care of us. Someone had to. And, after all, it was a serious issue.

That was the other girls' favourite line. "It's a serious issue!" When I first said it, they thought I was joking, since I do that a lot. I was actually serious. But once I knew they thought it was a joke, I just continued saying it—to staff, counsellors, nurses, therapists, and then it grew...about food, groups, TV, anything. Everything at Renfrew became a serious issue. And despite the propane, it brought some fun into the community. The community, after all, is a serious issue.

Getting my voice back is a very serious issue, and one that I am excited about.

Chapter 20
My Breaking Heart

Goodbye Hollywood, Hello West L.A. I am at Sam's and it is weird. Strange to be moving into another person's house when I have had my own space for so long. I moved in, mostly, and she poked around. After all, it is her space.

I tried to unpack as quickly as possible and make it tidy, but that wasn't the problem to her.

There were bigger issues at hand.

"Your eating issues concern me," she told me.

Why, because I'm a picky eater? And I don't eat a lot?

I told her, "I eat a lot of little things throughout the day."

"You're not anorexic, are you? I mean, I know you don't eat a lot, and you've lost a lot of weight. You've been having a hard time and people deal with issues in different ways. There's a fine line between being a picky eater and having a problem. I know too many people who have anorexia."

Great. An accusation. I told her I didn't, of course, because I don't. I just don't eat a lot.

"Are you still getting your period?" she asked

"Yes," I said, though I think it's been two months now without one. That happens with a lot of athletes. People who exercise a lot. I am not anorexic. I am healthy.

***

Our first night together as roomies, we got a Carvel Ice Cream Cake. I mentioned how I liked the frosting and Sam goes, "What? Lard? Now I know you're not anorexic."

Maybe now I at least have her off of my back.

She told me: "I'm not gonna watch you, but I'm just concerned."

That translated to "I am going to watch you." Now I have to make sure I show her when I eat. I hate having to eat when she does. I like to do my own thing. Tomorrow we're having a BBQ—hamburgers, corn, salad, and more ice cream cake. So many calories! In a way, I guess it'll be okay to increase my caloric intake, but ice cream cake two days in a row! Too much! At least she'll be back at work in a couple of days and I can detox a little.

I talked to Mom on the walk to the gym today and started crying. It was awful. She said, "Don't cry. I wish I could be there to help you. Don't worry. It'll get better. This is just a temporary living arrangement until you can sort things out." She asked me if there was any other reason I was upset. I told her "no," that I didn't know what was wrong with me and that it just seemed like everything hit me all at once. I don't know if she suspects something else is wrong or is just asking. I don't mean to be a baby and cry. I'm not usually like that, but things have just been tough on me and I don't know why. I guess the uncertainty of it all and the lack of friends and missing my family and just all the change has hit me in a weird way.

There was also the fact that I was on my way to the gym and didn't want to be going. I couldn't tell her that though.

Sam's friend Anna came over for the BBQ. Sam kept making comments about what I would eat and said how I eat a lot of fruit and Anna goes, "so that's how you stay so slim."

Slim?

Anna asked if I ate burgers and I said "yes."

Sam acknowledged that she had seen me eat. Then said, "well, you've lost like, what, 10 or 15 pounds since I met you last summer? Not that you were fat."

Anna goes, "That's a lot."

I wanted to say, "Actually, I've lost 30," but kept my mouth shut. Instead, I said, "I don't really keep track." We still have that stupid cake and she's gonna want it tomorrow and I can't do that. I already increased my calories today. I need to detox tomorrow. Making excuses is getting to be too hard. She will be gone during the day, so I will just eat fruit and do a long work out. I don't want to get to the point of looking hideously skinny, not that I ever would, but I don't want to gain weight. I'll get to 125 or under, maybe even 120. Or 119, 118, just to break the 120 mark, though that might be too low. As long as I can maintain a low weight without gaining. I don't want living with her to screw up my routine. It seems that she will be gone all day and not be back until late at night, so if I can restrict all day, maybe eat fruit, and exercise a lot, then I should be OK. If when she gets home, I have to eat, I can eat minimally, saying I already had dinner. That is a good plan.

***

123 pounds, which is technically underweight for me! It's so amazing to say that I am underweight, when I was overweight for so long. I am under the 125 mark, and my new goal is 120. I lost 4 pounds in a week.

Losing 4 pounds in a week is not good, especially when you end up in the Emergency Room. I guess that I worried a hospital visit might be coming soon, but I didn't expect it like that.

On Saturday, I was out with Sam, and I felt like I might pass out, but I had eaten so I didn't think it was that.

Sunday, we went for lunch, I had a sandwich, went for a walk later, and my pulse got really fast. I felt again as if I might pass out.

On Monday, I was really woozy. I ate my leftover sandwich and was about to go to the gym, but the whole time I was having chest pains. I knew something wasn't right. If I went to the gym, I didn't think that the staff there would be able to help me. So I called my friend Danielle, who is a nurse, and she told me I needed to go to the hospital.

I was scared because chest pains are not good and I knew that I hadn't been taking the best care of myself. The excessive workouts, the diet pills, the restricting—it could all lead to something wrong. Danielle told me to find an orange or banana because it would give me some potassium, but we had none. She thought that my electrolytes might be off. Luckily, Sam was on her way home early from work, and ready to take me to the Emergency Room.

***

My EKG was normal and my chest X-Ray was fine. They actually raved about my low heart rate, but I knew it wasn't because I was healthy; it was because my body was deteriorating. When I finally got into a room, the nurse was about to do my blood work to test my electrolytes and anything wrong with my heart, but then the Doctor came in and called him off. He asked me a couple questions and thought he knew the prognosis.

"We don't need the blood work," he said, to my alarm. "You're too young to be having problems with your heart. It is costo-condritis. An inflammation of the chest wall and ribs. You'll be in pain for a few weeks. It is extremely painful. But, you did the right thing by coming down here. Most people who feel this pain do think it is a heart attack."

That was it. I was let to go.

I spoke with Danielle later and she was angry. "I wish they had done the blood work because I think your electrolytes are all screwed up. I don't think this guy is right."

I didn't either. I had been working out for so long, why would this come on now? He did ask if I had a regular period, and I lied. I hadn't for a while, and of course, that was something I was proud of. It made me feel thin, not needing a period.

He asked about my workouts and I lied about that too. Just two hours a day. He thought that was a lot. So did Sam. If they only knew how much I really worked out.

When we got home, Sam told me to take it easy. She said "Usually, when we get sick, it's our bodies trying to tell us something. You've been working too hard. Take some time off for yourself."

I somewhat listened. I took a couple days off, hung out at the house, watched T.V., and lounged out on the couch. Sam was gone for two days, which gave me some time alone.

I also snuck off to the gym. I took it easy the first couple of days. I even ate more. Part of me thought that it could have just been the shock to my system of eating more those couple of days before I felt ill. After eating only fruit for so long, my body probably had no clue what to do with a sandwich.

A couple nights later, I started getting weird spasms in my legs. Waking up in the middle of the night. It freaked me out because then my pulse seemed off too. I was even more worried that something wasn't right.

I went to see my regular Doctor, Dr. Otis. The first thing he commented on was my weight. He told me I was wasting away, I'm too skinny and that I shouldn't let my weight get below 125. I should keep it above 125 and ideally, at 130. He also asked me if I had missed any of my periods and I was honest.

"That is a sign your body knows it is too thin," he told me. "It's preparing for famine, but once you put on a little weight, it will get back on track."

I am not gaining weight. I am not getting fat again. I have worked too damn hard to lose this weight. I just bought all these size 0/xs clothes. Who needs a period anyway?

He ordered some blood work but made the comment that the needle would probably go right through my arm, it was so tiny. He pressed on my chest and ruled out costo-chondritis. He asked me if I had been under a lot of stress lately. I said, "maybe."

"Stress and anxiety can cause palpitations. This matter could be a factor of working out too much, plus stress and some inflammation in the chest. I think that you need to tone it down a little, in all areas. I'll call you Monday with the test results."

I talked to Dad afterwards and I told him how the doctor said I could stand to put on a couple pounds. He said, "Yeah, you don't need to be doing these 5 hour workouts and eating just fruit. I'm sure this whole stress thing has something to do with it. It's awful for your health."

If he could only see me. I don't want him to worry.

I talked to Sam and mentioned the stress thing, which I found to be a bad idea. "What could you possibly be stressed about?" she asked me. "There are starving children in Somalia and they should be stressed."

"Maybe 'stressed' isn't the right word," I told her. "I've just had a lot of worries lately." From Popie's stroke to moving to this new job to financial stuff to my own health, and then missing my family and Dan going to college and Kelly's engagement...it takes a toll on a person. I've been depressed about it all and didn't handle it well. Then there's that whole lack of friends thing.

Sam mentioned again how my medical issues might be because of my weight loss. I am at 122 now. Exciting.

She said again that, "I'm a little concerned about your eating habits."

I wanted to ask her if she snooped through my stuff and looked through my weight loss charts. I should hide them better.

***

I went back to my doctor since I was still having weird feelings in my heart during the night. He ran another EKG and another blood test. He told me, "I want you to know that I'm doing all these tests. I don't want you to think I'm being neglectful."

"I don't think that."

"Have you been having any anxiety?"

"Maybe a little."

"Then we need to talk. What's going on? You can talk to me. Nothing will leave this room."

"I'm uncertain about things and whether I should stay here or go back home," I told him, though I wanted to say more.

He asked about my family, if I had made friends here, and told me it was hard to be here without a real support structure.

"But does that mean you should move home?" he asked. "No," he answered his own question. "Does that mean you should give up? No. I'm not saying you should hop on MySpace or go to Hollywood where they have their noses up in the air. But get out a little. Do your work in Santa Monica, in coffee shops." He also gave me the name of a counsellor/hypnotist that he said people love. "And you can always come here, once or twice a week, if you need to talk. Talk to us. You always have friends here."

It was so nice and reassuring. There was so much that I wish I could have just said, but I'm not ready. I know that eventually I will have to, but I just can't bring myself to do it yet. I'm not even sure what I would say if I tried. I don't know what's going on with me.

He told me to relax, enjoy myself and have fun, which is also what Dad said. And my friend Vicky, from Boston, will be here for a couple of days, so that might bring a little cheer into my life.

It still didn't stop my worries about all my chest pains and weird spasms I was having. I went online and googled anorexia and chest pains. Not that I have anorexia, but just to see. When the search engine was finished, the first thing that came up was: Anorexia—Number one cause of death, Cardiac Arrest.

Not too reassuring.

There was also a lot of information on electrolytes and how with an eating disorder your electrolytes become disturbed. Your potassium level is low, so your heart doesn't function properly, and neither do your muscles or nerves, which can cause spasms.

These things all made sense, but I didn't have any eating disorder. I ate, after all, just minimally.

I then found my way back to the pro-eating disorder website, where at least I knew I had some friends. I loved to look at the new methods to lose weight, "thinspiration," and even information on medical complications, which confirmed what I read on google. Everything I read was something I could relate too, even though I didn't have their problem. I had merely lost some weight and was having health issues.

It was a good resource though. I learned how to lose weight faster, could look at pictures of skinny people as motivation and then read about other girls' stories of weight loss. In addition, there was information on new diets, exercise and health issues. I joined the website and like most girls in my signature had my highest weight and current weight, which was my lowest. Then I noticed I had a message from one girl. She told me that she used to weigh as much as I did and was now losing weight. Her goal was to weigh as low as I did and she wanted to know how I did it. She was in her teens and I was filled with enormous guilt. One part of me was proud that my weight loss was acknowledged, the other wanted to reach out to her and tell her she was fine the way she was.

I merely told her: "Your weight is great at what it is now. Trust me, you don't want to lose weight the way I did. It's torture."

I stayed away from talking to people, but continued to use the website as a resource.

Vicky came to town and we went to a show in Hollywood. I hadn't seen her for two years and it was nice, just like old times. She first wanted to go out to eat, which I dreaded, but we had pizza and it was kind of nice. While we were talking, she mentioned going to "Knott's Berry Farm" in Anaheim. I hadn't done something fun in so long, so I said "yes," and the next day, off we were.

Dad told me to have fun, and those were the doctor's orders too, so when she stopped at Starbucks on the way down, I got myself a latte. I paid no attention to the calories and just thought of having a good time. That was only the start of the caloric intake, however. When we arrived, we got a sandwich. Then we realized we were practically the only ones at the park. Which was fine. We ran around like little kids looking for Snoopy, took pictures, and I laughed more than I had in so long. Then, we found a candy shop, and I loaded up. I told Vicky, "This is bad, once I start, I won't be able to stop."

I was right. I had been so deprived of the things I once loved, that once I dug into that bag of candy, I wanted to demolish it all. She told me to slow down, or we wouldn't have room for cake.

Yes, cake. Before were left, we stopped at this bakery to get cake, as a sort of celebration for seeing each other again. I got some yummy carrot cake, though I couldn't finish it and saved it for later. My stomach was throbbing and I could feel the sugar pulsing through my veins.

On the way back to L.A., we stopped at this sketchy casino, and then left quickly. Vicky wanted a taco but we couldn't find the fast food place, so it was 7-11 sandwiches for us. I wasn't hungry at all, but I figured since I was eating, I might as well keep eating, since I knew I wouldn't eat the next day. We went back to her hotel, I got my car, and that was that.

A day of fun and it was over. It was so good to see her, I felt as if we were 18 again. Fun was what I needed, but after those highs always come the lows. I was back to reality, and it wasn't a reality that I liked.

Back at home, Sam was on my case again. Her father is a doctor, and she asked him about me. She told him I was thin and he told her that could be causing all my health problems. Especially if I work out a lot. Now she is watching me. I had soup for dinner and while I was making it, she asks, "So how many calories are in that?"

"180," I tell her. "But it's squash soup and thick and filling."

"That's not enough calories. You're full because your stomach is so small."

I eat when I'm hungry, stop when I'm full. I'm not going to gorge myself, though I did have some of the leftover candy from Knott's. I ate so much this weekend. In addition to all that, Sam's daughter was in town and we went out to dinner. In a weird way, I felt better this weekend. I am not sure if it is because I ate more or because I had fun during my visit with Vicky. But when the weekend was over, I went back to feeling the effects of minimal eating and rigorous workouts, and my body just felt drained.

I want to take better care of myself. I went to the grocery store and bought more than fruit. I got cottage cheese, milk, cereal, some frozen dinners, yogurt and grilled chicken. I made an effort. Yet when I buy these things, they just end up sitting there, uneaten. Grocery shopping is a terrible chore for me. I am usually there for 2 hours and might come out with 2 items. I get my fruit, and then go up and down the aisles, looking at foods that I would love to eat, but I know I can't have. Even when it says "no fat" or "low fat," it is just too dangerous. I stare at the boxes, of maybe cookies or crackers or frozen meals, then take them out and read the nutrition label. 200 calories? How many grammes of fat? To a "normal" person, it is so minimal, but to me, I can't bear to do it. 200 calories is too much for a day, never mind one meal. I sadly put back the item and continue on, only to pick up a new one and stare at the label, brokenhearted that I can't bring myself to eat it.

Grocery shopping has become a bit more daunting since living with Sam. She has four cats and a dog, and part of our arrangement is that I do the grocery shopping and feed the animals. I buy all the cat food, but not just the canned stuff. She feeds her animals deli turkey and rotisserie chickens. I spend more money on food for the animals than myself. What is even worse is that when I feed them, I realize they are eating more calories than me. Part of it makes me laugh, part of it makes me sad, and part of it makes me pleased—the fact that I don't need to eat as much as a cat.

I am less worthy than a cat. But this less worthy girl now weighs 119 pounds. I have finally broken the 120 mark. I don't remember the last time I weighed this low, but I imagine it was in middle school. Early middle school.

My friend Charlotte had a show at the Hotel Café in Hollywood, and as always, she was amazing. Her music means a lot to me, as does she, and I had been feeling down again, so it helped to see and talk to her. Afterwards, I went up to her and the first thing she said to me was, "You're so tiny!" I had my arms wrapped around me and suddenly, felt like crying. I wanted to reach out to her. Even though I don't have a problem, she battled with anorexia, so I knew she could recognize the agony of not being able to eat.

"You've lost a lot of weight since I've seen you. You look amazing," she said. "I mean, I've just never seen you so thin. Though, people used to say that about me too."

I didn't know how to respond. I could feel my eyes welling up and I think something clicked with her.

"Are you okay?" she asked.

"Of course. Yeah, I'm fine."

"How is work?"

I gave her a quick rundown and she asks, "Is everything else okay?"

I kind of shrugged and tried not to cry and she said, "I can tell it's not."

That's when I started to get weepy. She took my arms and asked if she could say a prayer for me. I thought she meant at night, but she gave me a hug and I surrendered. She prayed to God to look after me, with my work, boys, life, happiness, the people around me, and that good things would come to me.

People always tell you they're going to pray for you, or that you're in their thoughts and prayers, but I have never had anyone actually do it for me right on the spot. I was definitely crying then.

I thanked her and she gave me a kiss on the cheek. She said she was my friend and always there for me and to email her if I needed anything.

The thing is, I've always thought of turning to her when "it" got bad, so the fact that she was quick to notice I wasn't okay made me realize that it'll be safe to ask her for help. I know I can trust her. On the other hand, she said I look amazing. But that's with loose clothes on. It's so bad right now. Technically, I'm underweight, but not by much. I do eat, though my habits are odd. During the week, I'm very healthy. Weekends, I tend to binge. I eat McDonald's. I feel disgusting because I haven't eaten like that in so long. I'm gross. My stomach is huge, I hate myself. I also know that my increase in calories should be a trigger for losing weight when I go back to restricting.

Is this any way for a person to live? I went grocery shopping and bought all these things, thinking that maybe I would start to eat "meals" again. I didn't touch them. I keep eating my fruit. I'm going to turn into a nectarine. I think back to the days when I didn't care, when I ate everything in sight. I was big, now I'm little—was I ever happy? I always thought the key to happiness was to be skinny, but maybe I won't ever be happy. Or I won't ever be skinny enough. That, or I won't be able to regulate my weight so that I am comfortable with it.

It's devastating really, it consumes you. Right now, I can feel my stomach growing. I know the fat I ate today will help me lose weight, but it's a hard feeling to sit with at the moment. During the week, when I don't eat any fat, I have to make sure I have a piece of fruit every few hours so I don't pass out. It's hard. When I go to the gym for four hours, I hate it. I always cry at some point. But when I look in the mirror and can see my ribs, I love it. I know some people think that's sick, but it's my accomplishment. I can see how far I have come. I was once 200 pounds. All fat. To see my bones now is beautiful to me. As long as I start to regulate it a little, it'll be okay. I'd like to be 115. That would be good. It will be tough to train my body to get back to a pattern of being able to eat normal meals, especially since I eat all non-fat stuff. Oh well, I really do like my fruit.

I emailed Charlotte to tell her how much I enjoyed her show and to thank her for caring and the prayer. She wrote back:
Hey Sweetheart,

Thank you again for coming to the show. I have to say when I saw you I just had these overwhelming feelings of mommyness. That isn't a word I know...but I could tell you weren't happy just from the first glance at your face. I meant what I prayed and I will continue to pray for you. You know God and I are tight and he loves you and we are both looking out for you. I will continue to pray for God to give you more direction and open the right doors for you and shut the wrong ones. I live so much by faith that I ultimately have to surrender my entire life to him otherwise I will go off the deep end. I'm living on that verge every day and I understand more than anyone how hard it is to move across the country without any friends and try to find your way. Just know that I love you and will be here for you no matter what....
Lots of love,
Char xoxxoxoxox

I was grateful for her support and to have a friend like her. I ended up seeing her again at a show in Santa Barbara. We talked after her set and she told me she was worried about me. I told her that there were some difficult things going on and medical issues and I didn't know what to think about L.A. anymore. She told me I could tell her anything. I think I might. When I'm ready...

Chapter 21
Renfrew:
Hard to Swallow

Crying came easily with my eating disorder, but I didn't know why. Now, I cry and I know why. I am aware of what has happened with my eating disorder and recovery has restored a lot of my emotions.

I know my Dad does not like to see or hear me cry, because he thinks I am hurting, but during a family session, I explain to him that it's okay, and he should let me.

"Although I was more fragile physically at the height of my eating disorder, I am more fragile emotionally now."

Robin jumps in and gives a good example of how it was good that I am showing my anger, like with the propane issues. Whereas when you are struggling with an eating disorder, you cut off all emotions, and don't have the strength to deal with your emotions. The fact that mine are coming back is a very good sign.

"I'll probably be crying a lot during this time," I tell them. "And whereas you seem to be inclined to stop me, maybe just let me go, because I need to cry. There's a lot to cry about and it actually helps."

With Robin's help, I tell them how I might be displaying more emotions, like sadness, anger, frustration or just crying randomly like a weirdo, but to just let me, or if anything, to hand me a tissue. Dad says he can do that.

We touch on the topic of L.A. and how after that visit home for Dan's graduation, I fell apart. I felt like I should have been home because there was so much going on there. I was missing out and wanted to be there for them. I also still wanted to be in L.A. The tears came, and I say, "In a strange way, I guess I thought that if I made myself sicker, eventually someone would notice and would say something to me. Would tell me that I had to go home. But no one noticed because I totally isolated myself until I did get sicker, and yes, then I did have to go home."

Mom jumps in: "Sometimes we rationalize things for what we really want."

How could I have had rationalized such a thing though?

Still orthostatic. I feel so dehydrated and my mouth is always dry. It's actually been causing difficulty eating, because it is hard to swallow food.

At lunch, we had to eat these diced pears, which I usually like. Until on the second bite of one, I realize it is lodged in my throat. My arm gets tingly, and I wave to the girls. As one of them runs over, I get the stupid piece of nasty pear down my throat, but am terrified. The girl, a resident, is also a nurse.

"I looked at you and you were so pale. I knew something was wrong. Are you OK?"

"Thanks for coming over. That was so scary," I say, coughing. "That was a serious issue."

All the girls laugh, and make sure I'm OK, and then we go back to eating. Except for me.

I stare at the bowl of pears, afraid to take another bite. What if it happens again? I don't want to finish them, but I know I have to, or else…supplement! So I do, bite by bite, and I chew each little piece about 50 times so I am sure I will not choke.

During Meal Support Therapy, I tell Eric, the counsellor, my dramatic story, and what does he do? He laughs.

"It's a serious issue!" I tell him.

The other girls laugh.

"No," says the nurse, "she was really choking."

"I understand," he says through his giggle. Then barely got out, "Are you OK?"

"Fine." I hide a smile.

"Go see the nurse after this."

So I do, and they tell me, "drink more water."

I am already drinking so much water. Water, Gatorade, milk, juice…any liquid imaginable. But it doesn't help.

Dinner is steak and broccoli, which I cut up into tiny pieces. I am sure they wrote down that I had a food ritual. I needed to do it so I wouldn't choke. It is still hard to swallow, literally and figuratively, but I did it. Now I have a new fear of food.

I have been here 28 days already—it's my original discharge date. It is also the anniversary of when I started my gym membership. What a difference a year makes. A year ago is when things really turned. When the battle with anorexia took over my life, since I started working out, which led to over-exercising, which led to the restricting, which then led to the fruit-only diet, that prompted the insane weight loss, that then caused the heart problems, which brought me to the hospital, where I had the realization that I had anorexia, that led me to try to recover, which brought me home, bringing about weight gain, then seeing that I was not really recovering, which then led me here, to Renfrew. A month ago. Wow. It seems as if all those terrors took place in slow motion, in a time much longer than a year.

The nurse told me that I might be permanently orthostatic, whatever that means, so they are taking me off the Gatorade diet. No! I love it so much now. She said I could come and get it whenever I felt like I needed some, so that is a relief. I think I should be able to start the exercise programme now, which will be nice. Finally.

People come and go so quickly here, just like Dorothy said in the Wizard of Oz. It is true. People I first met here are leaving, while we are getting a ton of new admissions. As I see both the newcomers and those ready to be discharged, I look at myself and see where I stand. I am glad I extended my stay because I know I'm not ready to leave. I see how much progress I have made. I can eat now. I was afraid to pick up a fork when I got here. I talk to people now—I'm not afraid to leave my room. I laugh again. I crochet. When I go on pass, I eat. Well, not when I'm alone, but I don't tell anyone that. When I go out with others, I eat. It's nice to have that comfort of eating with people who are just as scared as I am.

Myself and three others signed up for a pass during the week, so it was a shorter amount of time, but still a meal pass. Jamie, the sweet girl who helped me eat beans, was going and her Mom was driving us. Gertrude, my crochet friend, was coming, as was my first room mate, Amber. We all snuggle into the car and go into a different area called Manyunk. It was funny to see us squish in. Like how many Anorexics can you fit in one car? When we arrive and people saw us get out, they must have thought it was a clown car.

We walk around for a bit and then realize, "Shit, we need to eat." No one wants to make that first move, and of course, we can't decide on a restaurant. I spot a cute Irish Pub, so we go in and it's great. It's a little restaurant with cool seats and a great atmosphere. Very relaxed, so it took the fear out of eating a bit. We get the menus and all of us hemmed and hawed over what to eat. Really, who sends four Anorexics out to dinner together? It will take an hour alone just to look at one part of the menu, then another hour to decide. Menus are torture—looking at each dish, at what you want to get, but you know you can't because of the calories. So you look at what is healthy—a salad, chicken, fish, and though you may not always like your meal, you know it is better for your body. Like eating, menus are torture.

As we peruse the menu, the waitress puts a basket of bread down. We all stare at it. I am seated across from Jamie and we both know we should at least take a risk and try it, but bread is scary. However, there are raisins in it, so we kind of want it. She says, laughing, "How about we try a little piece, then eat all the raisins?"

I agree and we each cut tiny pieces, then go raisin crazy. The other two abstain.

The waitress comes back a few times to see if we have decided on a meal. We haven't. I finally opt for the salmon wrap with the mayo on the side (which I knew I wouldn't use), and I don't want the side of fries either. I knew my nutritionist, Nancy, would not be happy if I just got vegetables. Tonight was about taking risks, so I did. I got mashed potatoes. Unbelievable. I eat the mashed potatoes, which aren't even that great, but peeled off some of the wrap. It was too much.

After the meal, the waitress asks us if we would be interested in dessert. Jamie had to because her nutritionist told her to. I sort of want dessert, and figure it will look good to my nutritionist, so I use that as an excuse to get it. Besides, they have limited edition pumpkin cheesecake, and I sure do love pumpkin. Unfortunately, they were all out, so I get the next best thing—lemon cake. The other two also get dessert, and as we eat, we all stare at each other to see who is going to finish. Is it safe to finish? If she finishes, then I can too. It's a bit competitive, but more so, a comfort. It allows you to eat without being scared or worried about what someone will think of you.

I did eat all of my cake, but felt sickeningly full. Not that it was a big change. We were all full. We always were after a meal.

It was a fun night, yet it is clear we all still have issues. Gertrude and Amber didn't try the bread, Gertrude just got a salad, Jamie and I had our weird bread pact, and it took us all forever to order. We have of course made progress, but the eating disorder is still there, quieter, but there, and I wonder if it always will be.

After telling Robin about how my relationship with Kelly has altered, she suggested doing a family session with just her. She thought that there was so much I held in about childhood and how we weren't as close, but then how much I appreciated her being there for me now, and the new factor of how I would miss her when she moved to New Jersey after she got married, that it would be good to have an open talk. Robin thinks that now that we have a good relationship, we should talk about how we can maintain that.

I ask Kelly and she says "yes," but she can't come down because of work, so it will have to be over the phone, which is fine.

We get her on the phone and Robin suggests that I start with the history of my eating disorder. I am hit with nerves.

I describe to her how it was hard growing up overweight and I don't think she ever realized it. That she was the skinny sister, and it's not her fault, but people always made a big deal about her thinness and would make her extra food. It made me afraid to eat in front of people. They would know the big secret of why I was fat. We banter back and forth about how she had her issues also, how I thought she might be ashamed of me because I was overweight, but she thought our relationship in high school was just an age and sister thing. I even told her about the time we went to a concert together and were standing on the lawn when some guy trying to get by said, "move it fatso." I had never told her that, but it hurt so much then. I was in college.

I didn't feel I was getting anywhere. I jumped to the real issue, of the eating disorder, which I wanted her to understand.

"The eating disorder wasn't about the weight or food. It started that way, I wanted to lose weight. I wanted to be skinnier because I didn't like how I looked before."

"You don't look good now though." Ouch.

"I don't like how I've ever looked. I don't know what a normal weight for me is because I've never been at one. We're trying to figure that out."

"Kelly," Robin says. "How do you think her eating disorder started?"

"Control," she says, and I cringe. That seems to be the common misconception with eating disorders, but I never saw it that way.

"I think it was when she was in California and it was a time when she didn't really know what she wanted to do."

I step in and say, "I don't think it was about control, though that time certainly had something to do with it." I explain the "layers" to her and that my eating disorder started a while ago, but I was just afraid to call it that then. I've always dealt with my emotions through food, when I was over-eating and then when I began to purge in college. "I never considered that as an eating disorder, but it was." I went through the progression of the eating disorder in L.A., all of it, and then Robin asks if that made sense to Kelly.

"Yes, and I've heard some of it from my parents. Some of the pieces are coming together now."

"Remember when I was in L.A. and Dad first told you about the eating disorder. I thought it would be good to talk to you about it, so I called you. You asked what I had been up to and I said I had just come from the doctors. Your response was, 'Good thing you don't mind going to the doctors. I've had a cough since August and haven't gone.' That kind of hurt, and then I felt I couldn't talk to you seriously about it. Dad thought maybe you didn't realize how serious the eating disorder was. I thought things would change once I got home, but they didn't. You looked down on me—when I ate or exercised. I was sick, but you told me I was being ridiculous."

"It was ridiculous. I don't work out that much."

"I didn't want to be doing that stuff. I didn't want to be in a hooded sweatshirt working out for hours, and besides, it was much less than the 4 hours I was used to, so even that was hard for me to deal with. I worked out because I felt like I had to, as if I didn't deserve to eat otherwise. I hated it, but I did it."

"It was ridiculous, still. First of all, I thought that you should have been an inpatient when you got home, but no one would listen to me. So that made me mad. You were only eating some lettuce and cottage cheese in a teacup. You had a serious problem."

All that time, I didn't think she noticed, and I so badly wanted for her to notice. I wanted her to help. I thought she could have.

She went on: "It was hard to have meals with you. We would eat something and you'd join us, but make something different and then barely eat it. It was uncomfortable for me. You could have at least tried to eat what we had, even if you didn't finish."

"It was hard for me to make decisions during meals, that's part of the eating disorder. I was scared of the foods you were having. I ate what I was comfortable with and as I saw it, at least I was eating."

Nicole Roberge

Robin interjects and says that it was hard for me to sit there while they ate their meals too. Because I wanted to eat "normally."

"I know I wasn't eating a lot, but I couldn't help it and didn't realize how it affected you guys. Since I have been re-feeding, and am forced to eat other foods here, I should be able to eat other things once I get home. I'm sorry if you were uncomfortable. I didn't know. It was hard for me, but I'm glad you told me it was hard for you too."

After all the food talk, I brought up how I expected her to move to New Jersey once she got married, but I didn't expect that I would take it so hard, and actually cry.

She laughs. "Nicole, it's only two and a half hours away."

I laugh too. "I know, but I feel like we've got closer since I've been here and I appreciate you being here for me through all this. I want to be able to keep up with a stronger relationship, since we used to have some sisterly issues. You know, I was surprised to see you cry when you dropped me off. And your text messages and phone calls help me through the day."

"It's only a phone call."

"It's more than that. It makes a difference. You've made a difference."

That was the basis for our call, and we both agree to try and maintain a stronger relationship, which is good. Robin thinks she was a bit defensive at times, when it came to weight issues when we were younger, and I was a little hurt to hear that she didn't like being around me pre-Renfrew, but it was good to get it all out. It helped.

More progress. I got moved up to Fix Own (F.O.). This is where you go through the line as usual, pick whatever you want, and then fill out your food log. You have to make sure you meet all your exchanges during the day, and have four desserts a week, but it is so much more freedom. No more menus to follow. It's a little daunting, but nice. If I want a sandwich for lunch instead of some rice filled crap, I can. Also, no one checks you off in the beginning and end. They pretty much "trust" you. Now, that's something new. The first time was scary, but Amy was there to help me again.

F.O. is empty tonight. A lot of people are out on pass. So many, that it is only Gertrude and I at dinner. On F.O., you have to get one hot meal a day, either lunch or dinner, and since I didn't get mine at lunch, and neither did she, we were both stuck with fish, broccoli and a baked potato.

Neither of us wants the baked potato, but it is stupid not to get the whole meal because then it won't count as our "hot meal." So we get it. I do not like baked potatoes and Gertrude has a tummy ache. I take a couple bites and she goes, "I am not eating this."

Giggling, we both try to figure out how to hide it. So much for trust! Finally, she opens her milk carton, and smashes her whole baked potato (with the tin foil on it), into the carton. "Well that takes care of that," she says. It was a riot. I was hysterical.

Then, jokingly, I say, "Well what about my potato? Will mine fit? Yours needs a buddy."

She hands over the carton. "Here, try."

So I did, and I shove my whole tin-foiled potato into the tiny milk carton, with potato oozing onto my fingers. They both fit. The carton looks as if it might explode. It worked and I haven't laughed that hard in a long time. And to see her laugh like that was even better.

Being as cute as she is, she puts her butter container on top of it to give it a hat, because she said the carton looks like it had a face. Then she stuck a fork and spoon at the sides for arms and calls it "Mr. Potato Head."

As if stuffing two baked potatoes into a little milk carton wasn't hard enough, we had a real challenge ahead of us. We have to empty our trays downstairs, with the tray girls and counsellors all around. We go down and I stand guard while she threw it out. "BOOM!" The garbage can had been empty and our Mr. Potato Head sunk, loudly, to the bottom.

It was hysterical and I love that we had the freedom to do it because we are on F.O., and no one else was there. We didn't do it because we wanted to restrict, we just don't like baked potatoes in general. And it gave us a laugh, and what is better than laughter? At that point in recovery, fun trumps baked potatoes.

Gertrude made me a beautiful crocheted scarf, with little pockets on the ends. It is gorgeous and I know I will always treasure it, as well as think of our potato experience. She is such a kind woman, and funny, and I hope she fights this battle, because she brings life into every room she enters. She deserves a wonderful life for herself.

I hated to see her go, but her time at Renfrew is over. At the community meeting, we say our goodbyes, but she is offered the chance to say something first. She is too nervous, so they are going to move on, and I ask her, " Are you sure you don't want to? I know a lot of people care about you. Or, would you rather I say something for you?"

She thinks about it, nods, and I raise my hand. "I just want to let everyone know that Gertrude is leaving. She is a little nervous to say something, but I know how much she has meant to me and that she's meant a lot to many people here also." This is when I get a little choked up. "I just want to let her know what an impact she has had and how much I care about her and that she will definitely be missed." I can't say any more because I am crying.

She gives me a hug and decides to talk. She thanks everyone for their support and for never treating her like the old lady of the bunch. She says that her time here was special and she loves and will miss everyone. Now she is crying, and other girls start chiming in with their remarks, and more tears follow.

I will miss her. I got her a little teddy bear, since at one of the meetings she received the "Bear of Courage," but when we do those "Traditions," they are only kept for a week. I got her a book about "Knitting and Friendship" also.

Jamie is leaving as well. I got her a little necklace that several girls here have, called the "Strong Woman" necklace. I have one myself and it is to remind us of recovery, with just the shape of a woman on it. I tell her how encouraging she had been to me, for someone so young, and that she got me through one of the hardest meals of my time here. She is an inspiration and I know she will do well on the "outside." The outside. What a scary thought. I'm glad I'm not leaving yet.

Chapter 22
Put a Fork in Me, I'm Done

Sometimes, it is hard to talk. As in, literally get the words out. I was talking to Dad, and I wanted to respond, but I opened my mouth and it was as if tears were trying to come instead.

"Hello?"

"Yeah," I finally got out. "Sorry."

I now know what the phrase "choked up" really means. It's just physically hard to talk. And frustrating because I can't seem to speak. How did I get this way?

I can't keep living like this. When I first began having chest pains, I thought, is this it? And if it is, then I did it to myself. Maybe it's what I wanted. Some people call what I'm doing—over-exercising, restricting, diet pills—a slow form of suicide. I don't want to die, but I can't live like this. Perhaps it's just a cry for help.

It hurts to sleep. My ribs stick out so I can't sleep on my side. My spine pokes into the mattress and it burns. I lie on my stomach but my hips dig into the mattress. I'm in pain during the day and during the night. I think of food all the time during the day—when I will eat again, what I will eat, how my calories does each food have? —and then at night, I have constant food dreams. Sometimes, I wake up, and I'm exercising in my sleep. When I can't sleep, I lay there on my bed, and feel my ribs, then the droop of my abdomen, and slide my fingers up to my hips bones. I am satisfied then, and think it is worth the pain. Then I try to sleep, and cry. Nobody, no body, should be like this.

I talked to my grandfather, Buttsie, the other day to check in and see how he and Grammie were. He's always worried about me being out here and asks if I need a little extra money or anything.

"I'm all set, but thank you," I tell him.

"You let me know if you do. I don't want my little girl starving out there," he says.

If only he knew.

I began working at a Museum north of Los Angeles in Thousand Oaks. The drive alone was awful. Just sitting in traffic, hoping I would make it on time. A drive that should have been 45 minutes could turn into 2 hours. What made me more nervous was making sure that I would make it through the day. I'd have an apple before I left, and when I got there, I ate a plum in the bathroom, so no one would see. It was an "interactive" tour, where we walked on the grounds and I did storytelling. Some days, I just felt too weak. I had lost so much energy.

I would leave work and go home only to be frazzled about how I could get my workout in before Sam got home. I would check my emails and get changed for the gym at the same time. I also had to do my daily check of calorie websites, though sometimes I saved that for night, because, after all, I wasn't just counting calories, I was studying them. I memorized them and could have told anyone what the calories were in any item of food. Eating disorders, I realize now, are exhausting work.

People always thought I was strong, and I put on a good front that I am not so fragile, but while I wanted to be seen as strong, I was fragile, and wanted someone to recognize that for once. See that I needed a little more help than was apparent. Whether or not I would take it is another thing, and of course I would never ask for it.

Sometimes, random strangers recognized it. There was one time at J. Crew, when I felt frail and weak, and I was going into the fitting room. The girl who worked there gave me a water bottle. Just me, no one else. Which was good, so I didn't pass out from dehydration. I must have looked awful. Another time, I was in a novelty store, and began having chest pains. I put my hand on my heart. A worker there came up to me and asked, "Are you OK?" Embarrassed, I said, "yes," and walked along. I couldn't even go out, I looked so sickly. As I walked back home, I wondered what the people I passed on the street thought of me. I hated to think what was going through their minds.

It wasn't just people who noticed how my body was deteriorating. It was inanimate objects too. The love of my life at the time, the Stairmaster, hit a point where it would stop functioning when I was on it. It would stop and the screen would go back to the start menu. Aggravated, I'd re-enter my options and start stepping away, and the same thing would happen. I figured the machine was broken, so I tried another. It worked for a bit, then again, stopped. After trying every Stairmaster in the gym, and having each one stop on me, I was so annoyed that I gave up and realized what crappy workout equipment the gym had, and moved on to another machine. Even though I was mad that it messed up my routine, and I would now have to work out on something else for a longer amount of time, I realized the truth. I wasn't heavy enough for the machine to register my weight, so it couldn't function properly. Now my eating disorder was interfering with itself. I couldn't get my workout in because I didn't weigh enough. How was that right?

Then there were the embarrassing moments, like when the electronic toilet didn't recognize I was there. I'd sit on it and if I moved an inch, the sensor went off as if the person were gone, and it flushed, then kept flushing and flushing. People outside were probably like, "Who's clogging up the second stall?" Meanwhile, I hadn't even peed yet, but the toilet was flushing and spraying water all over me. Gross. At least I didn't fall in. But as funny as it was, I had to think about why it was happening. I was becoming so small that even the toilet didn't know there was a person there. Maybe that's what I wanted. To become invisible.

Several times with my doctor, I wanted to tell him, but I couldn't do it, and every time I left his office I was disappointed that I had to go on with the struggle. That he didn't notice I had a real problem, so I didn't have someone to rescue me. I would talk to my parents, crying, and say I was merely frustrated with work or L.A., but actually it could have been that I didn't get a good workout in or I was late for the gym or I felt like I ate too much or I was just miserable in my eating disorder that I didn't even acknowledge I had. They'd tell me I needed a break and, again, urged me to just come home for a bit. While that is what I wanted, I was too stubborn. That would mean that I failed, and I couldn't have that. So I cried, felt defeated by myself, and I think they felt defeated and a little helpless. I hung up, and that is when I whispered into the night: "Help me."

Someone heard my cries, literally. My friends in Boston, Erin and Danielle, knew I was somewhat depressed, and as an early birthday present, wanted to fly me to Boston and then go up to New Hampshire to our college for Alumni Weekend. I said it was too much, but they wouldn't have it any other way. I figured maybe this break would be good for me, and maybe I could tell them about some of my problems. So in October, I left L.A., ready to enjoy some quality time with my friends and fall foliage.

I got to the airport late because of traffic so had to get a new flight, which also meant waiting a few hours there. I poked around some stores and called Dad, who told me to relax and maybe grab a bite to eat. As I was speaking to him, I felt woozy and like I might pass out. "You're right Dad, I might go grab something to eat."

He kept talking and I could feel my pulse, and my surroundings, slow down. I told him I'd call him later, and went to the nearest food station.

Salads, pizza, sandwiches...yogurt. Only 60 calories. I could do it. I felt a little better afterwards. Shocked back to life.

The flight was worse and brought on more chest pains. I had tried not to eat much before I left for the trip because I knew I would have to eat with them. The flight attendant brought a snack pack, which I opened and then dissected—crackers, butter, cookies and raisins. I was in the middle seat, and the people next to me indulged in theirs. I ate the raisins because they were safe. I picked at them, rather, then broke off a piece of a cracker and nibbled on it. I can only imagine what the people next to me were thinking of me. I didn't want to eat it, but knew I needed something so the chest pains wouldn't worsen. I wanted to make it to Boston alive.

Erin picked me up at the airport and her first comment was, "Where is the other half of you?" I laughed it off. She hadn't seen me in a year, and Danielle hadn't seen me in two, so it might be sort of a change for them.

It was late at night, so we went to bed and the next day I ran errands with Erin. We go to lunch, I get a salad, which I can't finish, so I take it to-go. Then, Erin ushers me off to Danielle's because she has some things to do. Danielle wants to go out to dinner at the same restaurant Erin and I just went to. I ate the rest of my salad and wasn't that hungry. So we go, meet up with some of Danielle's friends and I order another salad. I was worried about having to eat, especially in front of them, and not working out. I was also a little discouraged that it wasn't just the three of us spending time together.

The next day was Alumni weekend in New Hampshire, which was nice because I got to see some familiar faces, and I was wearing my new size double-zero jeans. I was now less than zero.

Outside by the football field they had cookies and cider set up. I grabbed a cookie. It wasn't that great.

"What a waste," I said.

"What does that mean?" asked Danielle.

"If you're gonna have a cookie, you want it to be good and enjoy it." It's a waste of calories, I was really thinking. I hated myself for picking up the damn cookie. I should have waited until dinner. Danielle didn't get a cookie, so why did I? "Now I can't get dessert."

"Why not?"

"I just had a sweet."

"One cookie is okay, Nicole. You can still have a turkey club, like you always got."

"I'm still getting a turkey club."

"You just said you weren't because you had a cookie." She got defensive, trying to prove me wrong.

"No, I can't get a sundae."

"Yes, you can. Cut it out."

We moved from the football field up to the coffee shop, where we used to spend many of our days in college. It's connected to the pub, but we decide to sit and get something to eat and go in later with Erin, since she had a family function first.

Erin shows up and we order and I do get my turkey club. On wheat with no mayo, and when I eat it, I take out the middle piece of bread. I only eat half, and some fries, then excuse myself to go to the bathroom. When I am in there, I fill up my water bottle, and when I come out, it is obvious that they were talking about me. They were silent when I got back to the table. They must have thought I just puked.

"Did you just fill your water bottle up in the bathroom?" Erin asked.

"Yeah."

"That's so gross."

"Why? You used to do it all the time. It's just water."

I couldn't believe she seemed angry that I was drinking water.

"All you've been doing is refilling that water bottle. You're actually dehydrating yourself," Danielle said.

"But I'm thirsty," I told them, and we all just shrugged it off.

When we finally decide to go into the pub, we got a table and I actually finish my turkey club. Erin hadn't eaten there yet, because she had lunch with her family, so for the second time, I asked if she was going to get anything.

"In a bit," she told me.

"Like dinner, or a sundae?"

"Maybe both."

Part of me wanted that sundae, since I had already upped my caloric intake, and we used to always get sundaes. I figured I would wait and see what they did, because I couldn't eat if they didn't.

Since we were in the pub, we decided to get mudslides. I was nervous, because I hadn't drunk in so long and I knew my body wasn't in the best shape to handle alcohol. Besides, it has so many calories in it. But they looked good, and I had to prove I was nourishing myself, even if it was with alcohol. There was even whipped cream on it. I had forgotten how good whipped cream was.

Erin and Danielle decide to get calzones, but after my turkey club and mudslide, I wasn't hungry. I couldn't be the only one at the table without something, so I foolishly ordered another mudslide. It was good, until I started to feel sick. My heart raced a bit and I couldn't tell if it was because of not drinking in so long, or because my body was not able to handle it. Being that fearful, I figured I should get something to soak up the alcohol, so I ordered a grilled cheese, and then hated myself for being so full.

After that binge, we decide to check into the hotel. As we drove away from campus, I told Erin how full I was.

"The Nicole I know used to be able to polish off a turkey club and sundae, no problem," she said.

"The Nicole you used to know was huge."

"You were not."

"I'm not used to eating all that stuff now, I'm trying to eat healthily."

"Do you think you look healthy?" There it was.

"I don't know. I don't really look at myself or pay attention. Why?"

"You look too thin and don't eat a lot. You barely ate anything yesterday and Danielle and I weren't sure how to bring it up. My Mom thought you looked like Nicole Richie." That comment made me smile, being compared to a very thin celebrity, though I think her Mom meant it in a different way, since anorexia rumours had been swirling about her at the time.

"Danielle's friends made comments to her about you, her old room mates in the pub asked if you were okay, one kid in there didn't even recognize you, and our old friend Tom said to us, 'you're going to talk to her, right?'"

"Well, you just saw me eat…a lot. I usually eat mostly fruit and lean protein."

"You just don't look healthy."

"You haven't seen me in a year."

She dropped it and I was relieved.

When we get to the hotel, we check in and try to meet up with people at the bar. There was a long line and I was freezing waiting outside. The cold air went through my bones and hung on them, then created a wind tunnel in my chest.

"It's not that cold," Erin and Danielle both told me.

"I've been in L.A. for a bit. I'm not used to this weather." I didn't tell them I was freezing all the time in L.A. too.

We go into the packed bar, say "hi" to some old friends, but it was so crowded that we decide to just go back to the hotel and hang out.

I go into the bathroom to get changed. I sneak in a few crunches, and then go into my bag. I had brought candy for them from L.A. and had an extra. I opened it and tucked into a few pieces. I had already eaten so much food, that I figured I might as well indulge while I could. When I came out of the bathroom, they asked me if I got lost in there. They probably figured I was puking. Just the opposite—eating.

They were both lounging in bed, staring at me. I knew what was coming but ignored it. I hopped into bed and stared at the TV. They looked at each other, then at me. Danielle spoke first. "Okay, Nicole, we need to talk."

I was prepared.

I sat up.

"About what?" I asked.

"You know what," Danielle said. "You knew you couldn't come out here and we wouldn't mention how much weight you've lost."

Immediately, I became defensive.

"So, I've lost weight? You haven't seen me in like two years. Erin hasn't seen me in one."

"But this is drastic!" she said. "I was afraid to hug you when I saw you because I though I might hurt you."

"You look like you might snap in half," Erin said. "Your arms just dangle."

"You have a problem, Nicole," Danielle said. "Everyone has been coming up to me asking about you tonight. Strangers even. People we went to college with don't recognize you."

Erin finally chimed in with a blow I was not ready to take. First, she grabbed my wrist and poked it in the middle. "See that," she said, "it's just bone." She threw my wrist down and rolled over. "I can't even stand to look at you. I don't recognize you any more. You don't even look like my best friend."

I wasn't sure if I was more angry or hurt.

Here were my best friends, who, at this point, I wanted to reach out to for help because I was having a tough time, but the way they were treating me, I just couldn't.

Erin, still not facing me, continued. "I just don't want to get the call from California that something awful has happened to you. I couldn't live with myself," she said, and then had to throw in her celebrity comparison because she's addicted to "E! True Hollywood Stories." "It reminds me of the Karen Carpenter story. It's so sad. Your heart could just give out on you."

Danielle, a little more rational, but still blunt, picked up. "You're slowly killing yourself. Why do you think you're always cold? You have no body fat. Your electrolytes are probably so off. Your heart is so weak, and it can't take much more of this. You need help. You have anorexia."

Oh no, she said it. The "A" word.

"I do not," I told them.

Erin scoffed.

"I just eat healthily and work out a lot," I assured them.

Erin flipped back over. "But do you think you look healthy? Honestly?" she asked. "Your face is sunken in, your thighs don't touch, and look at your wrist—there is nothing there. Just bone." That hurt too.

"It's bags under my eyes. I haven't slept really in months."

"You even told me, you only eat fruit. That's not healthy," Danielle said.

"And do you have to go to the gym every day?" Erin asked.

I felt bombarded, and definitely cornered. "It gives me something to do," I responded, but felt annoyed by their attacks.

"See," Danielle continued, "you're depressed out there too. Maybe you should come home for a bit."

"Yeah," Erin added. "You're not doing what you wanted in LA and it's taken its toll on you. Just come home for a bit. We give you a lot of credit for going out there."

"Exactly," Danielle added, as the tag team continued. They were now trying the "complimenting while degrading you" trick. But the damage had already been done. At this point, I just wanted to get on a plane back to LA, but was forced to listen to them and respond. Danielle went on: "I'd be too much of a baby to do it. And you accomplished a lot. You can go back. But right now, you need to worry about your health and getting better, and if your family saw you this way, I think they'd agree."

Tears started to develop but I would not cry.

"I'm not leaving LA," I told them.

Again, Erin said, "Well, I just don't want to get the call from California that something awful has happened to you. We couldn't not say anything. You're having a tough time and people deal with things in different ways. And for you, maybe it's been food."

I started crying...and confessing a little.

"But I've always had issues with food, and you guys never said anything then—when I was overweight!"

"You weren't overweight!" they both yelled. "You were normal. And happy."

"I wasn't happy," I told them. "And even doctors said I was overweight."

"Well, you looked better then than you do now. You looked healthy then." Erin said.

"I wasn't."

"Well, if you wanted to lose 10 pounds then, fine. But you've gone too far."

Danielle stepped in again to tell me that it didn't help I was in L.A., the capital of eating disorders. "It made me so mad when you went to the doctor and they didn't do anything for you. I knew what was really the issue; you weren't eating enough and you were exercising too much. You have the patterns of an Anorexic and just from watching you these past couple days I can tell. You barely ate anything yesterday…"

"Yeah," Erin said. "You just pushed the food around on your plate."

"I did not," I said, because it was true. I ate it. "And I ate the rest of it in Danielle's car, because I'm classy," I said, trying to lighten the mood.

"You did not, I saw you. Besides, a salad isn't enough."

"Well you saw what I ate today."

"Yeah, and it was like you were putting on a show for us. When you did eat, you were panicky every time. I watched you. You were looking around, afraid to eat, wondering what everyone else was ordering. You were scared. It's like you can't eat in social situations. Those are the patterns of an Anorexic."

"And you couldn't order ice cream unless someone else did," Erin said.

"Well I ate other stuff."

"And then you complained about it."

"I'm just not used to eating that crap. I eat healthily, and a lot of small meals each day."

"Everyone needs that stuff. More than just fruit."

Danielle even went back and brought up the stupid cookie. I felt like they were trying to catch me on everything.

Erin, aggravated, finally burst out with: "The first step is admitting you have a problem. You just have to say it—I have anorexia!"

I didn't.

More calmly, Danielle said, "We're just saying this because we're your friends and we care about you. We want you to get better. We love you."

Danielle told me to at least go to a doctor when I got back to LA, and I told her I had been seeing one, and she told me to go and tell him the truth about things, and I said sure, just to get her off my back. Then she told me to see a psychologist about my depression and someone who specializes in eating disorders. Also, to get an echocardiogram and have my heart checked again, because the doctors were not doing their job. At least in that area, I agreed.

"We're so worried about you. It breaks my heart to see you like this."

I just stared at them, not knowing what to say at that point. I knew I had to say something though.

"Thank you for your concern. Yes, I have been a little down for a bit, but giving up on L.A. would be giving up on myself. I have got into a healthier routine out there and I'll try to eat more, I guess."

Erin rejected that. "I don't know how you have the energy to function, to go to work and especially to the gym."

They don't realize a lot of this is muscle. That's why I can lift so much.

"You're just too skinny." She was done, she threw in the towel. Danielle made another plea for me to go to the doctor's and I said I would, and that was that.

I could barely sleep that night. Were they jealous because I had lost weight? Perhaps mad because I was not the same girl I was in college? I had undoubtedly changed, and hopefully matured, other than just the weight. But I was upset that a trip I thought would get me away from constant thoughts and torments of food only increased them and created a rift between my friends and I.

Yes, I knew I had a problem.

Part of me wanted help.

But now, I had no one to reach out to.

The rest of the time there they watched closely what I did so that I did need to put on a show of eating, which was hard, because I had to figure out calories and fat. Plus, without exercise, it was frustrating.

The next morning we went to breakfast and they watched my every move.

I slipped a diet pill in my mouth before I ate, and they exchanged looks. No comments, but if they had, I would have said it was medicine.

Erin accused me of not putting milk in my cereal, which I had and showed her, though normally I wouldn't. Then she blew it off by saying how she drowns her cereal in milk. They watched the whole time, making the meal uncomfortable. When we were done, I said "goodbye" to Danielle, because I was headed back to Boston with Erin, but the three of us were to meet up later before I left. She told me to promise to see my doctor when I got back and to eat three complete meals the rest of the time here. I explained the smaller meals to her, but that I would eat.

That night I went out to dinner with Erin and a couple of her friends. It was uncomfortable, since I used to hang out with them when I visited Erin, and hadn't seen them in a long time. While I spoke to one, she went aside with the other, and they were looking at me and whispering. It was as if she just brought me for "show and tell." Later, back at her house, she told me that they had commented on my weight, and she indulged in it, claiming, "I told you so."

Erin treated me like a mutant the rest of my time there, but fortunately, that Monday, both she and Danielle had to work, so she let me take her car down to Rhode Island to visit my brother at school, which I was thrilled about. I wore my glasses, which I never wore, only to hide my apparently ugly and sunken-in face. I didn't want him to notice or embarrass him in front of his friends. I also put on extra makeup.

I pulled up outside his dorm and he walked out, Mr. College Student. I couldn't believe it. It was just so good to see him. He didn't look too shocked to see any change in me, but I was wearing a coat. October seemed so cold this year.

He first showed me his dorm room and then we went out to lunch. Apparently, he had told Dad that he wanted to take me to the restaurant we had been to when I was there for his Freshman Orientation because I liked it. I fretted about what to order, but since my calories had already been increased that weekend, I got a hot turkey sandwich. We had a great conversation and joked a lot, and when I only ate half of my sandwich (after picking off most of the bread), I asked if he wanted the other half to take back with him. He said, "no," so I was stuck with the remains.

At one point, I thought I saw him staring at one of my upper chest bones sticking out. Though, he could have been looking at my necklace. Or, it could have been my imagination, and me not wanting him to notice. We talked about his school, baseball, how he just had a visit home and about how long I'd be home for Thanksgiving. Then we joked about Kelly's wedding and what it would be like and how much fun we'd have. It was the same old Nicole and Dan stuff and it didn't feel as if it had been four months since I had seen him. It was nice, and I was grateful for the chance to visit him. It was just what I needed.

The check came and I went to grab it, but he took it first.

"No way," I said. "I'm not having my baby brother pay for me."

"Well, I walked across campus to the ATM this morning because I planned on paying, so I am." Later, when I talked to Dad, he told me how Dan had planned it all along. "You drove down here, that's enough." Dad told me that he was pretty pleased I was coming and excited to take me out. So I let the little tyke pay, but told him that next time, it was my treat.

We drove around and checked out some stores, and then he had to get back for a baseball meeting. I took him to his dorm, he gave me water because, of course, I was dehydrated, and then we hugged it out. He told me how good it was to see me. I said the same, and then offered him my sandwich again. I had no luck getting rid of the damn thing. Though only a few hours, seeing Dan was the highlight of my trip, which I told Dad on the drive back to Boston. I miss him, and my only wish is that I was a bit more like my old self. Maybe it's the anxiety medication my doctor gave me, or maybe it's just me. But I am not myself.

Hang In There... Wherever "There" Is

I ate some of my sandwich in the car on the way back, but chewed and spat out some of it. When I got back to Erin's house, she was there with Danielle, and they were waiting for us to all go out to eat. "I just ate," I told them. Another exchange of looks.

"Dan and I went out to a restaurant for lunch," I told them. Truth.

"Then he took me to the cafeteria before I left." Lie. "They had good chicken tenders." Another lie, but I knew couldn't eat again, especially after somewhat eating on the car ride back.

"Well, we're going for subs, so let's go," Erin said. We piled in the car and got to the place. They order subs and wait for me to order. I tell them my story of eating again, which I don't think they believed. I hated not being trusted, though this time, it was fair.

"Well, I'll get a cookie." But then I saw they had Baklava, which I do like, so I got that.

Back at Erin's, we all sit down and eat. Danielle picks at her sub. She always picks at her food. Who has the issue here? I start eating my messy Baklava with a plastic fork, and it's good, but I'm interrupted quickly.

"Did you just eat your fork?" Danielle said to me as I had just finished a bite of my treat.

I spit out the Baklava, and then began to panic, aimlessly searching my chewed up food for a piece of plastic fork. Danielle grabbed the fork and examined it while I frantically tore apart my Baklava.

Erin gently smacks her. "Don't upset her. Don't you understand how wrong that was to say?" she said, giving Danielle a knowing look, as if I wasn't in the room, across the kitchen table from her. Overwhelming fear. I hated being terrified of food, of eating situations, and most of all, of my body failing on me.

Danielle ignored her, focused on the fork, her eyes inspecting every edge. "Yeah, there's definitely an edge of this fork missing," Danielle decided.

I was beyond panic at this point. I feared death, I truly did. That damn piece of fork had to be in that now-mangled pile of mushy baklava that was slowly making its way through my body.

Erin grabbed the fork and examined it. "You did not eat the fork. Look!" she said as she pointed the fork out to me carefully. "Look at the edges, smooth and clean. All of them. The piece of this fork was missing to begin with. You didn't bite it off. You would have felt it. You just didn't notice when you got it. So eat the rest of your food, and Danielle, you stop worrying her."

Danielle laughed. "Sorry, I just notice these things," she said, as if her comments meant nothing.

The two of them started to pick up the wrappers of the subs that they had gotten, but I sat there frozen and remained in fear. The thought that there could be a minuscule piece of plastic fork making its way into my stomach burned in my head, collapsing me with terror.

They noticed.

"Nicole! It's fine! And you don't have to eat the rest if you don't want to."

But the thing is, I did want to. I liked it, and to allow myself to eat something I liked was a big deal. But the thought of the fork had consumed me so—a tiny piece of plastic in my body—how would my body, my heart, process it? My body could barely handle carbohydrates without me having to go to the hospital. The same with sugar. If plastic entered my digestive track and my blood had to try and, what, pull nutrients out of it, then surely, my body would shut down. Right? This was going to be the end of me.

I nervously finished up some forkless pieces, while Erin prepared to take a shower, and Danielle got ready to leave. As I was throwing out the remainder of my dessert-gone-bad, I heard Danielle say to Erin, "Do you want me to stay and watch her?"

"No, go ahead, I'll be quick," Erin said.

I became even more infuriated. I did not need a babysitter. What did they think I was going to do? Throw up my fork-infested food? I didn't do that any more. Erin never even knew that I did that when I was her roommate in college.

Danielle left, making me promise once again to see my doctor, and eventually, Erin went to bed, and I went downstairs to worry more. It seemed to be all I did lately.

But I made it that night. I of course made sure to take extra laxatives, but that fork did not get me! No, I would be okay for a few more days. Hopefully.

That night, I packed up my suitcase to head back to Los Angeles. The trip that I hoped would be relaxing and help me turned out to hurt me. I knew when I got back to L.A., I needed to hit the gym after all this food, but I also needed to relax a little. Eat some normal food—not too much, not too little. I know I have issues, but I don't want to be fat again. I like food, it's all I think about, dream about, all the time. I hate it. "It's just food," I always tell myself. But if it's just food, why do I let it run my life?

When I returned to LA, I did not feel well. I hit the gym right away, and was back into my regular routine. Later, Sam told me how she had hoped the getaway would be good for me, and that I'd come back happier and more nourished. But instead, she was terrified when I came back looking worse—she said I was a grayish green colour and walked very hunched over, without much to say, much like the "living dead." That was how I felt.

Chapter 23
Renfrew:
The Psychodrama of my Life

One of the groups here is called "Psychodrama," and is led by this hysterical lady, Claudia, who has been through her own recovery with other issues, and is so open and understanding. She's definitely a favourite here.

Psychodrama is when one person in the room is the protagonist and brings up an issue they are working on, and the rest of the groups acts out the aspects of the issue and their life—their family members, their job, their smile, their eating disorder—basically anything that comes up that is affecting them. I had thought about trying it, because I had seen how it impacted other people who had done it. Robin recommended I give it a shot as well. When I get into the group, Claudia asks for volunteers. No one raises a hand. She looks at me and goes, "You look like you're thinking about it."

"I am." So I go up there, oh so brave.

Claudia asks what I want to work on.

"My negativity," I say. "My therapist says that I'm too hard on myself, I don't look at my achievements as that and I see myself as a failure."

So she picks someone in the room to play my "Hope."

Then, she has someone in the room be my "Writing."

She asks me if I have any animals, and I tell her "Two English Bulldogs. Boomer and Molly."

"Let's get Boomer up here," she says in her gruff voice, which makes me laugh. This sounds like fun.

So there are three girls up there, Hope, Writing and Boomer, and then there is me, Nicole. I switch seats with Hope, and then suddenly, I play the role of "Hope," and the other girl is "Nicole." I have to act out my "hope," so I turn to the girl playing "Nicole," and have to give her, or rather, myself, some hope.

In my new role, I tell her/me, "I know sometimes you get down because of your writing and location and things not working out, especially because of the eating disorder. Things seem really tough, but trust me, they do get better. You will get better. You just have to have the strength and hope to get through it."

The group was like, wow, that was good. It surprised me too.

I switch back into my real role of "Nicole," and the girl who was me, goes back to "hope" and basically says to me what I had just said, but in her own words so that I can get a different perspective. It helps because I know I can say things and not believe them, but when someone else says my own words to me, they hit me in a different way.

Then I turn to my "Writing." I tell it how "Once you were my passion, but we lost touch during my eating disorder. Recently I got that spark back and I think we will have a bright future together because we are meant to be together and help each other."

Then there was Boomer, my precious, silly, adorable Bulldog. I got to be Boomer for a second and Claudia asked Boomer to describe himself. In the best Boomer voice I could do, if dogs could talk, I said, "I am lazy, I sleep on the couch most of the day and sometimes I'm grumpy."

Claudia asked, "What is your relationship like with Nicole?"

"It was good when she gave me lots of treats. I missed her when she was in L.A., so I was happy to have her back. I noticed that when she ate, it was very little, and that she fed most of it to me."

When I said that, it made me realize it was true. It had just come out of me, but it struck me what I had been doing and it was sad. I went back to my "Nicole" seat, and the girl playing "Boomer" stepped in.

She is funny to begin with, and got right into her Boomer role. "I still like my snacks, but I'd like it if you ate more too, Nicole. I miss you right now and can't wait for you to come home. We can take healthy walks together." It was adorable, and made me excited to see my Boomie again.

Then came "Negativity," which seems to loom over me at every moment anyway.

We switched spots, and I was in the Negativity's seat. I speak to myself like I feel. I told "Nicole" that "you are worthless, a failure, pathetic and that you set out to be a great writer and accomplished nothing. You turned to your eating disorder instead and you are going nowhere." Basically, all the things I really do say to myself.

So we switch seats, and the other girl has to say it back to me. She says a wimpy version of what I said. Claudia goes, "how was that?"

"Not mean enough," I tell her.

Claudia tells Negativity to try again, and she does, saying I'm pathetic and a failure, and I tell her, "still not mean enough."

She went again and told me how worthless I was. I start shaking. Claudia asks how it made me feel. I start crying. The girl feels bad because she didn't want to be mean to me. I tell her, "No, honestly, it still wasn't mean enough. But those are the thoughts going through my head all the time. I believe them, they're there, but the sad thing is if anyone else were up here doing this, I would feel sad for them and tell them that it wasn't true." So of course, here I am, crying in front of this whole group, but that's the point of this group. This is what is supposed to happen. I had no clue how powerful it would be.

Claudia decides to bring Los Angeles into the picture. She picks someone out of the group to be L.A. She sits in my seat and I sit where "L.A." is and speak to "Nicole." As L.A., I tell her/me that, "When Nicole first arrived here, she liked it, explored it, went to the beach, met people, took a class and was somewhat happy. Then she got tied up in her eating disorder. I wish she had taken advantage of all the things I have to offer, but because she was so sick, she only saw the negative side of the city, not the beauty. But don't view things as missed opportunities. There is a lot to see that you didn't, but hey, I'm still here, and so are you. I will welcome you back whenever you are ready, even if it's just for a visit."

I sound like a travel ad.

Then the beast comes out. My eating disorder. I speak as my Eating Disorder. "Nicole, we were good friends. I was there to comfort you and help you when your friends weren't there, or you were homesick. When you were lonely, I was always there for you to turn to. By eating only fruit, you were being healthy. Maybe sometimes, you didn't use me in the right way, but that's not my fault. It's yours."

"Look how manipulative the eating disorder sounds," Claudia says. "I mean, 'you didn't use me right.'"

Hearing things from a different perspective really does make everything more clear. Or scarier.

"When did all this negativity start?" she asks.

"I think it's always been with me, since I was young. Like 5 years old and overweight. I just kept it locked inside."

So out comes the family. She picks a girl to be my five-year old self, my Mom, my Dad, Kelly and Dan, in order to discover how I was unhappy but always smiling and seemingly happy, so no one knew of my unhappiness. We realized also that I was five when we moved into a new house and when my brother was born.

I sit in the 5-year old chair and talk. "There was so much going on that I never wanted to bother anyone with my problems. Everyone always said how I was smiling when they saw me, so that's what I did. It was tough being five. I didn't like being away from my parents. I liked doing stuff with them. They were busy sometimes with my brother, and my sister was older and didn't always want to hang out with me. I think I turned to food for comfort."

Claudia says how traces of my eating disorder were already there. "That eating disorder voice came in and said, 'let me in. I will give you candy and cupcakes." Which is sad, because that is what I turned to.

Then it's my family's time to speak. I sit in my "Dad's" seat and say how he's always wanted me to be happy and follow my dreams. "You were always my buddy and went for rides with me. I didn't always follow my dreams, and I want you to."

Back to the five-year-old, where I get very confessional: "I felt like I was always bigger. It was hard because I didn't understand it. Mostly, I just wanted everyone else to be happy. I was hurting at times, but I couldn't say that."

Then, as a five-year-old, I get to have a conversation with the girl in my seat. I talk to my twenty-four-year-old self. "Hi," I say, and get some giggles from the crowd. "I'm Nicole. I'm five."

"Hi," the girl playing me says.

"Sometimes I feel like I have no one to go to, even though I know I can always go to my parents, and they'll listen. It's weird and I hope I don't feel this way when I'm twenty-four."

Then, she and I switch places. I am back as myself, and this girl is my five-year-old self. I say to me at five that, "I know you're hurting and I can't change that now. In a way, I feel like you, this little girl is still in me, and I will work for both of us to work through this so we don't need to hurt any more. I know I can't change the past and it was hard for you, and I'm still struggling now, but I want to get through this and help me and the little girl inside."

Then I do some resolutions. I thank my acting parents for their support in the past and present. Even though I couldn't go to them when I was little, I knew I always had their love. The girl playing my sister apologized for not being there when I first came home from L.A., but she was scared for me, and is glad we're close now. The girl who played my brother says how he was glad he could be there for me during a tough time, but it's sometimes hard for him to express his emotions, and he was kind of scared too. "I'm a guy," the girl joked.

Then I got to tell all the other aspects of my life what I thought.

To my Negativity: "You have been in my life for too long and I want you to go away. I am going to leave you behind, here."

To my eating disorder: "You should never have been in my life, or in anybody's life here. You should go away because you are hurtful and manipulative."

To L.A.: "I'm sorry that I didn't take advantage of you like I could have, and I know I'm going home for a bit, but I also know that you will always be there and I can go back eventually."

To my Writing: "I have missed you. I am glad you are back in my life and I hope we have a great future together."

To Boomer: "I promise to keep giving you treats, but I will eat too, and then we will take walks together."

To my Hope: "Thank you. I am glad you are in my life and helping me through things. I hope you stay with me, because I know you are what I need to keep moving me through recovery."

Claudia asks how I feel. "It's hard because it really made me see things from a different perspective and listen to all the different voices coming my way, and there are so many it can be overwhelming. I realize how strong my negativity is, and how long it has been with me, and that I was just as scared as a little girl, and even worse, had eating disordered thoughts then."

It was totally draining and I did cry, but it was so good for me to get all that stuff out, and I learned a lot about myself. I can say positive things, but I know I won't believe them. That will take time. It's hard to accept them, but that's the negativity kicking in. I need to work on that, but this is a process.

Afterwards, I get a bunch of hugs and girls tell me how great I did and how brave it was for me to go through with that. For some, they say it really rang true for them, and they had the same thoughts when they were five and just realized it then. They tell me how looking at my life like that really had an effect on them and resonated with them. It was both cool and interesting to see how evaluating my issues had an impact on them, and how though we all come from different backgrounds and have different issues, we can all relate in some way.

I give Claudia a hug and thank her. I leave and run into Robin. I guess Claudia had already called her, because she heard all about it and was impressed with my work. She brings up my negative thoughts, and I find myself frustrated, unable to talk about it. I'm aware of my issues with it, and I know I am unhappy with myself, but I cannot just change those thoughts. Change is a long progression, I suppose, but one I hope to embrace and conquer.

I go to my mailbox and there is a card in there. I open it and it has a cute bulldog puppy on it. It is from a girl, Dana, who had been in the group, and read: "Nicole, great job during the psychodrama. I know that wasn't easy and you should be proud of your strength. <3 Dana P.S.-I thought the card would be remind you of Boomer.

How sweet is that?

Later I went to the art studio, where I decorate a stuffed doll. I make one using word beads. Since I had heard the phrase so much, I put "Hang in There" on the front, as a reminder to myself. Then, since I have never really understood how to do that, on the back I put, "Wherever There Is." Right now, it is Renfrew, and I am so glad to be here.

Chapter 24
The Confession
October 19, 2006

I was scheduled to work three days in a row after returning from Boston. I did one day, but I was so drained. The next day, I didn't want to go. Something didn't feel right. I didn't feel right. The night before I had called the other teachers on the list to see if they could cover for me. One was the wrong number, and the other one, the "head teacher," just couldn't do it, and said "aww," when I told her about my chest pains. Despite her "aww," I still had to work.

I couldn't ignore my obligation to the job. I knew that at 10 o'clock there would be a bus with students on it waiting for a tour of the museum and for some storytelling on the trail, and I had to be there for them. I got up, threw on some clothes and looked at myself in the mirror.

My eyes, I thought. Are those bags under my eyes, or are my eyes sinking into my face? I looked horrible. Pale. I didn't want to go back to bed or to the gym, and I definitely did not want to go to work.

I knew I needed some nourishment because I was the only leader on the tour. I ate a nectarine and brought a plum and some dried apricots for later. I get up to the museum, prepare everything, and shortly after, the bus arrives. I show them some things in the museum and then we head out on the trail.

Shortly up the path, I stop them so I can tell them a story about some birds and a tree. As I start talking, everything slows down in front of me. My heart starts racing and I realize I can't speak. I'm about to pass out, and I catch the eyes of one of the teachers and say, "I'm sorry, I don't feel well," and walk off to the side. A few of the chaperones rush after me.

"Just stay here guys," I hear the teacher yell, and he comes to check on me also. I stand there, trying to breathe while checking my pulse. It's racing. Some dried apricots, maybe that's all I need.

One lady asks, "Are you having a panic attack? I have Xanax!" The other chaperones shake their heads "no" at me.

The take me to a picnic table and sit me down. I was having trouble breathing, but was able to explain that I had been seeing a doctor for chest pains.

The teacher came over and told me they had been here before and done the tour and that they could lead the kids. That it would fine and for me to relax and take care of myself. They were amazing.

Then one of the chaperones tells me she's a Somatic Therapist and maybe she could help calm me down. She sat down with me on the picnic table, and the other chaperones went off. I had no clue what a somatic therapist was. I was both embarrassed and nervous about my health. She thought it could be anxiety or a panic attack, but I knew better.

She had me put my feet on the ground and do some breathing, while I tapped my hands on my arms. She told me to think about happy memories. I couldn't. Did I have any? No recent ones at least. I talked about my family—nothing specific. Just memories of us laughing together. Some thoughts brought me back to college, some fun times. Happy moments, yes, but never any true, lasting happy feelings. I began to cry and I didn't know if it was because I missed how things used to be or because I wanted them to be different now.

She didn't care. She told me tears were good, to breathe, place my hands on my knees and keep my feet grounded. Problem was, the tears brought on a runny nose and I didn't have a tissue. Embarrassing. I pretended to be wiping my tears. So gross. As if this moment hadn't been awkward enough.

We were there for a while and she asked if maybe I'd like to rejoin the group. I didn't want to but I said I'd try. We walked a little ways over and I felt sick again. Woozy, with palpations and that slow feeling. I couldn't do it. She thought it was because when I got closer to the group I felt sick. I assured her it wasn't, and that I had been having these pains for a while. She suggested I call my doctor. I did, and got an appointment. She said they would take care of the rest of the tour. I thanked her...for everything. I showed her the rock painting activity we did and was then on my way for the trek back to L.A., hoping I would make it there OK. What had just happened?

I get to Dr. Otis's office and check in. By then, I have calmed down a bit. They call me in shortly and I weigh in at 120, which was so disappointing. I had been 118, but I was wearing sneakers and I never wear sneakers to his office.

"120," the nurse says. "You look slimmer than that." She always has some sort of comment on my weight. She left the room and said that the doctor would be right in.

I figured that I had a couple of minutes, so I snuck into my bag and pulled out a cracker since I still felt as if I might pass out. I didn't want to eat it before I got weighed in case it made a difference on the scale.

Dr. Otis arrives and I explain what happened at the museum, that I was still feeling woozy and having chest pains.

Slightly annoyed, he tells me, "Your blood work came back normal."

"But that was about a month ago."

"It shouldn't change that much." *Electrolytes*, I remember Danielle saying.

"I've been having a lot of chest pain though."

"Your last EKG was fine. I guess we could do a stress test."

"Not an Echocardiogram?"

"That won't show us as much."

That was it. He was done with me and about to leave the room when I stopped him.

"Wait, there's something else I should tell you."

Nicole Roberge

He shut the door and sat back down.

I look down and start crying. He hands me a tissue. "I've been exercising too much and not eating very much." It was out. Sort of. I apologized for crying.

He said it was okay, and then, "I am glad you told me this and I think I hinted at it before." He took out my chart. "Does anyone in your family have a history of anorexia?"

Was he saying *I* was Anorexic? I don't think of myself as thin, even though I look pretty gross.

"No," I told him.

"Do you ever throw up after you eat?"

"No." Because, after all, it had been a while. I should tell him that I used to. I will. Eventually.

We talked for a bit and he said he was going to keep a close eye on me.

"I understand the problem, your past issues of weight, and being in LA now. I think you're a good person and can get through this."

He gave me the name of a couple of therapists and we scheduled an echocardiogram. He also gave me his big treatment plan: "Eat more and exercise less." Like that would be easy.

He was about to leave again and then poked his head back in. "Maybe some of the chest pain will go away now that you've brought this to my attention. You know, since you've got it off your chest."

I didn't think so.

I was happy to finally admit it to him because I wanted to tell him so many times before, in many different ways, but it never happened. I thought, this is it, let's get better.

I left his office and went to the grocery store, and instead of getting just fat-free items, I bought a variety of foods. I also got some lean cuisines, though the problem in the past had been that I would buy them and not eat them. Not this time.

I went home and then to the gym to do a quick workout. I had a snack of yogurt and fruit. Sam came home late and we sat down to watch TV. I felt uncomfortable sitting in the chair, and it wasn't because of the chair. Everything was getting slow again, and my pulse was off. I thought that maybe if I stood, I would feel better. I get up and go to the kitchen. A snack, I thought. That's what I need. I take a bite of a granola bar, but still, I don't feel well. It's food, why doesn't it work?

I sit back down and am woozy. It feels worse when I sit. I need to get up again. I don't want to worry Sam so I go back into the kitchen and lean against the counter. Without warning, my pulse quickens, until it is racing and my blood burns. My heart is beating so fast I think that soon it will be going so fast it will have no choice but to either stop, or explode. I panic, thinking, this is it. I had been warned, by both my body and friends. I am going to die. I had done it to myself. My head clears enough for me to think, "I'm never going to see my family again." They will never know what happened to me, or how much I really love them. With the fear that I only had seconds to live, I scream for Sam. She didn't hear me. I scream again. She runs in.

"Something's wrong," I tell her, shaking. She calls 911.

They ask her questions. She puts her hand on my pulse. "Yeah, it's really fast," she says.

She gets me to sit down, but I'm afraid to sit, so I sit and stand and rock back and forth.

She comes near me and I hear her say to the operator, "If you ask me, I think she doesn't eat enough."

I hear sirens, which scares me more. When they arrive, they are all over me, asking questions and attaching wires to me. I can't answer. I can't breathe.

My pulse has slowed but it much higher than the 40's it is usually in.

They ask if I am on medication. Sam goes into my room and gets it.

"You're on anxiety medication?" they ask.

"Only because I've been having chest pains and my doctor thought it was anxiety, but this isn't anxiety."

They call the hospital and tell them they are taking a female in who is having an anxiety attack.

"This isn't anxiety," I tell them.

"Just relax," they say.

Sam stayed home because she was leaving the next day for a business trip. When the paramedic asked if she was coming to the E.R., she said, "I've done this before," and then to me, "Give me a call when you know if you're staying."

They took me out to the ambulance and asked when my last period was. Could I tell them five months ago?

"I don't know," I said.

"But you're not pregnant?"

"No."

In the ambulance, he hooks me up to an I.V. to test for something, but I was so dizzy. I wanted to tell him what I thought was going on, but I couldn't. Maybe at the hospital. I needed to get to the hospital.

When I did get there, they left me on a stretcher for an hour in the hallway. When they left the chart on my stretcher, they let the desk know that it was just an anxiety attack. I was about to give him an anxiety attack.

They finally put me in a room where I waited for about another hour. I kept having palpitations and couldn't lie down, but couldn't sit up either. I tried to get the attention of a nurse, but they were all chatting. People glanced in my room once in a while, but no one came to help. I held my chest and prayed it would be okay.

Eventually, a doctor came. She barely looked at me, and then said, "So you're having an anxiety attack?"

"No," I told her. "Chest pains, dizzy, short of breath."

"Sounds like an anxiety attack. Plus, you're on medication for it."

"But I don't need the medication."

"Well if your doctor ordered it…"

"I really don't feel well."

"We'll run an EKG."

"They just did one."

"Well we don't have it."

It was as if she couldn't be bothered with me. She had "real" patients to deal with. Later, I would learn that a lot of doctors view eating disorders as a "choice" to be sick, but it's not. It's a disease, and a deadly one at that. Doctors don't have the knowledge of mental illness, and especially all the damage it can do to a person physically. If I had a broken arm, she would have attended to me, because she could actually see the pain, not just what I was telling her. So why should she believe me? She thought I wanted to be sick, after all. That is when I realized the true stigma that comes with eating disorders.

More waiting, and soon a nurse came in to tell me I am being discharged. Shock.

"I don't feel well," I tell her. "What did the doctor say?"

"Hang on, I'll go check."

I should have told her the truth. That I needed to eat, and probably could use an I.V. Most likely, I needed to be admitted.

The doctor arrives, frustrated, and gives me some Ativan for anxiety and a prescription for three more pills. Then, I am on my way. Alone, and Terrified.

I make my way to the pay phone and call Sam, who then picks me up.

I get in the car, and immediately, she says, "I can't believe they aren't admitting you." There was some silence, and then I tell her how scared I was. She tells me how I should be on an I.V. and feeding tube. "I know you don't want to hear this, but I think you're anorexic."

"I know," I said, crying. Finally acknowledging the eating disorder and not that I just had an "issue" really had an impact on me. But if the doctors weren't going to help me, I needed to help myself. I had no idea how I got into this mess of an eating disorder that had more of a hold on me that I've ever had a hold on anything.

We talked for a bit in the car, and she went over how she asked me when I first moved in if I was anorexic. She tells me how before then even, when we went out to a restaurant, she could see the panic in my eyes. 'Ultimately, this is something you need to do, but I am willing to help. It will be a long road back and you will try to sabotage yourself. But you're a nice girl with a lot of things going for you. You're too hard on yourself and you don't need to be suffering all the time."

I tell how it's hard to be constantly thinking of food. She tells me I need to increase my fat intake, but I'm so afraid of gaining weight.

When we got back to the house, my heart rate had settled a bit, but I hadn't.

The car ride home had seemed to take forever, even though we were just a few blocks away. The tears flew out of me, along with the confession that I knew I had a "problem." I told Sam about what had happened earlier—the chest pains at work, the visit to the doctor, what I told him and what he told me, and how it still didn't stop me from going to the gym.

"But you're aware you have a problem, right?" she asked me.

I knew I did. It was just hard to acknowledge it as an actual eating disorder.

"Yes."

"Because some people don't, so it's good that you can admit it. I've known for a while, I just didn't know how to bring it up. But I knew it was getting serious" she said as I collapsed onto a chair and she began poking through the kitchen. "I was even going to call your doctor and tell him. I mean, how could he not have noticed or said anything? I was ready to call your parents."

"He noticed the weight loss. I told him I worked out."

"Well, you're not going to now, are you?"

It's not that easy.

"I want to get better. I was so scared tonight."

"I know you were. Remembering how scared you were might be a good thing to make you want to work on recovery. The first thing is realizing that you have anorexia—"

I hate that "A" word.

"—the second part is actually wanting to get better, and not continuing what you've been doing. It's not going to be easy. I can try and help you, but I really don't understand this."

This was all too much. She was moving too fast. Pushing the issue when I hadn't even processed it myself. I was still coming to terms with the fact that I was alive right now, never mind that I was...sick.

"Thanks. I don't understand it either, really. Right now, I just want to work on staying alive. I do want to get out of this, because it's torture. It's like living in the prison of your mind. I cry on the way to gym, I don't want to be doing it. I want to be able to have real meals but I just can't. Tonight made me finally see what was happening to me, and the damage that has been done to my body, and it's not a place that I want to be. I never wanted this."

"It's good that you're talking about it and that you recognize that what you've been doing is bad and you want to get better," she said as she pulled out two pieces of toast from the toaster and I crossed my fingers that they were not for me. I looked around to see if any of her four cats were on

147

standby. Not that cats eat toast. They might. Well, her cats definitely might. She put some cherry jam on the toast and put the plate on the table in front of me and motioned for me to eat. I wiped off a little...or most...of the jam onto my plate and took a bite.

After a few bites of toast, I was done. I ate about a half of one piece and honestly, it felt good to eat something different, and I felt as if I needed to eat something to keep my heart going, but it made me so full to eat that much that I started to feel gross and filled with that familiar feeling of guilt and shame. I pushed the plate back.

"You're done?" she asked.

"I'm sorry, that's all I can do."

"That's OK, it's a start. I wanted you to get a little something in you. Why don't you go get some rest now?"

"Thank you for being so understanding and talking about the eating disorder stuff. It's nice to finally talk about it, even though I don't understand it."

She looked drained. I felt drained. I wonder what I look like?

"It'll be okay," she said.

I went into my room and couldn't climb into bed just yet. I was too nervous to close my eyes, and I needed to reach out to someone. I went to my computer and checked my instant messenger. My little brother was online. Not much of a surprise—he was in college. The only reason I had downloaded the program was because it seemed the best way to keep in touch with him. Unfortunately, he had an "away message" up. But I just had to tell him. I had to let him know. I clicked on his screen-name and a box came up. I started to type:

"Hey. I just wanted to let you know, in case anything ever happens to me, that I love you. I know I don't say it much, but I do, and I hope you know that."

Send.

I sat back in my chair, hoping he would get my message and know it was true. I hated myself for being so far from home, for not being there for the events in their lives, and for almost being taken away from them. They needed to know how much they mean to me. Through all this, if anything did happen to me, I wanted him to know that I loved him. To have him tell my family I loved them. That though I didn't know what was going on with me, with my life, I knew one thing was clear, and that the only love that existed within me was for my family. How could I have sacrificed so much?

A box popped up on my screen.

"What happened?"

He was there. He got my message.

Of all the people I could have talked to at the moment, it was my eighteen-year-old brother that made the most sense, and who I needed the most.

I didn't tell him about the "A" word, but I did tell him that I was back in the hospital with chest pains, and that the doctors didn't treat me. I told him how I thought I had gone overboard on the workouts and had not been eating enough and maybe lost too much weight, and my heart couldn't take it any more.

Being the baseball player he is, he tried to stress the importance of nutrition with protein and eating all of the food groups. I told him I thought gaining weight would be too hard for me, especially because I had been trying to lose it for so long. I said I didn't want to gain weight, but I didn't want to be unhealthy any more.

"Gaining a small amount of weight would be a start to becoming healthier," Dan said. "You just have to eat normally and gain some healthy weight."

What is eating normally? I was so far removed from it that I didn't know how I could get back.

"Especially because you work out so much," he added.

"That's part of the problem," I told him. "Everything I've been doing is damaging my body. I got really scared today, I thought I was done."

"This is just something you've gotta fight through. It's part of the struggle," the wise one told me. But it has *all* been a struggle. Does that mean that's all that's in front of me too?

"It all boils down to determination and will power. How much do you want it?" he asked.

"I do," I told him. "I want, and need, to get better. I can't keep doing this."

Talking to my brother brought some relief. When did he get so smart? I knew that the torture of the disease was hard, and the coming out was going to be very difficult. But after that, the recovery, this whole matter of trying to get better, that was unthinkable, even though I wanted it so much. How do you get yourself out of a lifestyle you've been dedicated to for so long? And will it, the eating disorder, let me escape?

When I got into bed I took a long look at a couple of pictures on my nightstand. One was of my brother and I from his high school graduation. He was like my little buddy, even though he towered over me now. What would he have done if something happened to me? Then I looked at one with all of my family. My poor parents worry enough just about me being in Los Angeles alone, I'd hate for them to be worried or upset about things now. I knew I had to call home though and tell them. I turned off the light and lay on my back with my arms out so my heart and lungs could have more room. I didn't know if it worked, but it made sense to me.

I will call home tomorrow.

But I prayed that I lived through the night.

Chapter 25
Renfrew:
Everyone Loses Their Head Sometimes

I have been feeling down the past couple of days, so I took this little St. Raphael pin I have out. Because of the day I was born on, he is my Guardian Angel, and was assigned by God to follow us as we search for real happiness. He also protects us from danger and brings good health—just what I need. I ask him for help, and explain that I don't want to be sick, I don't want to die because I love my family, but I don't know what to do any more. I put it in my name tag and when I was in the bathroom, it fell out. It broke when it fell on the floor and his head fell off. At first, I was bummed because it broke and I felt bad and was mad at myself. But now, I think that it was a sign. He gave me a response. He said: "Everyone loses their head sometimes."

Oh Raphael, you joker you. I pick him up and the head still fits, but it's detached of course, sort of like I feel mine is. There are ways I could put it back on—glue, tape even. It may not ever fit perfectly again, but it can go back together. And it's better that it doesn't fit right, because who wants to be "perfect" anyway?

Dad had emailed both Jason and Charlotte to let them know I was extending my stay and they both emailed him back.

Jason responded: *"I'm glad to hear she is doing better. It's a disease and a terrible one at that. My prayers are with you and her..."*

Charlotte wrote: *"Thank you for letting me know. I love your daughter so much. I had an eating disorder in my late teens and early 20's and with my strong family support, beat it. I'm praying for all of you and know she will be okay and get through this.... Let me know if you ever need anything at all."*

They are both amazing. It's bizarre how these two have been my best friends and supports while I'm here and going through this. I'd feel alone without them, even though I still feel alone. I had to cut Danielle and Erin out of my life for a bit. I told Danielle I was coming here, but not Erin. Her words were so harsh when I saw her in Boston, that I thought it might be good to take a break from her. I knew that talking to her, or both of them, would make me more frustrated and I needed to take the time for myself. I do hope to reconcile when I leave, but now is not the time. This is the time to focus on getting well.

I finally got to exercise, but I wouldn't call it exercise. We marched in place, jogged in place, did a few jumping jacks and some light abdominal word. I don't think that it will change my mentality on exercise. I know that I don't want to torture myself any more at the gym, but I want to get in shape again. Robin asked me, "What's to stop you, once you start again?" I don't know. It's a vicious cycle. The lady who led the group kept telling us to stop when we were tired, but I kept pushing myself because I wanted to work harder. No pain, no gain, right? I was finally exercising and wanted to do more. I don't know if this part of the programme alone can change my mentality, even though I want it to. I feel hopeless about a lot of things, and don't know how to fix it. There's gotta be a magic button somewhere. I just haven't found it yet.

Robin tells me she would like to see me extend my stay, and I think it's a good idea too. She suggests two more weeks, I say one. That will be a total of 7 weeks as an inpatient. Dad thinks I need more help than I am getting here, mostly to work on the depression, but he tells me if I need the time, take it. He also tells me that they can come down for a pass and we'll go out, which is good now, since I am extending my stay. I think it's the right decision. There are still issues to be uncovered. Also, I want to show them the progress I have made and prove to them that I am doing well. I am no longer the girl who ate lettuce and cottage cheese out of a teacup.

I was a little uneasy about my decision, so I head out to the Smoking Gazebo. We were only allowed out there a few times a day, for fifteen minutes, but it is a place of refuge. I am not really a smoker, but once in a while, it helps to relax me. To sit and talk with the girls there is fun. The rules do not apply in the Smoking Gazebo. We can talk about the crappy food, the stupid rules, stupid people and staff, and how our treatment sucks sometimes. We laugh, joke and, for fifteen minutes, forget that we are at an eating disorder facility.

I go out and sit next to this woman Barbara, who I crocheted a headband for. She loved it, but it was really a lame attempt on my part. I tell her about my pass and some of my Dad's worries, but explain that they haven't seen me and though, yes, I'm still not well, I have made strides. I feel bad when my Dad has to listen to the upset version of me. "He should take it as a compliment that you call him and talk to him about this stuff," she tells me. "It means you trust him and can confide in him. You've made so much progress, and only you know that. We can see it, and you should be proud of that."

It is so sweet of her. All these girls are amazing. I call Dad to apologize for being grumpy sometimes, but all is fine. I explain to him how I think of him as a friend, and that's why I go on about things, but I appreciate his support and am looking forward to seeing him. What I didn't tell him, or anyone, is that I have still been doing crunches in my room, and when I go on pass alone, I restrict, but lie on my food journal. I'm not hungry and still force the issue of "eat when you're hungry, stop when you're full."

That night, I went back out to the Smoking Gazebo. We all chat wildly as one of the girls, Marissa, is leaving the next day. She was the first one to say "hi" to me, and I remind her of that. She yells to someone down the path. "Ralph, are you gonna miss me?"

We all look, and it's Ralph, the cute little old man who does maintenance for the building and locks up at night. He's so sweet and we love to chat with him. He tells her that of course he will, and he misses all of us when we leave because we're like family. He is so kind and probably cares about our well being more than some of the staff. He gives us pep talks often too, and does one now. "If you feel yourself sliding back," he says, "then get back here, because you don't want to get back to square one." We all nod. "You're beautiful young ladies who should live to be beautiful old ladies. You've got too much life to live." We get tearful. "When life beats you up, bite it in the butt." We giggle, and Marissa gives him a hug and says, "You always have the best advice."

"Seriously," he says. "You girls are like daughters to me. It hurts me to see all of you here because you don't realize how much you have to offer."

Ralph is so great and makes more sense than most people here. His words touch us and he's right. I don't want to be 60 and still battling this. Then I look at the 14-year-old girls, and it hurts to see them here. I feel like a big sister, but how can I give them advice? I am struggling at age 24. I could be their future. After all, I was taking diet pills and skipping meals at 14.

***

I met with my psychiatrist and we talk about my antidepressants and how they aren't really affecting my mood. She tells me that when I came in, I was "superficially perky," which makes me laugh, because I think I was so stunned to be here, I just rattled off my story in a robotic way.

"When was the last time you were really happy?"

"I don't know," I tell her.

"It's good that you're down and this is your mood. It's okay. We need to peel back the layers and find different emotions."

"That's what I want too. I know my parents just want me to be happy."

"You're in treatment. You're going to be miserable. You're going to have more bad days than good, and that's okay. Happy stresses people out. Be miserable and work through it. That's what treatment is. Finding the sources that make you miserable, and figuring it out."

She's great, and I know she understands. She just puts it right out there.

I left that meeting and went to a large group meeting. Meg and I decide to cause trouble by sitting in the back. She had gotten a whoopy cushion on pass. After the therapist spoke, she let one rip. Brittany, the musician, was cracking up, and tells her how she needs to make them sound differently. "No two farts are alike," she says. "They're like snowflakes." Farts and snowflakes…and eating disorders, I think. Each one is different and unique. We're hysterical, so of course everyone knew where the toots were coming from, but we didn't care. It was fun.

We continue our trouble causing the next day. We have a lame group to go to, but we don't want to. We want to watch a movie. Usually, when we go to a group, we have to get our schedules stamped, and then we hand them in at the end of the week. It just so happened that Meg had a "Curious George" stamp, so we all hand our schedules to her, get them stamped, then get comfy in the living room to watch a movie. I'm beginning to think everyone should take a mental health break once in their lives. Just check in somewhere for 28 days, even if you don't have an issue. It can be life changing.

Mom and Dad are coming. I check my phone to see if they had called, but had a text from Jason, asking how I was. I tell him it's draining, I extended my stay, but it's for the best. He says: "I can't imagine how tough it is. Hang in there. Food is your friend."

Yes, hang in there. He's great but has no idea how great he is.

Before I can respond, Mom and Dad arrive. I run down and give them hugs. It is so good to see them. They sign in and I bring them through to the living room and they meet some of the girls, then I show them my room. Dad was relieved that it did not smell of propane.

We go to Chestnut Hill and browse the shops. Mom gets some fabric for quilting and then they take me to the knitting store to get yarn for me so I can crochet. They think it's a good coping mechanism. I didn't want them to pay, but Dad says, "That was the point, we wanted to get you something and take you out to dinner."

"Thank you. And crocheting is good for all that idle time."

"It's not good when Nicole has idle time," Dad says.

"It's not that I really had idle time. I had stuff to do, I just didn't do it. Other things took over..."

We walk over to the Chestnut Hill Grill. I got the Salmon Salad again, which is good, and I had plans for dessert.

Dinner was strange, in some ways. It was like having dinner with them back in normal times, but also surreal because I knew the circumstances. We chatted, but there was no eating disorder talk. Once in a while we'd bring up the girls or the facility, and I don't think it's that we were avoiding the real issue, I think it's that we were out for a meal and just enjoying it. Enjoying a meal? Food?

We all got dessert and then I was quite full. When we left the restaurant, I say to Dad, "See, I put dressing on my salad."

"I didn't even notice. See, I'm not watching."

Part of me doesn't want them to watch me like a hawk, but part of me wants them to notice how I was doing better. I'm sure they were also treading lightly, not knowing what comments would upset me. Like when people say, "you look healthy." Here we all think that healthy equals fat. Stinkin' thinkin', I know, but it's the truth.

Before I knew it, the pass was over and we were back at Renfrew. More hugs and I thank them so much for coming.

"We can't wait to have you home," Dad tells me. Oh, the waterworks. Seeing them made me realize how much I miss them, and though I feel safe here and need the treatment, I want to be home with my family. I had missed them for so long, it is tough being away. I know it will be hard when I leave, but best not to think about it yet.

Our visit was nice and makes me less scared to go home, whereas if I didn't see them and went straight home, I think it would have been more difficult. I am glad they got to see me eat a meal—it had been so long. I now know I can go home and work things out and not have to stay in this bubble. It's home and I love it. I love my family. Yes, I need time for recovery, and will continue that there. Renfrew is really the start of my recovery. The real work starts when I get home, and I know I have my parents' support, even though a lot of it is up to me. Courage is being able to do it on your own...or something like that.

I go to a group on "Getting Your Needs Met," and we talk about how most of us feel like a burden but we need to put ourselves first. I keep quiet the whole time and then the group leader asks if I have anything to say. So I blurt out: "Not really. I just know that it's not going to be a quick fix."

"Why do you say that?" she asks.

"I can be very negative about myself and what I do. I think that there's no future for me and I know I can hear these positive things and know to put yourself first but I don't and can't feel hopeful for myself."

"Thank you. I give you credit for taking it all in and then sharing with us. That's admirable that you knew to do that." I had no clue what she meant. She probably didn't either.

Then this girl Tina, who was kind of new, spoke up. "Nicole, I love hearing you talk. You always sound so positive and I really look up to you. You're such an inspiration to me and a lot of the other girls. I think you're amazing."

Barbara added to the sentiment: "I never would have thought those things about you by looking at you because you're so proactive in getting things done. That's what we all admire about you." It was nice to hear. I had no idea that they thought those things about me.

It is strange, because a lot of the girls who were here when I came in have left. I have seniority now. I went from being a newbie to the head honcho. People look up to me, for some reason. I talk to the girls whenever I can, and try to help the newcomers and chat with the ones who have been here for a while. After all, we are all in this together. I hadn't realized what a change had taken place in me—from the scared, crying girl on the first day, to the fighter against propane, to the trouble maker with the fart machine, to the gal who could now eat a meal and dessert. So this is progress, huh?

The Flu takes over Renfrew. It sounds like a bad movie, and it kind of is. All the girls have it and I am stuck in bed, with a high temperature and some bad tummy issues. After some visits to the nurses' station, and a psych appointment (she came to my room), I was left in bed. All alone with my thoughts, just staring at the ceiling, with nothing to do. I try to read but I can't. I can barely move, I'm so sick. So it's the ceiling, my thoughts, and me, which isn't a good thing. It makes me realize why they keep us so busy. Down time is not a good thing.

My mind wanders back to past experiences...to thinness in L.A., and I crave once again the dark world I once admired. I think about how I would smile as I stood in front of the mirror naked, seeing bones protrude, knowing that I had accomplished something, and now I want that body back again. Especially when I would put on a cute XS dress and it would just drape over me and I stood there, frail yet elegant, fragile yet damaged, wanting yet rejecting. Then I cry. I cry at the thought of me then, the thought of me crying then, and especially the thought that I have changed so much since then. Worse, that a big part of me still wants to be tiny and bony in a little dress. To go down to the Farmer's Market and have that guy tell me again that I was the "prettiest peach here." I don't think that day will come again when anyone will think much of me. If I'm not tiny, people will be able to see me, and they won't like what they see.

I yearn for someone to see me, but I am afraid of what they think. Being left alone all day with my thoughts hurt so much. I cried all day thinking about where my life went wrong, and what I could have done differently. But if I hadn't done those things, I would never have been tiny, and then where would I be? Worthless still, in another sense, I guess. In a different body. Nobody.

I start to feel a little better, so I have to meet with Nancy, my nutritionist. My weight went down a bit because I was sick, but she doesn't mention that. She wants to know why I still don't eat foods that I like, and says that it's "self-deprivation." I explain to her, for example, this turtle cheesecake at the restaurant.

"It's good, sure, but it has no nutritional value. So why have it? What good is it to you? I can have one bite, get the taste, and be just as satisfied. I don't need the whole thing."

"You can, and you should eat things you enjoy," she explains. "Food is nourishing, but it should be fun too. Perhaps your self-deprivation of foods you enjoy mirrors your own life? Can you do things in life that seem meaningless but make you happy?"

"Yeah, sometimes just strolling around, looking at shops makes me happy and I guess that's good. But eating all those foods wouldn't make me happy. It would make me feel worse afterwards. Guilty. Gross. Like I didn't need it. It would have done nothing for me. They are empty calories with no point to them, and I would be mad at myself for doing it."

"I'm just trying to play Devil's Advocate here. There are things in life like that, and perhaps you do the same thing with life situations, deprivation-wise, as you do with food. It's just something to think about."

I hadn't thought about it before, but I think she's right. I leave her office with my own thoughts. With the eating disorder, I was so consumed by the thought of food and by the eating disorder itself, that I deprived myself of all the things that I once enjoyed. Now, I don't even know what I enjoy any more.

Chapter 26
In Limbo

I have Anorexia.
I am Anorexic.
I have an Eating Disorder.
I need help.
I am getting help.
These are just some of the thoughts swirling through my head as I try to recognize this disease that has been tearing me apart, and now, how I will begin to recover.

Sam had to go away on business for the weekend, so I was left alone and scared. I tried to eat, but when I did, my heart would race again, as if it wasn't accustomed to the food. When I slept at night, I kept the phone on my pillow in case I had to call 911. I kept a granola bar by my bed and would break off a little piece when an abnormal heartbeat would wake me out of a sleep. I'd have a little bite, thinking that might save me. Just a bite of food, yes, that was all that my body needed. And that is the anorexic mind. I am sure, at that point, that my body needed more than 10 calories...much more...to regain a healthy, operating heart. But the calories were just too scary. Calories versus heart—my low weight won out.

I had known for a while that I needed help, but couldn't ask for it. I finally wanted to reach out, but had no one to reach out to. My friends confronted me in what I felt was an insulting way. I didn't feel safe communicating with them. I had to be scared before I could tell my doctor, and then reach rock bottom before I was ready to start recovery. It was the ER, the hospital, and others that were required to validate that I truly had an eating disorder, so that I knew this wasn't just some phase. This was no rut I was in. I had a serious and life threatening disease. I was, in fact, afraid I was going to die. I was never sure if I might, and always afraid that once my heart felt "strange" again, it might just happen. This might be it. I'd take that small bite of food, thinking it would save me then—but food was too late to be my saviour at that point.

I wanted my heart to keep beating. It was one of my greatest fears, that my heart would stop. I used to say to myself, "I eat to keep the beat," and even though my eating was so minimal, I thought I was pretty clever. I was truly scared then, but it's even scarier now to look back on that. It's heartbreaking, really. If I had seen someone else in my state, I would have thought how tragic and painful it must be, and would have done anything I could to help and stop the torment. When I think about how it was me, I can recognize the situation, remember the feeling, and somehow feel detached from that girl I was. I know how helpless she felt, but I can't reach her. She is too far gone now.

I waited all weekend to call my parents. I needed the right time and I wanted to make sure I didn't sound too awful. I sat, teetering on the edge of the bed, not sure whether to sit or stand. What would make it easier? Would the words find their way out better one way or the other? I decided to sit, in case I passed out. I called my Dad and we had one of our regular chats. I was getting more anxious by the second. He was about to say "goodbye," when I stopped him. I told him to wait, and that I had something to tell him and Mom and if he could have her pick up the other phone. She did. They probably thought it was good news, like I sold a script or something.

"Okay, we're both on," Dad said.

Before I could get any words out, I started crying. I couldn't speak.

"What is it?" Dad asked, and I could hear the concern in his voice.

"I had to go to the hospital again," I said. "To the E.R. By ambulance."

They were somewhat silent, but I could hear their breathing, their nervousness. I kept talking, tears still coming.

"I know why I've been sick," I told them. "I know why I've been having chest pains." Then I erupted into full-blown crying. "It's because I have an eating disorder. I have anorexia. I don't want to be this way, but I am and I can't help it. I just wanted to lose some weight, but then I couldn't stop and it took over and now it's torturing me. It's all I can think about. And now you know why I'm always grumpy. It's because I'm probably thinking about how many calories I'm going to eat later or when I can get to the gym..." and then I couldn't talk any more. I wanted to get it all out while I was brave enough, but the crying was just overwhelming. It was all so overwhelming.

"Oh honey," Dad said. I couldn't remember the last time he called me "honey." "We were so scared that something like this had been going on, or something was really wrong. Things didn't sound good with you and we knew how much you go to the gym. I was worried you weren't eating enough, and then I saw those pictures of you from when your friend visited. You looked so skinny."

"I think I sent you those pictures because part of me wanted you to notice."

"I wish you had said something. I didn't want to go around you, but I asked Dan if when he saw you he thought you had lost more weight since we had seen you last in June. He said he didn't notice."

We both laughed.

"Boys," I said. "Actually, I've lost 20 pounds since then." Dad sighed.

"I was worried you were anorexic when you were home in June," Mom said. "I should have said something to you then."

"No, I probably would have denied it. It's just got so bad and I need and want to get better."

"You don't need to eat stuff that's bad for you," Dad said. "You can eat balanced meals. You just need to eat."

I talked to Mom for a little bit afterwards and she told me that I just lost too much weight and I don't realize how thin I am. The eating disorder whispered in my head, "But you never hit your next goal weight!"

They were so supportive and loving. We talked about treatment and they just want me to get better. It was a relief to talk to them and know they were there for me. That I wasn't alone in this, because I had been alone for so long. Even though it was out in the open, that didn't mean I was cured. I was going to try and recover, but I knew it was a lot of hard work, and the eating disorder was still very much present, even though I didn't want it to be there. I was up for the biggest fight of my life, and though I had a lot of people in my corner, I knew ultimately I was the one who had to throw the final punch.

I talked to Dad later and he said that I really scared him. I told him that I really scared myself. He also suggested things to eat.

"Not eating messes with your kidney function and your organs. You have too much to live for. I want to keep you around for a while. Since you were focusing on this all the time, you weren't doing any of the fun things that you liked."

He's right. All I thought about was food. Constantly. I wasn't writing, which is the whole reason I'm here. I'm so glad I can talk to them about this. I booked my flight for Thanksgiving, though they wish they could see me sooner. Mom offered to come out here but I told her "no" and not to worry about it. Dad said she is worried though.

I feel like now that it's out, I have some control. If I hadn't admitted the problem, I would probably be getting worse. I'm hoping to get better and eat something more of substance, not just fruit. But I am still going to work out.

Mom talked to Sam on the phone, and Sam said they will both be on my case, which is somewhat upsetting, because in everything I've read, it says not to be "policemen." I know they mean well, but I can't be pushed. Since I have admitted my problem to others and myself, I am not going back. I want out and I know I have a lot of support. This will definitely be a learning experience.

I went to see Dr. Otis the next day. It was time to get serious. The nurse weighed me in at 117. "You're losing weight, Nicole," she said.

"Last time I had sneakers on."

"Sneakers don't weigh three pounds." Yes they do, I thought.

Dr. Otis came and asked how I was doing. I told him about the talk with my parents and that I was going to an eating disorder support group. I couldn't say "anorexia" yet.

"That's the first time I've heard you use that word, 'eating disorder,'" he said. "I'm very proud of you." I was a little bit proud of myself too. Even though I had already admitted the problem, I was truly naming the problem here, and it was a bit of a release.

I told him how I know I have a problem, but I don't want to gain weight.

"I promise you, you're not going to balloon up. You can put on muscle by doing weights at the gym. Body building. Take protein shakes. Then you know that the food you are eating is going towards building muscle."

He also wants me to increase my caloric intake to 800 and keep a food journal. 800? That will be hard, since I was only eating about 200, and that was all fruit, and occasionally yogurt or cottage cheese.

"UCLA does have an inpatient program, but for now I think we can handle this on our own as an outpatient. If it gets worse, there is always that option. You'll probably still feel weak and tired for a while, just because of what you've done to your body."

I brought in the supplements I had been taking so he could look at them and what was in them. He was appalled. "There's so much caffeine in here, and some of this stuff can damage your thyroid and cause osteoporosis. I can't believe they can sell this stuff." He sounded like my Dad, but I realized then that the caffeine had been the only thing that had kept me going. I was merely living off caffeine and fruit. The supplements were bad for me, but in a way, they kept me alive.

He told me to work on a food journal and building muscle, and as he left the room, he pointed at his chart where my weight was circled. "Watch this number, okay? We want it to go up, not down."

I nodded, but didn't agree. My goal was 115, just 2 more pounds. I know it's bad that I'm still trying to lose weight, but that is my goal and I need to reach it. 2 more pounds. I have been working out at the gym still pretty intensely, but eating, even though it's still not a lot of calories.

I like my bones. I don't want them to disappear.

I'm afraid of how much weight I will gain over Thanksgiving.

The pride I felt earlier in the visit had only lasted a brief moment, and the fear came again, because, after all, what would I be without my eating disorder? It was all I knew. It was how I existed. My anxiety increased. I worried about everyone, everything, all the time. I was a recluse, with no joy in life. I was once filled with laughter, and now I had become so silent that I forgot what my laugh sounded like.

I was scared to eat in front of people. Putting together meals was difficult. I told my Dad about the visit to the doctor and the 800-calorie meal plan. Though still worried, he is glad that I am taking the right steps. He jokingly told me, "I could do that in just one meal." I knew that most people probably ate that and didn't even think twice about it, and could easily do it in one sitting, but the thought of having that many calories in one day terrified me, and I tried to keep it as minimal as possible, or just to the 800 mark, with many fruits and vegetables and lean protein, though I did incorporate other things.

Hang In There... Wherever "There" Is

I went to the gym later and was on the treadmill. Some dude came up to me and goes, "You know who you look like? Karen Carpenter. You have her eyes and features...when she was younger. She died of that anorexia, you know? Awful. They tried to revive her. Man, I loved her." Then he walked away. I wonder if he was trying to tell me something, like "get off the treadmill before you have the same fate as her," or "you have anorexic eyes," or if it was just a sign saying to get off the treadmill and go eat. I picked the latter and went and had a snack.

Eating has not been easy to begin with, but Sam is trying to dictate what I eat. She tells me I need more fat, more protein and that if I eat fruit, I can't have it alone, I have to have cottage cheese with it. I don't like cottage cheese with fruit. She tells me I shouldn't even bother with the fruit then. Isn't it good that I'm eating at all?

She has me measure things, which drives me mad. She watches as I make meals. I pour cereal and she tells me it's not enough. One morning, she said, "You need to eat peanut butter today." What if I don't want peanut butter? Isn't it better to eat something I feel like? Won't that create a bad association with food if I am forced to eat things? She also counts the calories of everything I eat, which makes me anxious. Sometimes, by the time she's done counting, my dinner is cold. Scrumptious.

I told Dad about my frustrations and he thinks she's just trying to help. Which I know is true, and I owe her a lot for letting me stay with her. But eating is stressful enough, and all her added stuff makes it worse. He told me to be patient, and that I don't have anyone else to do this for me. Then he said, "I wish you'd just come home."

It caught me off guard. I'm not if sure he truly meant it or was just saying it. Then he continued, "That way, I'd know what was going on."

"I like my doctors here though."

"I have no clue about your doctors there, but it might be better if you were here."

He has a point. Something to think about, I guess.

In a surreal way, I feel like I have recovered, though I am nowhere near that. I am eating, probably too much. I feel like I'm binging, especially when I break out the peanut butter. Sam tells me I think I'm eating a lot, but that's my perspective. If someone else saw me, they'd still realize how little it was.

Dr. Otis noticed the same thing at our next visit. I brought my food journal to him, and he was literally shocked at how truly minimal 800 calories was. What seemed like an enormous amount to me really worried him. He told me that if this is what I am eating now, he hated to think of what I had been eating before. "I don't know how you are alive," he told me, truly nervous. And while that should have been what shook me, it was his next statement. "I'm increasing your caloric intake to 1000." I was petrified.

Then he got angry. "Are you still doing cardio?"

"Yes."

"Didn't I say just weights?"

"Yes, but I can't stop." It's like telling an alcoholic to stop drinking. I can't do it right away. I feel so lost in this recovery, like no one is really guiding me.

"You have to trust me and trust that it will work."

I don't know what to trust any more.

I woke up the next morning and Sam had already left for work. I went to grab a glass of water when I notice the mop is out and next to it, a note. It read: "Please vacuum and mop the kitchen floor. You only need a little cleaner. You have to eat at least 800 calories today—combine foods, drink milk, have snacks, measure foods—stop with the bullshit excuses. If you won't do it for yourself, do it for your parents and all the really starving people in the world!"

I slumped down next to the mop. She had been mad at me the night before because I hadn't eaten enough calories. It was true, because I had a stomach ache. She counted what I ate during the day and rounded it to 450. I told her I would eat when I felt better, but she didn't want to hear it. Feeling guilty, I ate some Halloween candy that night, and then felt gross. I left her a note so she knew I ate. That was her response.

I called Dad and explained the situation. "Calm down. I don't agree with her note or her methods. I know she is trying to help you, but in a different way. You have to understand this is hard on her too. She let you stay in her home and didn't expect any of this. Maybe you should sit down and explain to her how you're feeling, what your doctor said, and what this is really like for you."

I had told him that the doctor said no measuring foods and counting calories because it makes me more anxious. Also, that Sam thinks if a person is sick, then they should recover in a day. She doesn't understand this disease. It isn't a cold that I'm just going to get over. I know she wants to help, and I feel like a burden, but I cannot go on like this. The stress is making me more sick.

"You're coming home soon for Thanksgiving. That will be a break for both of you. What you want to do from there is your decision. I know this is tough, but not as much as you know. No one does."

"Sorry to keep calling like this."

"If it were up to me, I would have had you come home 2 weeks ago when you first told us."

"I know. I just thought I could do it here. And the weather does help."

"Whether you get treatment in Connecticut or L.A. is up to you. We just want you better."

"Me too."

"Okay, stop crying."

"I'll try. I have mopping to do," I said with a laugh, and then got to it.

I had sent Charlotte an email to let her know about the eating disorder, since she had been worried about me and wanted me to keep her posted, even though I think she had an inkling of what was going on. But as anyone who has had an eating disorder knows, you have to wait for the person to admit it. I thanked her for being there for me when I was having the tough times, explained to her my troubles, and that I might go home...or not. She was on the road, but wrote back:

Hey sweetie,

I want you to know how concerned I am about you. I've been praying for you a lot, and I'm super proud of you that you are seeing a doctor and facing this eating demon. And it's exactly that, a big nasty demon! How are you? Are you getting better? How is your family? How is California? I am glad you went home and your friends confronted you. I didn't know what to say. I just was so shocked at how thin you were at the L.A. show. I understand how emotionally consuming it is when anorexia takes a hold of you. I am just so happy you are realizing it. I did a lot of damage to my body by not eating for years. It's the reason I still to this day suffer from a very low immune system and always get terrible infections. (I am actually getting over a sinus infection that I got on the tour.)

I will pray for mental clarity, strength and that food has no power over you. You don't have to worry about gaining weight. Food is not the enemy...

You are a beautiful, amazing, unique woman. I am proud to know you and I am proud that you are taking control of this. I know it's a fight... but keep fighting it. It's your life, and your life is important to more people than you will ever know. You are important to me.

I love you...

Write soon.

Char

Her words were comforting and just what I needed. Knowing that she beat this "eating demon," as she called it, and is living a wonderful, healthy life now gave me inspiration. It's also nice to have someone to turn to who knows what it's like to suffer through this. I am lucky to have her as a friend and a motivator to get healthy.

Another motivation was the support group. I was excited for it because it was all people in recovery—even the facilitator had recovered from anorexia. There was only one other girl there that night, a binge-eater, but we could relate on so many levels. Kristyn, the facilitator, talked about the eating disorder being an "entity," what it will and won't let you do, which is the truth. It tells you to do things.

"Right now," she said, "Everything is black and white, but when you recover, it's all colour." In a weird way, I understood that. It was the all or nothing attitude. If I went to the gym, I couldn't do just an hour; I have to do the extreme workout. She was also a compulsive over-exerciser and said that now she has to force herself to go to the gym.

"After I stopped going so much, it was like having another day within a day. I had so much time to do things that I wanted to do."

"I know," I said. "I feel like all I do is workout, and it's so stressful because I have to build my day around gym time and I get anxious if I'm not there at the right time or I don't get enough time there. I hate it. It's so consuming."

We talked about the guilt of eating, and how now, since I'm eating more, I feel like I have to work out more to rid myself of the calories. But it's the whole mental thing of what the eating disorder tells you to do, and how negative it is. Like there's the eating disorder voice and then the rational voice, which is Nicole, and I want that voice to get louder.

We talked about food and I said, "I don't know what I would be thinking about if I weren't thinking about food all the time.

"Exactly," she said. "What would you be thinking about? There's something that you're avoiding—whether it's your life, work, friends—you're using the eating disorder to avoid the real issues you have. You need to figure out what that is."

Then we got on the topic of food and I tell her that the things I used to like, I don't now. "Nothing interests me any more."

"It's funny you say that because I think you can look at a menu and things do interest you. You want them, but you won't let yourself get them. When you say 'nothing interests me any more,' it's as if you're talking about your life."

It shook me because it was true and scary.

I weighed in at 116. I was so excited, though I know I shouldn't be. I'm still losing weight here, though I am eating, but I feel so sick, achy and tired all the time. My bones hurt, but I can't stop exercising. It's making me wonder if I will get better or worse if I stay in L.A.

My parents wanted me to make my own decision, but I knew what they thought was best, and in my heart, I knew what was best too.

I missed home—that was part of what had been tearing at me for a while, and I knew that is where I would get my best support. My parents and friends tell me I can always come back, but I don't think I would. I don't know if it's because it would be too hard to go back and live with the ghost of my eating disordered-self wandering the streets, or if I just wasn't meant to be there to begin with. If I tried it, and this wasn't the place for me. I couldn't see myself doing it again. I had to make a decision. I wanted to pursue screen-writing, but how much writing had I been doing? Nothing in six months—the only thing I had been pursuing was my eating disorder. I also knew that I wouldn't be able to do anything while I was sick. Getting healthy was my number one priority, and the longer I stayed in LA, the worse I would feel.

I decided to call Dan, who, for a little brother, is wise beyond his years. For some reason, I know I can always turn to him, and he'll steer me the right way.

We talked on the phone for about an hour, which is a miracle, considering this kid hates talking on the phone. He told me little things like, "I didn't think you were even gonna stay in LA for that long," and bigger things like, "I think everyone's kind of worried about you and would feel better with you home. You just need some time to rest and get better." And in between all that, he listened to me go back and forth between the pro's and con's of moving home. When I was done rambling, I asked what he really thought I should do, and my oh-so-wise 18-year-old brother said right to me: "When it's time to go home, you'll know."

He was right. When it was time, I would know, and I think I was getting to that point. I soon knew, and that time came.

I had a talk with Sam that night, and aside from telling her about my food battles, when I told her about my frustrations about whether to come home or not, she came up with this brilliant idea: since I was going home for Thanksgiving and Christmas, then why didn't I just extend my stay, and leave my stuff at her house and go home for a bit. Relax, work on getting healthy, and then decide what I want to do. If I feel more comfortable there and end up wanting to stay, then I can come back and get my stuff. If I go home and realize that LA is the place for me, then I can return and continue living there. What a relief! It sounded like an easier and less stressful solution. So I had two weeks to wrap up in L.A. and then I'd be heading home.

The two weeks flew by, and my health deteriorated. My chest bones ached more and I went to see Dr. Otis.

"Stress fractures are normal in your condition," he informed me.

He checked my food journal and told me it was good stuff, but still not enough. He said I also need to understand that an appropriate weight for me would be 130, at the low end. How could I gain weight when I've been trying to lose it for so long?

"Just keep adding a little bit of food each day. It'll be slow, but you're making progress."

I know he wants to help, but he never did blood work again or appropriate tests for someone in my state, which worries me.

I tell him that I am going home for a bit, for both holidays, to be with my family and get more support and he thinks it's a good idea. He tells me to stay in touch, and when I'm back to schedule an appointment.

"You're a nice smart girl," he says. "I know you can get through this."

I hope he's right.

I talk to Mom on the drive home and she tells me that the important thing now is to get healthy and that she doesn't want me to get worse. And not to worry about where I'm living. That shouldn't be my priority.

"There was so much I wanted to do here that I haven't taken advantage of yet. I've just been wasting time…at the gym, fruit stands. Think of all the things I could have accomplished in the last five months. I could have done so much, instead of wasting away."

"You've still got time for all those things, but you can't do anything if you're sick."

I go on to tell her how I had started out good with the recovery stuff, but this week wasn't as good.

"You're not going to fix it in a day," she tells me. "This didn't happen overnight and you can't fix it overnight. You will get better. I know you will. I'm always proud of you, for everything you do. It'll be okay."

I had been emailing back and forth with Jason, and when he asked what was new with me, I decided to tell him. I mention that I am having some health problems and might go home for recovery.

Immediate response back: *"Are you alright? Is it serious? Is there anything I can do?"*

I write back and tell him the real deal. I know I can trust him with it and he won't judge me. Then I joked that he was probably sorry I asked, since I went on so long.

He wrote back*: "I'm so sorry…about asking the question I mean. Kidding. Look, first and foremost is your health. I know it's a cliché, but without it, we have nothing. So if going back means getting better, then do it. California will always be here.*

Food is good. Remember, a man likes a girl to eat with him. You have a lot going on for you…you're a talented writer who works a lot. That's so much more than I can say about ¾ of the people I know out here. Honestly. Get yourself better. If you need anything, let me know."

I think he really is one of the most kind and amazing people I have ever met. I was very touched, and I don't mean that to sound cheesy.

I wrote back and explained the eating disorder a little and my gym habits, then told him to vent about whatever he wanted. It only seemed fair.

"No venting here," he said. *'Just enjoy eating. It's one of the greatest pleasures in life. Working out is great too. I couldn't live without it. But, 3 hours a day is what out of shape actors do to prepare for a role. An hour, hour and a half is perfect. Don't run yourself into the ground. You will always be welcome back to L.A., but right now a strong support team will do the best for you. I know it's insanely hard, but you have a lot to look forward to."*

Hang In There... Wherever "There" Is

I thanked him for the advice. It's incredible how supportive he has been—from when I first moved here and he gave me tips on where to live, to referring me to a doctor, to reading my script, to even setting up interviews for me. And we met just because I did an interview with him. Jason is one of those people that you meet in life and wonder how you got to be so lucky to meet him. I'm glad I did.

Getting close to home time. I called Grammie and Buttsie to tell them I'd be home for a bit and they were glad. Buttsie said I needed some TLC and it's important to be with family, especially around the holidays. He was in the service and knows what it's like to be alone, so can imagine what it's like for me.

I talked to Meme who said it would be good for me to come home, take a break, think about what I want to do and then sort things out. "It's your life and you can do what you want."

I told her, "I just need a break and time with my family. And I can do my work at home. Since I had been sick, I've been needing to rest up a little."

"You're still not feeling well?"

"Better, but a bit run down."

"Are you eating enough?"

I paused, then said, "I don't know. I don't cook a lot."

She asked if I still went to the gym a lot, and I told her yes.

"Maybe you need to take a break from that."

"Yeah, you're probably right."

She said something to Dad the next day about my coming home and how I had been sick, and maybe it's because I lost too much weight.

"You have to be careful," she told him. "Because of that anorexia."

"I know," Dad said.

I sent Jason a bouquet of baseball cookies as a thank you—for everything he did while I was here. That night, I got a call from him to thank me for the cookies, but he didn't know why he deserved them. I told them they were just a little something, but I wanted to thank him for all he's done for me, and his support.

"I haven't done anything!" he said.

"Yes, you have. And I hope you like cookies."

"Of course I do, especially baseball ones. How are you doing?"

"A little worse actually. I think it will be good to go home."

"Yeah, just to be home, spend some time with the family, work on getting better. How long have you been dealing with the anorexia?"

"Well, it's been building up for a while. It got really bad this summer and then it just got out of control. 4 hours at the gym, eating only fruit and living off caffeine supplements."

"Geez. How much do you weigh?"

I paused, because I didn't want him to think I was fat.

"You don't have to tell me," he said.

"No it's fine. I like to think I'm a smart anorexic, because I tried to keep on a lot of muscle, which weighs more," I said, trying to rationalize. Smart Anorexic, who says that? "I weigh 115, but I'm 5'9, so I should be 135 for my height. 130 at the lowest. I think the average is 145."

It wasn't an intrusive question, from him at least. He had a genuine curiosity. He went on to tell me how he just watched a documentary on eating disorders. I had too. It had been on after I told him about mine, so I had to wonder if that is why he watched it.

"I just want you to get better, and hopefully being home will help."

"Me too. I think it's gonna be a long road though."

"It'll be hard, but you've gotta keep at it and you'll get there. And I will see you in December when I'm home."

"I'll have put on some pounds by then."

"Pounds are good. I want you to come out the other side of this."

He told me to have a safe trip back and to keep in touch and let him know how I was doing. I was surprised at his real interest, not only in my health, but also the disease itself. He didn't look down on it, yet wanted to learn more. If only everyone could be that way.

Time to leave L.A. Very anticlimactic. Sam doesn't like goodbyes, so she wished me well and told me to have a safe trip. I packed my bags, which I could barely carry, and took an early flight. Soon, I would be home. This had all been such a whirlwind. I was sad to be leaving L.A. behind but happy to be going towards my family. What rested in between that was me, and I don't know how I truly felt about that. I would soon find out.

I tried to prepare myself for home, but apparently, my family had been preparing themselves for me. While I wore plenty of layers—a t-shirt, a long sleeved shirt, a sweatshirt and a coat—it didn't hide the truth of what was beneath. When my dad picked me up at the airport, he was shocked. My mother had tried to warn him. Later, he would tell me that I looked like a skeleton and he was trying to hold back tears. I had no idea.

I was so happy to see him. I had been rescued. While waiting for my luggage, I grabbed my heart at one point. The palpitations came on because I hadn't eaten all day, and I could see the worry on my Dad's face. He asked if I was OK, and I assured him I was. Strange, how accustomed to pain I had become.

We got into the car and I mentioned how if I don't exercise, I don't feel like I deserve to eat. He couldn't understand that. Neither could I. We passed a McDonald's and he asked if I wanted a Diet Fry. I told him that I want that stuff, I just can't have it.

"That's why you really need to find someone to talk about this with," he said.

"I've been looking."

"There's this place in Connecticut, and they have lots of programs. Have you thought about residential treatment?"

"I've thought about it..."

"I'm not telling you what to do. We're just talking..."

"I know. I have thought about it, but I'd rather handle it on my own, especially because I'd be afraid of entering something like that where they force you to do things, then coming out and relapsing. Whereas if I try it on my own, I can work through it gradually and hopefully stick with it."

We stopped at the grocery store. That dreaded mall of food. I bought a lot of fruit, yogurt, cottage cheese, cereal, turkey, chicken, milk and the usual stuff. We were there forever, and he truly saw how daunting it was for me to be around food and worry about calories. It was painful for him to watch. If he hadn't been there, I would have been shopping for another hour.

Mom came home later from work and wanted to know how I was feeling and what my doctor was doing for me. She told me I really needed to see my doctor here, and a therapist. We watched TV for a bit and I knew I needed more to eat, so I had a snack of peanut butter and bananas, which would soon become my nemesis.

The next day, we went to pick up Dan from school. It was so great to see him, but I hadn't eaten anything, and was so weak, I passed out on the ride home. When I got home, there was a card from Meme that read: "I'm so glad that you're home." She had asked Dad how thin I was and he responded, "pretty thin." He said she looked very concerned, that she's pretty worried about me and she probably knows what's going on. He said he couldn't believe how thin I was, just looking back from June.

It was the first time he had mentioned my physical appearance. I had been wondering what they were thinking.

Kelly asked me to be a bridesmaid at her wedding. We went wedding dress shopping at one place but all the dresses were circa-1980, so we left and went to lunch. I ordered a salad, which I picked at. I had a doctor's appointment and didn't want to weigh more.

Mom and I left and went to the doctors. I go in alone and the first thing he asks is, "How long have you been having issues with your eating?" Now that's a loaded question. I weighed in at 117, but I had heavier clothes on here, and had eaten a bit, so I say, minus 2 pounds from that.

I gave him the whole run down and he agreed that the other doctor didn't totally treat everything. They are doing blood work again and he wants me to work towards 130 pounds. He says I need to do therapy and he's going to keep a close eye on me. Where have I heard that before?

"Your low body temperature is bad because your basal metabolic rate changed, so we need to get that back up."

Though he was helping, one of things he said made me cringe. "So, did you catch on with that L.A. diet trend?" I guess he doesn't understand either.

When we got home, Kelly said that our cousin, Katie, asked her what was wrong with me. That I look too thin and I didn't eat anything at lunch. Kelly told her she didn't know. I asked Kelly if I really looked that bad.

"You don't look healthy," she told me.

"My face, or just everything?" I asked.

"Your face, yeah. And, I have thin arms, but yours are really small. Sorry, I'm not trying to be mean."

"I'd rather you be honest." At least I have a realistic view of what I really look like, whether I believed it or not.

My birthday and Thanksgiving landed on the same day. I did not have a cake. I wasn't ready. Thanksgiving dinner was OK. I tried a little bit of everything, though Dad was not too impressed with my portions. Later, I had a ton of peanut butter and bananas. Then I had a piece of pumpkin pie, and then candy and more crap. It's this weird thing that I cannot eat in front of people, for fear that they'll think I'm eating too much or too little, and I hate being watched. I'll binge in private later and feel totally gross about it. I haven't worked out in over a week and I can feel my fat cells expanding.

Out of boredom, I began going through all my old journals, and my one wish was to always be skinny because I wasn't, I was overweight, and I thought it was the one thing that would bring me happiness. I never thought it would actually happen and of course, it ultimately did, in the worst way, and brought me despair. At times, it brought me a false sense of happiness, but it wasn't a true kind, it was a narcissistic kind, or where I wanted to believe that it was how I should be, and other people would like me more that way. When I would look into the mirror, I'd admire the bones that I never thought I'd be able to see. I'd smile, then ultimately, the tears would start running into that smile and I'd realize how my quest for thinness, for happiness, had turned into my demise.

My bedroom is downstairs. I was back in my old room—the room that I had left a mess before I went to LA. It was downstairs where the dogs can't go, so there were gates set up at the top of the stairs. I felt like, "here are the gates to keep Nicole in. So we can keep a watch on her." I was very secluded anyway. I had my gates, but I didn't try to break out. Didn't want to. Had no need to. No life, just me. Me and my gates. What else in life did these gates protect me from? Did they also serve as a barrier to keep others away from me? I am sure that there are those who did not want to be around me and probably did not need to be, and that was most likely a good thing. It was scary enough to have to deal with myself, never mind the outside world. I isolated myself so I wouldn't have to deal with it, and they wouldn't have to deal with me. I was scared to be around people, because I wasn't comfortable with myself. I felt fractured, broken in places that I didn't know to fix. How could I enter the world again? The gates may have been there for the dogs, but it was easy to pretend they were there for me.

One of my first quests when I returned home was to go to my brother's baseball sports banquet. Though he was out of high school, they had been State Champions the year before, and were recognizing that accomplishment during the winter break.

My parents told me I didn't have to go. My brother told me not to—he didn't even want to go. After all, it was my first week back home facing an illness so hard to recognize, so how would I be able to face a large group of people I once knew that might not recognize me?

I wanted to be there for my brother, no matter how scared I was of a dinner and facing a lot of people who knew me as a much heavier and more jovial person. I was filled with anxiety and a panic that no one should have to feel when attending a high school dinner in small town Connecticut. Not even the kid giving the speech.

My parents reassured me that it would be okay. We'd all be sitting together and there should be something I liked to eat there, at least a salad. I'd come to hear that often.

We arrived and I slunk behind my family, not wanting to be noticed or questioned, not even wanting to say "hi." I wanted it to be over with and go back into hiding. I didn't want to embarrass my family. My Dad told me I was never an embarrassment. Yet I was embarrassed by myself.

We made our way to the table and a couple of the other dads came over to say "hi" and talk to my Dad. I put on the smile and answered their LA questions, only this time, I said I was taking a break and didn't know when I was going back. Judging from their looks, they knew why. A smile cannot hide everything. Neither can a sweater.

After some waiting, I became more anxious, wondering why we got there so early. Before I could rest easy at our little family table, another set of parents sat down with us, rounding out the group. I was unsettled, because it was one of the more nosy mothers, and one, unfortunately, who had relatives in California.

"Oh my gosh, look at you! How are you?" Nancy yelled.

"I'm good," I replied, keeping it simple. "How are you?"

"Good. So how is California? How long are you home for?"

"I'm taking a little break," I told her. "I'm not so sure I want to stay out there."

She stared at me, shocked, almost annoyed.

"How could you not like it? It's beautiful. I miss it. I can't wait to go and visit my family soon."

I wanted to drop it because I knew she wouldn't give up, but I had to give an answer or she would keep pressing. "I just don't think it's for me," I told her. "I didn't meet a lot of people out there."

"How could you not meet a lot of people?" she yelled back, somehow not realizing that I was sitting right next to her. "There's so much going on there."

Anxiety level—increasing.

She gave me a weird look.

"Well, I thought you would have liked it. Maybe you just need to give it another shot."

Nice. Another person who barely knows me telling me what's best for me.

Then she hit me with the big one.

She leaned in and said somewhat quietly, "So...my gosh! How did you lose all that weight?"

I wanted to reach out to my family for support, but they were all talking to someone else.

I was mostly honest. "Diet and exercise."

"You must work out a lot."

"Yes."

"I've gained some weight and I can't seem to lose it. You'll have to give me some tips," she said, seriously, and I slunk down in my seat. *You don't want to lose weight the way I did*, I thought.

Instead, I told her, "You don't need to lose weight. You look great."

"Stop! No, I don't. So, what kinds of things do you eat?"

Why is this conversation happening? Since I had been so focused on food and exercise, I realized how body-conscious "normal" people are. The first thing they say to you when they see you is about your looks, your weight—it's all superficial. Shouldn't things, anything, matter more than that?

"I just try to eat healthily," I said, feeling helpless.

"But you lost a lot of weight," she told me, nodding, as if I didn't know.

I gave up. I didn't respond, shrugged it off. I didn't need this. If Rational Nicole had been in control, she would have told Nosy Nancy that, "Actually, I'm suffering from an eating disorder and am really struggling to get myself back together and move into recovery. So I'd appreciate it if you'd refrain from your obsessive and negative food and weight talk. It's not healthy."

Rational Nicole would kick ass.

But Rational Nicole was not in control. She was barely hanging on and instead was buried beneath layers of anxiety, fear and shame. Irrational Nicole was not in control either though, because the eating disorder was not on in full force. There was a focus on food, but because it was the first big dinner in public and eyes were focusing on me, and mouths were chirping, my mind was not filled with eating disorder thoughts. Instead, these two Nicole's were at war—wanting to acknowledge my strides to become healthy, and fearful of the food I would have to eat soon, especially without having had exercised. But better to be in a constant war than already defeated.

Nancy leaned over the table and asked my Mother how she was, so I decided to escape. I walked towards the bathroom and saw the mother of one of my brother's friends. I smiled at her, and she just stared back with a puzzled look. Embarrassed, I pushed open the bathroom door and was glad to find the room empty. I just had to catch my breath and regain my composure before I could release myself back into the hoards of these people. I looked to my left and found myself staring back at myself in the mirror, but it wasn't me. At least, I didn't think it was. For the first time, I saw and realized the changes that had taken place to me physically. I was somewhat hard to recognize, beyond my mental condition. I looked—as I never thought I would—tiny. Fragile. I was thin. *Thin*. How was that possible? How come I never noticed that happening? I certainly looked tiny tonight, though I never tried too hard to hide it. I wore my tightest jeans to show my stick-like legs, and a green sweater that was a little looser, but couldn't hide my emaciation, especially when I wrapped my arms around myself to keep me warm from the cold—which usually wasn't cold to anyone but me. I looked sickly, my face especially. The bags under my eyes. I just thought I was tired before. Was my face really that sunken in? I looked like I could cry at any moment and the truth was, I might.

I had to stop staring at myself in the mirror—this mirror of truth—because I knew how dangerous that was. The obsession of details and focusing on the different pieces of me. The broken pieces. Could I ever be put back together?

I also had to get out of the bathroom. I had been in there too long. I left and there were still people mulling around. Again, I saw the woman who pretended not to know me, and this time, she stopped me.

"Nicole," she said.

"Hi. How are you?"

"Good. Sorry, I didn't recognize you before. You passed by and I was like, 'Who was that?' And then after a minute, I realized it was you. Guess it's been a while."

"Yeah," I said with a slight laugh, and we each went on our way.

I was no longer invisible, I was worse—unrecognizable. Maybe that's what I wanted—to go unnoticed, to disappear from my life as, not I, but others, had known it. Now, not only did they not recognize me, but I didn't recognize myself either.

I sat back down at our table where I resorted to mostly silence. When it came our time to get in line for the buffet, I stuck close to my Dad. There wasn't much that I could choose from, so I went with salad and two little pieces of ziti, one of which I tried a bite of, but didn't like. Then came the cake, and the battle grew. I wanted that cake, but I knew what it really was. My eating disorder told me that I shouldn't have it, but Nicole wanted it. She wanted to sit with her family and enjoy cake like a "normal" person, and beyond that, prove to them that she could. But the war raged on, and while I tried a bite and liked it, then I resented myself. I continued to pick at it throughout the ceremony; not wanting anyone to see me, even though they had probably already noticed my behaviour.

Everyone else had eaten theirs, except Nancy, who had a bite and left it at that. I felt like I shouldn't eat it because she didn't. How would that make me a good anorexic?

But I do really like frosting.

Finally the waitress came to take away the plates, and as I looked at the mangled piece of cake in front of me, I gave her my plate so the frosted mushiness wouldn't torment me any more. I commented on how it was good. It was, but I hated myself for it.

After the awards, there was some mingling. I began to feel sick with heart palpitations and some dizziness. I knew I hadn't eaten enough all day, but I also knew that the sugar overload wasn't good for me either. Placing my hand over my heart, as I had done so often before, I thought it would help. This time, no one noticed. They were busy doing what they should be doing, enjoying themselves. I wondered what that would be like.

I figured that I could hang on until we got home, or at least hoped so, and knew I couldn't leave until I said "hello" to a former teacher who was there. I went up to him and he looked at me, shook his head and stepped back.

No "hello."
No "how are you."
No "good to see you."
No hug.
He just said: "Are you eating?"
"Yes," I lied.

I called this place, the Renfrew Center in Wilton, Connecticut, about therapy. The person I spoke to suggested that I do a complete evaluation, since the outpatient program is only a few days a week for four hours, and is a two hours' drive each way.   The residential program, they say, might be better for me. The only thing is that their inpatient facility is in Philadelphia, and the usual stay is 3-6 weeks. There are 3 staff assisted meals a day, with meal support therapy after, individual therapy, group therapy, art therapy and family therapy. Did I mention there's therapy? She told me it's a good program that helps to get over the fear of food and of gaining weight, and deals with issues such as depression. I tell her I have been eating since I've been home, but I can't eat normal meals. I also mention I am nervous that once I gain weight, I will relapse and lose all of it.

Dad is excited I am doing this assessment. He reiterated the fact that he wants me around for a few more years and told me, "Your body can't take another hit like that," which I'm afraid I know. He told me that I need to gain 50 pounds though, and I told him, "no, then I'd weight 170, and I'm not going back there."

"There's no way you weigh 120."

"117, plus, I have muscle."

He didn't believe me. He told me that I'm half the size. Even as I gained weight, day-by-day, week-by-week, he didn't believe the weight gain. I offered to step on the scales, but he didn't take up my offer. I see my protruding stomach, but no one else does. Maybe my face still looks gaunt, but the scales don't lie. Number by number, my weight went up, and I knew why. I couldn't during the day, but at night, after everyone had gone to sleep, I crept upstairs into that peanut butter jar, and I couldn't stop. Food! Finally. I could eat in secrecy and peace, and then, the guilt would come, and in the morning, so would restriction.

I went with Dad to bring Dan back to school. I slept most of the way there. I'm just so exhausted. I realize now the effect that the caffeine had on me. We stopped at Dunkin Donuts on the way back and I got a latte. Dad got a cookie, so I did too. I couldn't eat it all, but saved it for later.

We had a good talk on the way back. I told him how I couldn't imagine having to go back to L.A. the next day and that I'm really glad I'm home right now. He said he was too.

"I think this is where you need to be," he said, and I agreed. He has been an amazing support and I know he doesn't really understand everything that's going on, and neither do I, but he's trying, and that's incredible in itself. I love him and Mom so much, and I am so happy to be home right now.

I got an email from Sam. She opened it with talks of Thanksgiving and then got right into it. About how she's realized she wants to be alone, that she needs the solitude, and she knows I'm trying to sort things out, so I can leave my car there for a month or so and then maybe go out to get it and stay for a few days.

I wish she had mentioned that earlier. We had this plan and now it feels like it fell apart. She was the one who didn't want me to leave, and now I am being kicked out. I am faced not only with my recovery, but finding a future in Connecticut, because I know, for my own well-being, it is not safe to be in L.A. on my own right now. It was disappointing news, but it is her house, and she did a lot for me, so I do respect her wishes. However, my anxiety is going through the roof.

I went out to dinner with Dad and bravely tried a few of his fries. I told him how freaked out I was.

"That's why you need help," he told me. "It's just three fries."

I try to explain that it's not about the food, it's not a choice and I don't want to be this way.

"You're trying to rationalize it," he tells me.

"I know it's not rational thinking, but I can't help it." It's frustrating. I know that they are concerned, but they see it as not eating. They don't really understand the illness. I'm not happy. I don't have a real life or existence. I left L.A. and my dreams behind. I don't like who I am and I don't know where I'm going. I was just trying to be small. As small as I felt.

Everyone wants to know, "What's the matter with Nicole?" I suppose it's a valid question. I went with Dad to get his hair cut, at the place he's been going to forever. The barber said, "Wow, you got so tall and thin. Don't they feed you out there in L.A.?" I felt bad because Dad was standing right there and I don't want him to get upset when people say those things. It's not about me, it's about how it affects my family. I worry about them.

My Aunt came over the other night to bring me my birthday present and called my Mom the next day. She asked if I was okay because I looked so thin. Mom told her I just worked out a lot and was being healthy. Yeah, that's what I used to say. Secrets, secrets, secrets.

Grammie even went so far as to ask Dad if I was anorexic. He told her I was eating now, but he couldn't say what my eating was like in L.A. Meme asked if I was eating okay now. Apparently, everyone is concerned. Dad told me that I don't realize how thin I am.

"There's a difference between being thin and too thin," he told me. "You look unhealthily thin, and I'm not saying that to be mean, I'm just being honest. You are way too thin. You arms are like the size of my fingers." Sadly, that made me proud.

"I do want to get better but there is still the eating disorder voice telling me to lose weight. And…I started taking diuretics again." That flipped him out. He couldn't believe I was taking that stuff here and hurting myself like that.

"If you're going to keep doing that stuff, you're ruining your kidneys. It's like committing suicide. If you died, I'd have that void in my life forever."

I felt awful. I don't want to hurt them, but the disease is still pulling at me. He went on to tell me how he couldn't believe I was doing those things still, and it was hindering my chance at getting better.

"The fear of gaining weight takes over, and I don't want to do those things, but it's like I need to take control to lose the weight."

That spurred discussion of a ton of issues—my depression, I have no real job, I'll never get married or have a house and I feel as if my life is going nowhere.

"You're young. You don't need to get married right now. You've had a lot of accomplishments. Everything will sort itself out, but you need to get your health back in order first. I'm worried how you're thinking mentally and I know you need help. If you keep doing this, you won't be around for much longer."

I just shrugged, not knowing what to say or how to feel about that.

"If you have that kind of attitude, then you really need help."

This all led up to my assessment with the Renfrew Center—an hour-long mental health assessment. There were questions about my past issues with depression, hopelessness, anxiety, history of anorexia, what I want out of treatment, family stuff, etc. I told them I was doing better since L.A., where I was really extreme, but I still need help. They asked, on a scale of 1-10, how much do I want to get better. I was honest and said 7. I want to be normal, whatever that is, and healthy again, but I've been losing weight for so long, I don't want to gain it back. She is going to evaluate the assessment and call back to let me know what my level of care should be.

The call came soon and she said, "The team had decided that it would be in your best interest to come down here, to the Philadelphia facility, for inpatient treatment of 28 days."

"Not outpatient?" I asked. "Even though I've gained a little weight, am eating more and doing better?"

"Yes, because of your history with over-exercising, restricting, use of laxatives and diuretics, and because you are still underweight."

"When would I have to enter?"

"They want you to come down as soon as possible."

"What about Christmas?"

"You can have your family come down during visiting hours, which is a couple hours in the afternoon."

What kind of Christmas would that be? I came home to have my family as support, and there was no way I would be away for Christmas.

"Can I come in after Christmas?"

"We'd like to get you in soon, but your assessment is good until January 1, though spots fill up fast and sometimes there is a waiting list. Talk it over with your family and get back to me."

I talked it over with Mom and Dad and told them I'd be devastated if I woke up Christmas Morning in an eating disorder clinic. I had come home to spend the holidays with them and I feel like I'll go in with a negative attitude right now. They understood and said they want me home too, but, if I keep taking pills and hurting myself, it'll be better for me to go in sooner. As long as I keep eating and stay on track, I could go in after Christmas.

I am worried about going there, now that it's a reality. I am anxious about gaining weight and the whole process of eating and therapy. I hope to come out better in the end, but I am afraid that I'll put on a lot of weight and then I'll feel like I have to lose it all.

I talked to Dan to let him know what was going on, and he said to me, "I understand you want to be home for Christmas, but you need to focus on your health. It's going to be hard, but you have to see what's important right now. You first need to stop taking those pills. You can probably eat enough to physically get you through Christmas, but it would be a good idea for you to go to this clinic. You see yourself as healthy, but everyone else sees you as too thin. You think they're going to be drill sergeants there, but it's going to make you better, mentally and physically." Boy Wonder, that kid is.

"I don't really know how I'll come out of all of this."

"I think that you'll come out happy, and truthfully, I don't think you've been happy before all of this."

"I don't remember ever being happy."

It's great that I can be open and talk to him, but I don't want to bring him down. Dad talked to him later, and said he sounded concerned.

"You two are so close, and if anything were ever to happen to you, he'd be devastated."

I don't want to be hurting my family. I don't want to be hurting myself. I know I need help, I'm just scared to get it. I never wanted to be anorexic. No one does. It's not like that.

No one gets into this disease by waking up one morning, stretching, letting out a big yawn and then saying, "You know what, I think I'll try that anorexia thing that's going around."

Nope. Anorexia is a disease, not a choice. It's a tortuous, insidious, life threatening disease. It has the highest mortality rate of all mental illnesses, and I was almost one of its victims. It's ruining my life, and I have to work incredibly hard to get it back. There are millions out there who are suffering from this disease and more whose lives have been touched by it—friends and family. There are even more who know so little about the disease that it is damaging to those suffering. Again, it could be those close to the sufferer, but in my case, it was those I sought for help from the nightmare. It was the doctors who almost let me die. So would this treatment centre be any different?

I feel so fat. I weigh 124 pounds. I had noticed some weight gain, but started using Kelly's elliptical machine and yoga, and my pants got loose again. I could even see my pretty bones start to come back. So maybe I gained some muscle. I'd rather be 115, or better, 110.

Jason sent me a text message to see how I was doing and I told him okay and that I had gained some weight, which made me nervous. So quotable, the writer that he is, he told me: "Success is one pound at a time." Cute. I used to think it was losing one pound at a time. I don't think that's what he meant.

***

Alone with Dad, I sat on the couch and watched T.V. with him. All was well until we hit a commercial and I chose to talk.

"I've been thinking about this inpatient thing and I don't know if I can do it," I told him.

"You've got to do something,' he told me.

"I know I need therapy and I want treatment, but I have gained more weight. I am 126 now."

"I don't see where you've gained any weight. I saw you last night and you looked like a skeleton in that t-shirt. From behind, the back of your arms were barely there."

"I've gained ten pounds since I've been home, and my general health is better than it was."

"I know you say you're better, but I don't see where your habits have changed."

"I just ate two cookies."

"That's not healthy."

"I had half of a lean cuisine pizza for lunch."

"That's the thing, you're still eating baby portions. You don't eat the things you used to eat."

"My tastes have changed and even before I got into this, I was trying to eat more healthily. Honestly, I don't know how I will deal with 28 days of isolation and being forced to eat things that I didn't want to eat before. Like butter on vegetables, and sauces and that kind of stuff. I know I'm stubborn but I don't like being told what to do."

"Look how far you got doing things your own way."

"I've been crying the past two days over this and I know I need treatment. That part of me thinks this will be good for me. The other part is so afraid."

"We'll talk it over and if you are better by that time, then we'll see. Ultimately, it's your decision, but I do want you to get help."

"Me too. But I am no longer underweight."

"Doesn't look like it. You look like a skeleton. In June, I thought you were too thin. Now, your face is sunken in."

"That was only because of how I used to look. It was a huge difference to you because I had lost weight. When I saw the picture you sent from Dan's graduation, I didn't like how I looked."

He stared at me for a second and said, "There's not a thing I'd change about you. You're a great person and everyone thinks so and I wish you would realize that."

Of course, surprise, surprise, I start crying. I'd like to know when I developed such massive tear ducts.

"I don't know why I'm doing this," I tell him.

"That's what we've gotta figure out. We suspected something was going on for a while and we didn't know what to do, and then our worst fears came true. I don't know what I would have done if I had lost you. You know you're my little buddy, always hanging out with me—even when you were little. I love you and I don't know what I would have done if I had got the call from California that something had happened to you."

Now I'm bawling. How I have the ability to speak at this point, I have no clue. "That night I went to the hospital, I thought it was the end."

"It was probably pretty close."

"All I could think was that I wouldn't be able to see you guys again and I couldn't even imagine it. I was so afraid that I had done something really stupid and this was it."

"There are a lot of people who care about you who would hate to see anything happen to you. I hope you realize that."

Damage to myself and damage to others. The only way to make up for it is to get better. So perhaps Renfrew is a good idea. Sort of like a mini-mental health vacation. I know I have issues. Many built up from over the years that I need to work on. It would be good for recovery, which is ultimately what I want. I'm worried about packing on the pounds. Dad is worried about me being miserable. What is more important? I don't know any more. Why is it so complicated? Why do I have to worry about it so much? Why can't the nutrients I need just be in a quick little pill and there be no food necessary? Oh wait, I've tried that route before…and look where it got me.

I am doing better, though I struggle. When they think I am better, they are happy. When I am honest, such as with the diuretics, they are mad. The more I try to hide it, the more it torments me. People may have thought I was better, but I was just better at hiding it. It makes it worse because then I'm really isolated with no one to turn to. I feel like I'll be stuck with this eating disorder forever. It is so tormenting. Secrets really do make you sick.

The admissions coordinator from Renfrew called me, wanting my decision. We worked it out so I could come in a few days after the cut-off period—January 5. That was my admission date. I was accepted at Renfrew. That's like, almost as good as college!

After I hung up, I sat on the floor in front of my mirror and cried. Not just tears, but audibly loud, insane crying. This was the final straw; I was going away. It had been decided and I didn't know if I was ready.

Mom heard me crying from upstairs, and came down to check on me. I explained to her what happened and then went on a tangent of "I hate myself," "I'm a failure", "I've ruined everything," "I haven't done anything with myself," and "Nothing will ever get better." I let it all out in a big release. I was hysterical.

She told me how much I have accomplished and that that is something to be proud of. Regarding weight, she couldn't see where I've gained it, which slightly annoyed me, because the scales don't lie and I can see the fat in my once-concave stomach.

"You can be thin, but you need to be healthy," she said.

"I hate being like this."

"Does anything make you happy?"

"No."

"It's a disease, and you'll work through it. Talk to the Renfrew Center about your concerns and we'll go from there. It's only 28 days. It will be so much better to work through this and get healthier. There is so much you can do in your life but you can't do it when you're sick like this."

"All I think about is food all the time and it's such a stupid thing to always be thinking about. I can't even work. The admissions person asked me what I did for fun, and I didn't have an answer. I don't know any more. There's so much I'd like to do, but I don't have the energy or focus. I can't do this for ever. I want to get better. I want to beat this. I know I need to do this, so I need to go in and just do it."

"It's good that you've accepted the fact that you're going in."

I will go in, and come out much better.

Christmas was nice and I was glad I didn't wake up in the morning on a cot somewhere. It was great to be home with the family, after being and feeling alone for so long. On Christmas, Meme asked me what my dress size was. She kept guessing and going down until she got to a 0. "Yes," I finally said.

I had a quick talk with Dad about my anxieties over treatment. He told me "I'll miss you for that month you are gone, but I know it's the best thing for you. It would be easy to overlook things and hope it gets better, but that's not going to beat it, and I want you to get better."

"I know. Even though I have gained weight, it's not about the food, and I have a lot of other issues to work out."

"This will be good for you to go over these issues and really work through them and come out having worked on yourself and focusing on you more. You have to start focusing on yourself, not because other people want you to. If you feel obligated to do something because someone else suggests it, just tell them 'no' and that it's not the right thing for you."

It was soothing to hear because that is one of my biggest issues. I've always done what everyone else wants me to do, and every time I try something for myself, I get entwined in their things, whereas treatment will enforce the idea of me doing my own thing. I want to lead my own life and become my own person—whoever that is. If I can start to discover that in 28 days, here's to anorexia.

My goal is to come out of there and to finally have my (belated) birthday cake. And Dad threw in, "beer and pizza at Mr. G's," a good restaurant near us. It's the little things that count, he mentioned.

I am scared. I had thought that coming home would "fix" this. Dad said I had been eating more but it doesn't erase the problem or mindset, and he's right. I need to get back my life. A life.

I needed to tell my grandparents, because it would be strange if I disappeared for a month. I wanted to confront this disease head-on. They had their suspicions anyway, and I didn't want to be ashamed of what I was going through. I didn't want to be this, 'it just happened'. Somehow, right before my eyes, I became ill, and now I was seeking recovery. That, I thought, was the one good thing to come out of this.

I called Meme and told her I was coming over because there was something I needed to talk to her about. As soon as I entered the house, we went into the kitchen and sat at the table. She was so open to sitting and talking with me. I told her how I know she was worried about me when I first came home and thought I wasn't eating enough, and the truth is I wasn't.

"I have an eating disorder," I said. "Anorexia." Then I started crying again. I really don't know where all these tear have been hiding. It's like I have a hose stuck to the back of my head. Meme took my hands and said, "And you don't think you can handle it on your own?"

"No," I said, and explained the whole situation of what I had been doing and why I came home and that I was going to Renfrew.

"You're a smart girl, Nicole. You will get through this," she said. Whenever she spoke, it was in such a wise and profound manner that I believed her. I held her hands in mine and didn't want to let go. If Meme said I would get better, then I would, and I wished that was all that would have to happen. If she said it, it would be so. Yet I knew there was so much more work that had to go into it.

"If you decide to go back to L.A. or stay here, I will support you either way. Just get better, take care of yourself and then worry about all of the other stuff," she told me.

It was nice to have her behind me as well and be able to talk openly about it. The shame and guilt had been lifted, and I was so grateful to have such a supportive family. I knew they would be an intricate part of my recovery.

I walked into my other grandparents' house and sat on their couch opposite them. Each of them rested cozily in their chairs, and I hated to disturb them with my news. How could I tell them that their granddaughter had anorexia and was about to go to an inpatient facility to get "fixed?"

I had called ahead of time and told them that there was something I needed to talk to them about, and Grammie said to come on over. She had known something was wrong. In fact, she probably knew exactly what was wrong. When I first came home, my grandfather, or "Buttsie" as we all call him, told me that I looked good, but "maybe missed a few meals." I smiled and assured him I was making up for them now. Grammie just said that I looked tired. She was right. I was so tired—of it all.

Grammie went on telling me stories about what was happening in all of my cousins' lives, and I asked what was going on with them, and then they asked how it was to be home. Buttsie got up to use the bathroom and Grammie said that he'd probably be going to bed soon.

It was time to speak up.

"Okay," I squeaked out. "I don't want to hold you up, but there is something that I wanted to talk to you about."

"Yes, you said that with your phone call. How are you?"

I took a deep breath.

"I know that when I first came home you were worried about my health, and thought that maybe I wasn't eating enough."

She nodded. "Oh, I was so worried about you, even when you were out in L.A. And when you came home and I saw you the first time, I was just shocked at how thin you were. I told your father, 'I hope she didn't see the look of shock on my face.' Because I'd never want to hurt you, you know that?"

I nodded, and the tears I had been holding in were slipping out of my eyes. She got me a tissue, then sat back down.

"What I want to tell you is that I have an eating disorder. I have anorexia."

Grammie kept nodding and I was a little shocked at how calm she was. "I thought so. Even when you were in L.A., and before I knew you went to the gym so much, you just didn't sound like the same Nicole on the phone. I knew something was wrong. But you look better. You're doing better now?"

"Kind of," I said. "I want to get better but it's really hard. I'm going down on Friday to Philadelphia for 28 days of inpatient treatment."

"You don't think you can do it on your own?"

"I've tried and it's so hard. They'll have counsellors, therapists and nutritionists there, and they'll help with meals. I want to work on recovery and move on with my life."

"That's a brave decision to make."

We both looked up when Buttsie sat back down. He must have caught a bit of the conversation.

"So, have you get your appetite back at all?" he asked.

"No, Buttsie, she has the anorexia." she told him.

Oh, my. Please don't explain it. Not "the anorexia!"

"Oh," he said. "Are you feeling better?"

I told him I was, but that I had to go somewhere to get treatment for a bit. He reiterated the fact that when he was on the phone to me, it didn't sound like "his" Nicole. Not the "jolly" Nicole he was used to.

I flinched a little, those eating disorder thoughts creeping in, thinking that "jolly" meant "fat."

Grammie pulled out a STAR Magazine from next to the table. It had Mary-Kate Olsen on it and in big letters said, "Anorexia," and then next to it, "Is she relapsing?"

Oh no, this can't be good.

"I get these magazines," she said, "and when I saw this one—" and she pointed at the cover and the word *Anorexia*, "—I thought, *that's my Nicole.*"

Great, that's exactly what I want people to be doing—pointing at pictures of emaciated celebrities on tabloids and comparing them to me.

I didn't respond. She put the magazine away.

"You think this place will help?" she asked.

"I hope so. It'll be hard, but I need that."

"28 days isn't really that long."

I nodded, because in the scheme of things it's not that long, but when you're battling this disease and will be far from home, it will seem long.

"You know," she continued, "I know it's hard to go through these things, and I don't judge anyone. When you see someone with a broken arm, you know where they're hurt and that they're in pain. But when someone is hurting inside, when they have pain in here," and she pointed to her head, "people don't realize that and they don't take them seriously. But not me, I know that pain can be worse."

She gets it. Tabloid covers aside, my grandmother gets it. She gets me.

"I knew someone who was an alcoholic, and he used some drugs too, and I asked him why he did it. He said he didn't know, but the pain of not having it, the drink or the drug, was too much. He would have been much happier if he didn't have to have it at all. He would have given anything up at the time just to get his hands on some drugs, and that wasn't any way to live. He's sober and clean now, but all that he went through, people don't understand that," she said.

"It's not a way to live," I replied. "That's how I feel, and I want to get my life back."

"You will, honey, and anything you need, you just call us. And get me your address when you get down there, okay?"

I thought it was Buttsie's bedtime, so I said goodnight and goodbye and Grammie told me again how brave I was for getting help. I left feeling a little bit braver too. With their support, I felt stronger. It was nice to have family behind me that weren't just saying they were there for me, but who truly understood. Who cared.

I still felt like I was disappointing others, and I didn't want to be. They said I wasn't, they just wanted me to get better. Then I knew that I was scaring others. I was scaring myself too. Fearing that your heart is failing is the worst feeling. You're scared all the time for yourself. Your loved ones are scared, they think you have no idea how worried they are, but you can't dare tell them how terrified you are every second. That you live in fear. You're afraid to go to sleep in case you don't wake up. Every strange feeling you get, you question. You wonder what damage you really did to your body and of course you don't trust the doctors. What did they miss? You wonder. Shouldn't they do blood work again? I was running from my life by using my eating disorder and suddenly, I had become afraid of my life, when it was really the one thing I was trying to hold on to.

Eating disorders are exhausting work. I didn't want to, but I kept secrets from my family, friends, my room mate and myself—and secrets make you sick. People say that those with eating disorders are manipulative, but I hate that word, because I don't like to think that I was cruel—I was scared. Scared of being caught and what people would think of my odd habits, scared of what I was doing to myself, and what would happen if someone found out. I never had any intentions of manipulating people, except perhaps myself, which I did often by telling myself I didn't need to eat or I had to exercise more. But I would never manipulate anyone I cared about. The eating disorder might try, but I wouldn't. And I hate that there is that stigma, that label. If people don't understand the agony of an eating disorder, how can they tell you your actions are manipulative?

I had to be "manipulative," I suppose. I had to keep secrets, lie about what I was doing, to isolate myself, to keep my eating disorder for myself, and a secret from everyone else. Because what would I do without it, and what would people do if they knew I had one? People with eating disorders aren't "manipulative," we're just as scared as our loved ones. It's the eating disorder that is manipulative, not us.

My parents were glad I was going to Renfrew. They were sad to see me go, but knew it was the help I needed. My sister was taking me down, and we left the night before to stay with her boyfriend in New Jersey, and would head to Philadelphia the next morning. I knew how stressed and worried my parents had been, and I didn't want to be doing that to them. My parents loved me and I knew they were afraid I was going to die if I didn't get help. I was afraid too. So with some teary goodbyes and "I love you's," I hopped in the car and to Renfrew I went.

Chapter 27
Renfrew:
Saying Goodbye

People coming and going; I can't keep up. It is sad to see people go, but I am trying to welcome the newcomers. Amy is leaving. She is the first one who helped me through a meal, and reminded me that food is so much better than supplements. Boy, was she right. At 16, she was wise beyond her years. I bought her a necklace and wrote her a quote by one of my favorite singers, Matt Nathanson, to hang on to: "I'll learn to get by on the little victories." Which is so true, because it's step by step and day by day, and truly, meal by meal. They are all little victories.

I met with one of the counsellors, Colleen, who told me that after seeing my parents, I should be relieved of some of my anxieties for when I returned home. How I shouldn't listen to what everyone told me about having to write in L.A. I should find what makes me happy and do it where I want. It was sweet and encouraging.

I realize how hard it will be to leave. The transition is going to be more difficult than I thought. I knew it would be bad, but I'm devastated, not only for the loss of L.A., but the loss of connection with people there, the loss of independence, of my surroundings, and loss of self. I am regressing and that's scary. Where do I go from here? And don't say anywhere, because it's not that easy.

Though eating has been hard, as well as the realization of what my eating disorder is and all the pain it has caused—not just to myself, but also to others—another terrible thing has happened. After 9 months, I have got my periods back. It sounds ridiculous to be upset by it, but not having my period meant I was thin. My body did not have enough fat to produce estrogen. So now that I have it, it means I am fat again.

I freak out and go talk to Lindsay, a young nurse who I have bonded with. I explain to her what is happening, and that I know it is healthy to get your period, but it scares and upsets me.

"It's a good thing," she tells me. "Does it really bother you?"

"Yes," I say. "It means I'm fat again."

"You are not fat. I know I can sit here all day and tell you that, but you're not fat. I don't know what you're body percentage is but you don't look near it, and for your height, I don't know...130?"

I didn't tell her I was just over 130, but that I was close to the percentage of a normal body weight.

"Oh! Normal!" she says, and laughs, and so do I. "Normal is good. Normal is healthy. What about this, do you want kids?"

"Yes, and I know it's important to be getting a period. It scares me because I haven't had it for so long."

I didn't say this, but I feel like it means the end of the eating disorder.

Hang In There... Wherever "There" Is

"You're still sick. This doesn't mean you're better, but it's a good sign."

It was good to talk to her because she understands how strange the physical changes of recovery can be.

The next morning, it was evident that it was my period and not just some spotting. I'm angry with myself for letting it come back. I know it's because I'm no longer malnourished, and that's a sign I am getting better, but the idea of being healthy when I was so sick for so long is bizarre. It's the eating disorder slipping away. What will I do when it is completely gone?

Jamie, my bean buddy, who already left, sent me a package. I open it and it's a kid's book about a Chihuahua who likes beans. It's hysterical and brightened my day a bit. She enclosed a note and told me "it's OK to break up with Ed." 'Ed' being the "Eating disorder." She's so sweet, I hope she is doing well.

My contact at night is Lindsay. She tells me she makes the schedule so she made sure that she got to see me. She asks about my period and how I was doing. I tell her it's a full-on period now.

"How do you feel about that?"

"Normal Nicole knows that it's okay, but the eating disorder wants it to go away."

She comments on how when she was writing her notes, I had thought that a period meant being both healthy and fat. We both agree that it makes no sense. I tell her that I am getting fat, she says I'm not, and I tell her I can show her.

That is when she brings up redistribution, which I did not know about.

"When you first gain weight back, most of it will go to a certain area. For a lot of people, it's the stomach."

I nod, as my arms are already tightly wrapped around my stomach, which now protrudes over my pants.

"You're gaining weight, so the body needs somewhere to store it. But as time goes on and your body recognizes that you aren't going to go back intro starvation mode, it will redistribute the weight you have gained—to your legs, arms, etc. As you continue eating healthfully, everything will go back to a 'normal' state."

"Are you sure? My stomach won't be like this forever?"

"Trust me. It all just takes time to even out."

"That does make me feel better, even though I feel so uncomfortable now."

"Re-feeding is hard, it does take a toll on your body. But think of the toll the eating disorder takes on your body. It's all working hard now to restore itself to a better state so you can be healthy again."

"Healthy? What's that?" I joke.

I am glad I got to talk with her again. I will definitely miss having these contacts when I am home, or at least having someone to talk to.

My room mate was caught water-logging. Before she goes down for weights in the morning, she drinks of a ton of water so that on the scales she weighs more. They had suspected this though, so they weighed her during the day and the two numbers were completely off. She keeps saying she is better, but she is still so stuck in her eating disorder. They put her on contract and she's upset, but also kind of happy she got caught. It was bothering her and it was getting to be too much work.

I leave soon and I'm terrified. I think people expect me to be cured when I go home, but this is no quick fix. Renfrew is just the start of my recovery. It is safe here. I go for meals when I am supposed to. I have therapy and a nutritionist and plenty of support. When I go home, I will be on my own. No counsellors telling me it's time for dinner. Just me and the broken pieces of my eating disorder. Will that voice get louder again? How will I protect myself against it?

I try to explain my fears to Dad. He says, "What, are we so hard to live with?" We both laugh.

"No," I tell him. "It's not you, it's me. I'm afraid of what I'll do and how I'll be on my own. I am already wondering what my first meal is going to be when I leave here. Food, food, food—it's all I think about. It's awful."

"You'll get back in the routine once you get home, and you can make your own meals separate from what we have. But you can't be using diuretics again, and no more lying. I can't have that."

"I don't like that either. I never wanted to, it was the eating disorder. I was two different people."

"I understand that, and I know more about eating disorders now, but you have to realize how hard it was for me to see my daughter starving herself to death. I'm just being honest. I thought that was what you wanted."

"Yes. It still hurts, but I am sure everything I say hurts too."

The girls here are telling me how much they are going to miss me and what a source of inspiration I am to them. It baffles me, because I don't recognize that. All I do is talk to them. If they saw me when I first came in, they wouldn't be thinking that.

In Community, we do traditions—the Bear of Courage, the Blanket of Comfort, the Bracelet of Faith and the Book of Wisdom. We do these each week, and I have never got anything. I sat in Community like always and Traditions came up. To my surprise, I was given the Book of Wisdom from Barbara. I felt honoured.

Hang In There... Wherever "There" Is

In it, each person who has it writes on to the next person why they are giving it to her. She first wrote a quote from Ann Landers: "Expect trouble as an inevitable part of life, and when it comes, hold your head high and say, 'I will be bigger than you, and you cannot defeat me.'" Then she wrote to me:

"Nicole,

I am in constant awe of you. Without saying too much, I know that you doubt yourself. But you have already accomplished so many of the things that I dream of and hope of for myself. I hope that one day you will be able to see yourself as I, and the many people who love you, do: accomplished, poised, ambitious, courageous, charming...I could go on. You have been a source of inspiration to me since I first met you. When I think of the 'strong woman' charm symbolic of Renfrew and the women here, I think of you. You are the epitome of a strong woman. Stay strong! The fight is a bitch but worth it.

Much love,

Barbara

Never would I think these things about myself, nor believe anyone else would. It was nice to receive. It was touching to get and I appreciated it.

My last day here and I feel sick. Literally. My temperature is 98.5, whereas it is usually 96 or 97. Sore throat, aches, you name it. I talk to Maura, my team nurse, and ask her if my immune system would be more susceptible to these things because of the eating disorder. She says, "yes," that I may get sick more easily. Great.

At medication, she had better words for me. "You did so well here, Nicole. You've really come a long way and truly blossomed. I wish you the best of luck and really think you'll do well in your recovery. You better find me before you leave tomorrow!"

Her words are encouraging, but it's sad to hear the word "leave." That isn't the last time I hear it though. We have a community meeting and I have to say my "goodbyes." It is a difficult thing to do. I tell the group, "I cried on the way in, and here I am, crying on the way out."

I continue, "At first, they told me I'd only be here 28 days, but that turned out to be just a funny Sandra Bullock movie. My time here has meant so much. I am glad I came, and yes, I struggled, but I am coming out so much stronger. To the new people, it does take time to adjust, but you will. I remember coming in on trays and calling my family, all upset about how they made us eat everything on the tray and how I didn't understand the system. They told me to be patient because it would work, and they were right. It did. It's easy to doubt yourselves, but then when you succeed, you'll feel that much better for it. I wish you all so much luck and thank you for your support during my time here."

They all clap and then two people are allowed to respond. One is this girl who is newer, Tina. "Well, I know I've said this before, but you are such an inspiration to me. I feel like we have a lot of the same issues and you were always there for me with guidance. You are strong, brave and always willing to fight, not just against the eating disorder, but also things like propane, and to raise awareness about eating disorders. I'm definitely going to miss you around here."

Then, my room mate, Diane, gets to speak. "I am still in denial that you are leaving me. I know you like your quiet, alone time, and I am always gabbing away, yet somehow, you put up with it. I appreciate all the advice you have given me, especially when I was going through a tough time with my family. You could always talk me through things and give me advice and just make me feel better." I had no idea of the impact I had on her. I thought I was just her roommate.

Then the therapist, Margaret, closes and says, "I will definitely miss you in all of the groups." There was a resounding goodbye and I thank everyone again, still shocked that this was my last Community. I remember my first meeting and hearing people do their goodbyes, having no clue what was going on. The newcomers probably had no idea either or didn't care, but one day, it would be their turn, and they would. All I could do now was wish them well and hope their journey through recovery would be a strong one.

I call Dad and tell him that I don't think it will be too bad going home. He tells me it will be good to have me home, but of course I am still nervous. But like everyone says, they would be nervous if I wasn't. It will be a change, and like Dad says, a way of life, and I just have to get myself into a routine like I had before—only this time, a good one. I can stay with them as long as I want, and then if I want to move out, it won't hurt their feelings. Hopefully, I can allow myself to enjoy the things I like to do and get back on track. I know I am still in recovery and not everything will be perfect.

I have one last contact with Lindsay and we go over all the issues—food, family, L.A. and bread. Yes, bread. She tells me that I need to find things I like and that real bread (as opposed to the "lite" bread I eat) is not going to make me fat.

"I am so sure that you will do well and just remember, it's okay to have a slip up or make a mistake. It is just a mistake and then you'll get through it and know that it's normal. It's a slip up and you'll come out of it."

She had tears in her eyes and so did I.
"Now you're making me cry," she says.
"No, you're making me cry!"
"I can't go out there like this!" she laughs.
"Neither can I!"

Hang In There... Wherever "There" Is

We hug and take a moment to compose ourselves. We talk about Gatorade and vitamin water and how I will continue my regiment of electrolytes. I give her a thank-you card that I wrote for her and we walk out and decide to say our official good-bye later. I have more cards to write and I am sending flowers to the nurse's station.

The night wore on and soon it was morning—my last day.

My last meal at Renfrew. I think back to how scared I was at the first meal there, and now, I have the option to eat anything, but I decide to go out with a bang. I choose the full meal that is being served: French Toast. Yowza. I would normally have yogurt, granola and fruit, but I wanted my time here to come full circle. So I get it and I eat it. That, my friends, is progress. I was not even scared.

I become a little tearful because I remember when I first got that meal and how afraid of it I was. I was barely able to complete it, and I thought about how terrified I had been of food in general. How just looking at food on my plate would scare me. Not today. I ate it, and that was accomplishing something.

I was all packed and then Dad arrived to pick me up. He told me I looked good, and I am sure it was a huge difference from my old skeletal self. Then, we went for our last family session with Robin.

She jumps right in, validating the fact that 7 weeks may have seemed like a long time to him, but it wasn't to me. This was not a quick fix and recovery is a long process. I am still going to struggle and mess up. She brought up anger and emotions and that it is good when I let them out, because bottling them up contributed to the eating disorder. We talk about changes that will need to be made at home, such as not arguing about what to have for dinner, no calorie talk and not focusing on the meals. It was good to get that out there, because those things make me anxious and could hinder my progress, and Dad understood that.

We wrapped it up, and I had a gift for Robin. With my wonderful crocheting skills, I had made her a baby blanket, because she was pregnant. It wasn't perfect, but what is? She said she loved it, and being my first real creation, I was a little proud of it. But just in case I had tanked, I got her some toys and stuffed animals for the little one.

Dad and I get my stuff and leave my room. All the girls are having lunch. I say "goodbye" and get a few hugs. They wish me luck and thank me for my guidance. I say goodbye to the counsellors and then to everyone at the nurses' station. I find Margaret, my team nurse, and she wishes me well and hopes that one day I can come back and talk about my recovery. I hope so too. That means I will be in a better place.

Dad and I hop in the truck and drive off, leaving Renfrew and my home of seven weeks behind. It was odd, and sad, to leave. I learned so much and made a lot of strong connections. To think that seven weeks ago I was in a room by the nurses' station, crying on the phone about how I struggled over lunch—a whole sandwich. It's amazing how different things were and how far I have come. I am proud of myself but I know I still have a lot of work to do. At Renfrew, I was "forced" to do those things. Outside, I am responsible for myself, and that is scary. There's an open kitchen so I can eat or I cannot eat. I don't want to binge or restrict, but I don't feel as if I have control. I do sort of want to restrict. It's Nicole versus the eating disorder and I hope that the tools I gained at Renfrew will let Nicole win out.

At Renfrew, I found out that the symbol of recovery for eating disorders is the butterfly and the colour is purple. It is the whole idea of transformation with the butterfly. There was a quote I got in a journal that read: "Just when the caterpillar thought the world had come to an end, it became a butterfly." It's true. I had thought that my world had come to an end, but I've made it, and I hope the day comes when I can become that sort of butterfly. Maybe I already am one.

Part II

Finding Home

"If I ever go looking for my heart's desire again, I won't look any further than my own back yard.   Because, if it isn't there, I never really lost it to begin with" – Dorothy Gale, The Wizard of Oz

"Your body is a temple, but only if you treat it as one" - Astrid Alauda

Nicole Roberge

Chapter 28
Taking the Leap

Being an inpatient was hard, but leaving was harder. I left the comfort zone and took the leap, or the plunge rather, and kicked through the air, uncertain of where I would land, just hoping that I would. I looked down into the unknown, and hoped that eventually I'd come to the point of looking out. Right now, it is a struggle. Adapting to being on my own is difficult. I'm in the "real world," and that is a big difference from the secure boundaries of a treatment centre.

Eating disorders are hard; not everyone can do it. Which is a good thing. They take a lot of energy, but I didn't have a lot of energy because of my eating disorder. My focus and coordination was lost. I had to be strong-willed and determined to have an eating disorder, so hopefully, I can be strong and determined in recovery. But eating disorders are very hard to do, which means recovery is very hard as well. Hopefully, just as I came into it, I can come out.

When I left Renfrew, it was a tricky situation. I had begun to feel sick when I left, and on the drive home it was worse. When I got home, my temperature was 100.3. The next day, it was 103.6. I could barely move when I was taken to the doctors and he told me I had pneumonia. It was awful. I had to wait a week until I went to day treatment (which my Dad accidentally called "day care," not realizing the meaning of what he actually said, which I found hysterical), which was an entirely different experience. I did actually see some recognizable faces from Renfrew, but the program itself made it feel like I was regressing. They checked my glass to make sure I had enough milk in it, and checked me to see I ate all of my meal. I had already done all of that, way back on trays. The thing with outpatient day programs is that everyone is on a different level, and I felt as if I had accomplished many of these things. I stayed for a week and was done. The groups were not helpful at all. Plus it was a two-hour drive for me, so we talked it over and decided I would follow up with aftercare locally.

So now it's a therapist, nutritionist and support group on my own. Things are okay, though I'm actually having a tough time, but that all ties into the adjustment of being home and not in LA, and also some of the weight gain since I've been back. It's hard in general, and I wonder when life will ever be back to "normal." I know it's not going to happen overnight and I've got to keep up the fight. I hate feeling this way, it's so depressing. It's hard because I do miss LA, but what was I doing when I was there besides the eating disorder? I don't have any friends here and I just stay inside all day. It kind of sucks, coming back to bills and the "real world," but I guess that's what we were being prepped for. It's difficult when you actually have to step into it. I was good when I got home, keeping up with it and all, but I've been slacking off lately. It's strange when you don't have boring groups to go to all the time where you can just knit and crochet away with a blanket wrapped around you.

Nicole Roberge

I think of it as training wheels. Recovery and going out "on your own" from residential treatment is like taking off your training wheels. I'm still on the bike of recovery, but I don't have those extra supports under me. When I came home, I got my own support team—they'll be the seat, wheels, pedals, steering wheel…BRAKES! But those training wheels, they were an important part of my treatment and recovery process, and like learning to ride a bike, they can be hard to let go of.

I remember the first time I tried to ride a bike without training wheels. My Dad took the wheels off, but I was not ready to ride the bike on my own, even with those other supports, without those training wheels. I would do the thing where you sit on the bike, hold the steering wheel, and then push yourself along the ground using your feet—never allowing them to touch the pedals. One day, my sister and I were out on our bikes with my grandmother. We'll call her "Meme," because that's what I call her. I was doing my thing, shuffling along on my bike, and Meme said, "you know how to ride a bike, don't you, Nicole?" She gave me a push on my back, and before I knew it, I was moving. I had no choice but to pedal, and to my surprise, I was doing it—I was riding a bike. It felt so good to be riding my bike down the road, my feet on the pedals, and no training wheels to guide me. I was afraid to stop, because I thought that maybe it was just a one-time deal. But it wasn't. I eventually stopped, and then was able to give myself a little push, place my feet on the pedals, and ride away—the happiest biker on the road.

So that's what leaving treatment is like—taking off those training wheels. Yes, it is scary, I didn't want to do it, I was afraid of what would happen when I did—but I had to think of the ride that lay ahead. Yes, it will be bumpy. That chain on the bike might get loose. A tire might go flat. Should I tell you about the time in fifth grade when I fell off my bike and broke my wrist? Darn that bikers' confidence. But just because the training wheels come off does not mean that everything is going to be okay. It won't. I still have a long road ahead of me, with lots of work to do. Those training wheels were there for guidance, and they were great support in that initial phase of treatment. I needed someone to take a little bit of responsibility for me, because I wasn't doing it for myself, and that's okay. Now I have the tools I need to learn more about the disorder and how to get my life back. I can kindly ditch the training wheels, plant my feet firmly on the pedals, and start moving towards the future. I have plenty of other supports under me, so no need to worry. And even if I fall, I know by now that it's okay, and to get up and try again is the braver thing to do. And with each scar, I'll learn.

Chapter 29
Post Renfrew: Month One
Scary Therapy

No one can be responsible for me but me. No one can support me like me, even though I need them to. I know I'm used to doing things on my own and prefer to do them on my own and now they tell me, strictly—I can't do this alone. It's a whole new way of thinking. As much as people tell me they want to support me, it doesn't seem totally there. I am in this alone. When I'm alone, I am beyond alone. When they're there, I have to face alone the fears in my head. No one can do this for me, no matter how much love and support surrounds me. So while they tell me I can't do this alone, and my need to isolate is partly how I got here, the scary truth is that, to get out of this dark well, I can't reach up and pull on the ropes people are throwing down. I have to strain and struggle and climb with all my might to get the hell out of there. I have to fight—just as I always have—alone. While this notion is probably what people are constantly in fear of, I'm afraid too.

No one knows how much pain I'm in all the time. I shifted from being in so much anguish from the eating disorder, to now dealing with the pains of recovery—the anxiety, the depression, and worst of all, the food. It's all the same, just in a different way. No one knows what it means to give up an eating disorder. It was essentially my best friend. The thing that was always there for me. And though it was an abusive thing, it is now as if a huge chunk of my life is leaving little by little, and I feel empty and hollow, without anything to replace it. The isolation is still there, and I know that I can't turn to the eating disorder. They tell me it is healthy to feel depression and it is a sign of recovery, because all the things I felt before the eating disorder, that I used the eating disorder to mask, are coming back. Now, instead of using the eating disorder, I have to deal with them. That is a difficult task. I have to deal with...life.

I question the decisions I have made, how I ended up here, and I wonder how it all happened. And then, I am stuck in silence, waiting for the answer.

Treatment is basically a bunch of people making me feel like shit—more than I already do. I know I'm in trouble. I know this is hard. I know what I did was bad. I don't need you to tell me that, thanks. I meet with my new therapist, near home. What a beast. Her name is Doctor Cagore, and she seems nice at first, and takes down my history, but as we get more into it, she keeps referring to me as an "anorectic," which I suppose is the appropriate term, but then compares me to her other "anorectic" clients.

I have my meeting with Dr. Ligorski, who was the psychiatrist at the Renfrew Outpatient Center in Connecticut. He is great, and I continue seeing him. I tell him how upset I am about gaining weight, how my clothes don't fit right, that my stomach is enlarged and even if I go up a size, it is disproportionate to my legs, so my body just looks weird.

He tells me "You just have a warped image of yourself," and I know what he is saying but I am sick of hearing it, because my reasons are true. If I went naked, people would see it. He continues with, "The way you feel then, you might as well go off to Kabul and wear a sheet over your body." Hmm, not a bad idea.

"Is there anyone you would trust to take you clothes shopping?" he asks. "That would be honest and helpful?"

"I guess my sister." I don't have anyone else.

"You need to take someone with you that will go," he goes on, and then his humour seeps in. "Look, you're retarded right now, you don't know what looks good, you need someone to take your hand and take you clothes shopping and go in blind and tell you what looks good because you have a distorted image of yourself. If you went in alone, you'd try things on and get aggravated, hate yourself, and walk out of there and not eat for 3 or 4 days."

I hated that he said that, but I know he is right—it's true. I'm mad because he doesn't understand what I am trying to say when I tell him about my disproportionate body and how my stomach is larger than my hips and it is hard to find clothes that fit. He insisted that it's in my head. It pissed me off and frustrated me because he doesn't believe me and told me it's the eating disorder in my head. Yeah, I know that I'm totally irrational about some things—a lot of things. But this I knew I was right about. I could have shown him my flab and how bad my clothes fit. That's what I hate, what makes me feel worse, because I feel so uncomfortable in my clothes and that is what makes me feel more fat. I am scared to get to a size 2. Even though my 0's are stretched out, it still seems as if a 0 is so perfect. You are supposed to be a 0. Once you go up to a 2, it's adding something to that perfect number, and that's just bad. You should want to stay at that perfect number, even if you have to really suck it in and have flab hanging over. Gross, I know, and totally irrational, but welcome to my awful, sick, twisted, scary, sad, and devastating world.

Mom and Dad are heading off to Arizona for Dan's Spring break, where he is playing baseball for a week. Dad feels bad, and said that I seem depressed, but I tell him that I was going to be depressed whether they were here or there, so not to worry. They went. And that began my restricting and taking pills again. One is supposed to cut 25% of carbohydrates and turn it into fibre and the other burns 40% more calories. Two sets of pills, again. So very "Alice in Wonderland." I also started using Kelly's elliptical again and doing crunches. I have to lose that weight! I couldn't believe how much I had gained. After the day program, I was in the 140's—not acceptable. I need to get back down, but I hate this. Thinking of food all the time, letting it rule my life. Why can't I just be normal?

Hang In There... Wherever "There" Is

I have sunk into a different depression. Crying at night. I don't know if I'm missing L.A., hating what my life has become, or myself, but I'm miserable in this half-life. It's not a pleasant way to function and I would not wish this hellish disease on anyone. It is going to be much more of a struggle to get out of this than I imagined. Renfrew gave me the tools and now this is the real start of recovery. I know that I could have stayed at Renfrew forever, but that would be avoiding my life. The big challenge was to leave, and damn, this is some kind of challenge. The eating disorder is hell, and in treatment they try to draw you out of that. To truly recover you have to go back into that hell and dig deep to find why you were there to begin with and fight your way out. Not that Renfrew was easy, but there's no one holding my hand now. I have to make a conscious effort to eat, which seems like a chore, and I am not doing such a good job of it right now. Lapses, side-steps, they are all part of this, and they told me that would happen. I just didn't realize it would be so soon.

It is awful because Rational Nicole knows I should be fighting this harder, that I should be sitting down for these meals and stomping out that eating disorder voice. That eating disorder voice is still there, telling the anorexia in Nicole, "welcome back!" and enjoying the fact that I can still restrict. But even with those two voices combined, there is a power within that wants my life back, a life, and to be happy. I hope that power will be strong enough to carry me through this.

I feel weak. After I eat the little I do, I am having palpations again and feel as if I may pass out. It may be the diet pills or the restricting. I try the gym and I cannot work out like I used to. My weight is down more, and so is my energy. Kelly noticed I wasn't looking good the other night and asked if I was OK. I'm not OK.

I see Dr. Cagore and she asks how I'm doing with my parents gone. She explains her concern after I am truthful with her. "You are just on the cusp of being ready for outpatient treatment," she tells me. "You probably could have stayed as an inpatient longer, or definitely should have been in the day program an extra week, just to have more stability. With your restricting and barely eating any fat, by the end of the week it will have taken a serious toll on your body."

Then, she says to me, so casually, "You are still an anorexic."

I tense up. No, I am not. I am in recovery from anorexia.

"It still has a hold on you. You still have that mindset. My job is to keep you from returning to the inpatient facility."

She goes on, and I fade out. She treats me like I am just admitting I have an eating disorder. I don't look like I have one, though I know that's never the case. It's not about looks. It makes me wonder, with her acting this way, what was the point of being an inpatient? I was there for seven weeks, doing all that work, and I could have stayed longer, but I had to be ready to go some time. Leaving is the real challenge, that is what takes strength—not going in as an inpatient. Being an inpatient is submitting—saying, "okay, I have an eating disorder and I can't fight it on my own. I need help and I'm going to get it." I don't like how I am being treated now, but I guess I just have to trust it. I hate it and struggle, but I'll learn. Then I'll just hope and pray that I can take all that I've learned and apply it to the real world and my life.

I am up for the challenge, though I hate every moment of the day. The nasty eating disorder is creeping back into my life and there is no fun group to take my mind off of it, or 30 other residents to talk to about it. I will not go back to being an inpatient again. I know too many girls who had been in treatment multiples of times. I am focused. I will fight this, and I will prevail. I will prove to my therapist that she is wrong about me.

I took the diet pills again and felt sick. It's not worth it. I am stopping. I ate a small but well-rounded breakfast. Focus. Determination. I surprise myself sometimes. I went out and bought Ensure. I am giving myself supplements. What the hell? I need the nutrients. I want to be healthy. Whatever it takes.

I don't want to get to the point of being so far off track that I can't see the track any more. Having these experiences of "slipping" makes me realize that recovery can get very slippery at times. Though I am klutzy, I can catch myself, and I truly do have support to grab on to. If I am alone, I might fall, and it may be difficult, because I may be tempted to stay down there—to restrict, to over-exercise, but that's when I can pull myself back up. I'll think back to that night when I almost died, and I knew I did not want that, so I'll pick myself up and eat. Though scary, I know it is the best thing for me. It's such a simple thing, it seems, eating, but I still have to treat it like medicine.

The whole idea of side-stepping came from Renfrew. It is not a relapse, but a lapse. A quick blip in the radar. You're doing the dance, but not the right way. It's the electric slide gone awry. I never did know how to do that dance the right way anyway. Is it to the left first or the right? Now slide? What? Either way, I was sliding or side-stepping, but that's normal. It happens. I'll have good days and bad days, and if I side-step a little, that's to be expected. I'm not going backwards, which is very good. I'm just not quite moving forwards. I'm going off track for a second. Maybe I didn't hit my meal plan quite right. Maybe I over-exercised. Maybe I purged. My symptoms came back. It was a difficult day and hard to get through and, as my coping mechanism, I used my eating disorder. But just as I took a step to the side, I can step right back. I was learning to do that. Get back on track, keeping forward, maybe step off again…oops…but that's how I learned. The side steps became fewer and further between. I realized how little I liked stepping off track.

Dr. Cagore calls me and tells me she's afraid I might have a heart attack because of how little I'm eating and the diet pills, which of course scares me and makes me try harder. This world outside the bubble of

Hang In There... Wherever "There" Is

Renfrew is tough. It's so much easier to slip back into the "wrong" things, even though I know they are bad. I am scared for my health, but I still do things I know are wrong. I hate feeling and looking fat, and then constantly having that number on the scales telling me I am. I don't want to be fat again, I want to be thin. I want to be tiny. I loved feeling so tiny and small...fragile.

Now I feel big again, my fat spilling out of my clothes. That is when my mind tells me that something has to be done. Severe measures need to be taken. Restrict! Diet pills! Exercise! Ah yes, the key to weight loss. I can do these things, I know them so well. That's what Mr. ED tells me. Then Rational Nicole reminds me that I didn't lose all that weight overnight before, and I can't do that now, so I am relieved and know that it is possible to lose a little weight in time. But is Rational Nicole fuelling the eating disorder?

I talk to Melissa, my buddy from Renfrew who I was admitted with, who is having some struggles also, and we make a pact. When the eating becomes difficult, pretend you are eating for someone you love. If I don't eat, I am hurting myself. But if it is lunch and I want to restrict, I should pretend that meal is for my Mom or Dad, because would I do that to them? Never. So I eat. On top of that, I know they would want me to. So it helps. I think of my loved ones and that familiar feeling of not wanting to hurt them any more and not wanting to hurt myself. The idea was very encouraging and the hope she had in me instilled a hope in myself.

My nutritionist, Holly David, understands me the most. I am so lucky to have her and can be open with her about my eating, for the most part. We develop a meal plan to try and follow that doesn't seem so daunting. It actually includes foods I like. The only aspect I don't like is that she and Dr. Cagore work as a "team", so they each report to each other. The worst part is that Dr. Cagore wants me to do "blind weights," where I stand on the scales backwards so I don't see my weight. I never had to do those at Renfrew, I explain to her, and Holly doesn't see why I need to, but my psychologist thinks it is good so I don't focus on my weight. I weigh myself at home anyway, so what does it matter? I'm not supposed to be doing that though. I get weighed once a week there so they can make sure it doesn't go too low. I hate being judged by a number.

The way Dr. Cagore put it to Holly is that they are "taking control away from me." That only frustrates me more. She meant it in regard to the blind weights and food. Why can't I just eat what I want? It's always going to be the same thing, and that is what is so aggravating. They can make up any meal plan they want for me, tell me how many starches, fats, proteins, dairy, fruit and vegetables I need, but I am still going to insert the foods I like in there, what I feel safe with. Even those foods, though I am comfortable with them and they are healthy, are starting to bore me. I don't know what else to eat. I have forgotten how to eat. When I was an inpatient, we ate different foods, but that was because we had to. I'm not going to eat other things now just to eat them. I feel no real connection with food. I don't really want these things, I eat them because I have to, as if they are on a check list.

I wonder if I will have to go through meals like this for the rest of my life? What is more torturous—planning what not to eat, or planning what to eat? This is exactly why you start eating as a baby, so you don't have to deal with this crap. And of course, the whole nutrients to survive thing. Re-learning to eat is an insanely hard task. Once you get out of the habit of eating, it is very hard to get back in. I know I need to nourish myself and if I think of it that way, it's okay. There is part of me that knows it can be enjoyable, and people have told me that. I would like to get to the point where I can go to a restaurant again and have fun, not fear what is on the menu or if I'll be able to find anything "safe" to eat. Even just to sit down with my family at dinner and not feel anxiety. Some day.

I went to an eating disorder support group, but it was small and I didn't connect with the girls like I had at Renfrew. The therapist who led it was nice and recovered herself. They talked a lot about the "right mind." I don't think I have one. If I did, I wouldn't be so screwed up. But as we spoke more, the therapist told me that my actions did show the "right mind" because I was trying to do what was best for me, even though it was hard. I wanted treatment and to get better. That was the right mind. What I really wanted was to be out of this hell and to have a true "right mind." Can I buy one of those somewhere?

Jason checked in with me to see how I was doing, and I tell him I'm struggling a bit and it's been harder than I thought. He said, "*I had a feeling. Sorry to hear that. I can't imagine how hard it is. Are you trying the protein shakes? On a lighter note, opening day is coming up fast. You need to get yourself in playing shape.*"

Only he can be helpful and make me smile with a baseball reference at the same time. I'm honest and tell him I haven't tried the shakes, but I will. I tell him that I had gone back to the diet pills and working out a lot again just to lose a little weight.

He replied, "*Remember, working out like that only does harm to the body. The body needs food to grow, otherwise you are burning muscle. Bad. You need carbohydrates, protein...all of it. Carbohydrates are important for the brain, protein for the muscle, but I'm sure you know all this. No more diet pills. Eat bananas. Grill chicken and steam vegetables. This gives you all you need with no fat. All good calories. You can do it.*"

So I make the protein shake, but one of the "lite" ones, and even toss some banana in there. It was actually good. I email him and tell him he should be my nutritionist.

"As a nutritionist," he says, "more French fries and less ketchup."

Hang In There... Wherever "There" Is

It's nice to have a voice, other than my treatment team, that cares, and one who I can talk to. Funny that I take his advice more than theirs. Maybe because I trust him more. He knows me better and understands that it is hard, without just pushing me like they do. Yes, I have my ups and downs, my good days and bad days, and that's how it is right now. It's amazing the curve balls life throws at you and what we have to do to get ourselves through the game. For now, it's protein shakes...diet protein shakes.

I do hate that as soon as I'm feeling great, something can suddenly set me back. That thing would be trying on bridesmaids' dresses. Trying on dresses and having to not only show people, but also stand in front of a mirror in a busy store while people stare. A recovering anorexic's nightmare.

I had to do it. In a way, I thought it would be a step in the right direction. Making progress. My sister made a date with the dress place to look at dresses, and I wasn't going to be the jerk sister who said no because I was afraid to look at myself in a dress or see what size it was. There were Kelly, my cousin Katie, and I, and at first the deal was that I would go to help pick one out, but just Katie would try them on. That way I wouldn't have to deal with the stress of it, since I haven't tried any clothes on since I gained weight. Feeling like a jerk turned into feeling left out, as Katie went in and out of the dressing room with all sorts of gowns. My huge fear was, what if I take a dress in to try on and it is too small? What if I can't zip it up? I am too fat and have to go up a size? I knew that would be the worse thing for my mentality.

After all of the dresses we looked at, it finally came down to two—one was long and green with a halter-style top, and the other was light blue, strapless and long. Either way, the colour would be burgundy, but those were the styles. Katie tried on both and Kelly said she wasn't sure. I tell her I like the green style. Finally, I found my courage and said that I would try on the green one so she could see them both.

I skulked into the dressing room, making sure the curtain was closed on each side so no one could see me. I pulled the dress on, sucking myself in the whole time, and luckily it zipped. It was actually loose in some parts, but I was angry that the waist mostly fitted. I was afraid to come out of the dressing room because I had been hoping it would be way too big, just to show that I was still thin. I knew I couldn't stay in there forever, and so I pulled back the curtain a little so Kelly could see.

"You look beautiful," Katie said. I covered myself with my arms.

"I think I like the green one, but try on the blue one too," Kelly said.

So I did, and it made me look frumpy. With hands held over my stomach, I yell out to Kelly that I had it on but didn't like it. She peeked in and agreed that the green one was the best style, and we all think it will be lovely in burgundy. I am relieved of dress duty and jump back into my real clothes. I was surprised that I tried it on and Kelly told me she was proud of me, but I was also uncomfortable. The dress was a size 12, but wedding dress sizes are different, not on a normal scale. The lady who was helping us asked Kelly about the other bridesmaids, and, referring to Katie and I, asked, "are they all as tiny as these two?" That was nice to hear at least. Katie got her measurements done for the dress, but I was definitely not ready for that. I needed to be a little more comfortable with my body first, so Kelly and I will go up another day. I told her I just wanted to lose a couple of pounds and inches.

"I don't think you need to lose any weight," she told me.

"I do. I've gained weight since I left Renfrew."

"That's good."

"No. I was maintaining at Renfrew. I don't need to gain any more."

Sometimes, I think people want me to be fat ol' Nicole again.

My car arrived from L.A. by truck. Talk about depressing. It's very sad to see it in the driveway when it should be in L.A. I am having a tough time with that. Sam put some of my clothes and bedding in the car. My things. My L.A. things are back in Connecticut. Bit by bit, my L.A. self is returning home, and I hate it. The girl who set out to be something is returning in pieces—damaged and wilted—the remnants of her dream now just a dusty car in the driveway, three coffee-stained scripts, and a girl who has been broken, stitched up, and is now falling apart at every seam.

Where did I go wrong?

Chapter 30
Post Renfrew: Month 2— April
Jump start

My car will not start. We had to jump it. It had, after all, just been sitting in a driveway for months, so it had really old fuel in it, and not a lot of it. I viewed that car like I view myself. What I had been functioning on before was not a lot. Sometimes, when I was fasting, there were probably only minuscule amounts of food that my body was trying to hang on to. If you compare your body to a car, it needs fuel to function as well, and consistently, not just once in a while. So, like my car, I had problems starting sometimes too because I was out of fuel, or had been stagnant for a while. Maybe what I need now is a jump start of sorts. Something to jolt a little bit of life back into me.

I want to help myself, but I want to help others. Perhaps by helping others, I can help myself. I pitched an article on eating disorders to a teen magazine I write for and my editor loved the idea. They are actually basing the issue around it, making the theme "personal strength." So I will tell a bit of my story, interview some teens, and then write about recovery, including the struggles and hope. Struggling is part of strength, and really where the strength comes in. When you prevail over your struggles. I may be wading in them now, but I have become a bit more optimistic.

Until I have therapy at least. That seems to bring me down. Dr. Cagore wants me to stop keeping a journal. Why would you tell a writer to stop writing?

"I think it hinders therapy," she tells me, in her over-the-top monotone voice. "You are putting everything down on the page, writing letters to yourself and then trying to analyze that. I can already tell you are a person who doesn't like to let anybody in, so it's a way of closing the world out. You are putting everything down in a journal instead of bring it up in therapy, and trying to work it out yourself."

"I like to write. Thoughts that come up, about anything. They could be totally unrelated to eating disorders. Maybe writing accomplishments, or things I want to write about. A writer should write every day, they say, no matter what it is. I don't want to stop doing that."

"You need to. Try reading or watching a movie. Give your mind a rest, because it's always going, it's always analytic. That is the anorexic mind. Writing the journal, especially chronicling everything that has happened, is obsessive compulsive and just goes to show your need to control things. Which is why you ended up with the eating disorder, and not other reckless behaviour."

I have low blood pressure, but I could feel mine rising. Her, making assumptions about who I am and what I do. She was completely off target.

I try to explain to her that I have always written in a journal and it is just a way for me to either work things out or remember things, and in general, I just like writing. It has nothing to do with avoiding therapy. I've been pretty open.

"Stick to the freelance writing, because at least that has a purpose."

So do my journals.

She went on: "That writing is controlled and will be put out into the world for others to read. And you have to do it at set times because you have a deadline."

She pisses me off because she tells me that she doesn't recommend any of her patients to keep a journal. Well, how many of them are writers? I have always been told that if you are a writer, you need to write something for yourself, otherwise you will get caught up in your work. That will bog you down and writing won't be fun any more. That did happen to me before, with the eating disorder. I don't want that to happen again. I'm not going to take her advice, so it doesn't matter, but it does anger me.

I feel as if she wants me to stay, or be, anorexic. She asked about the dress shopping and I told her how at points it was uncomfortable and she says, "There's that anorectic thinking." She said it twice actually. I thought maybe she would have been encouraging of the fact that I actually tried the dresses on, since she told me not to. She brings me down a little when she tells me those things, and that I'm not getting better, or I'm stuck in the thinking. Yes, I have negative thoughts, but I am nowhere near where I was. I feel positive, actually, until I go into her office.

That's unlike Holly, whose office I leave feeling positive, though I am anxious when I enter. It's the scales though, those damned scales. She wants me to get rid of my own so I don't weigh myself at home. I tell her that will be difficult, but I'll try at least not to weigh myself. She doesn't even want me going to the gym, because she's afraid that I'll fall back into the trap of a 4-hour routine. We talked weights, and while she wants me to be at 140, I said 125, but I could do 128. Then I said, "Okay, 130." She still cringed. She wants me to be at an okay weight, where if I get sick or something and lose weight, I won't be at risk. She also thinks if I am at 128, then that 125 will look seductive, and then I'll want to go lower and lower, and she is probably right. I guess somewhere between 130-140, though I told her that the 140's scare me.

"I can definitely hear both voices in you," she says. "The rational voice and the eating disorder voice. That's better than just hearing the eating disorder voice, because six months ago, that was probably all I would have heard, and you probably didn't realize it."

She tells me that I am still stuck in the eating disorder and she's worried about me. "I don't want you to end up in the hospital again. With the pills you were taking and the exercise, you could have a heart attack, and you were pretty close to it before."

I tell her I stopped taking the pills and will be conscious of my workouts.

"You've been in this eating disorder for over a year and it's not going to be a month or two and you're fixed. It is going to take time for recovery, but it's possible."

She wants me to keep a food log and try a "risk" food this week—something that maybe I used to eat or like that I'm afraid to try again, but would enjoy. Not to think about the calories or fat in it. It will be a good step in recovery. She is also glad that I have my periods back; otherwise she would push me to gain more weight or eat more fat. Phew! I guess getting it back was lucky for that reason. She knows my fears though, and tells me that she will not let me get fat.

"I already feel fat though," I tell her.

"You're not."

"I am. I have fat on me, and it's enough."

"You need fat on you, everyone does. It's protects your organs, it helps your body function. And besides, you can't feel fat. Fat is not a feeling. So you can't say that any more."

I still feel fat.

I make the trek across the state to see Dr. Ligorski, my psychiatrist, who is pretty cool and good to talk to. First he wants to know how things are going. I tell him how I'm struggling with the extra weight.

"It's probably where your body needs to be. Can you accept that?"

"I don't know. I was maintaining at Renfrew, then I came back and it changed."

"Your metabolism was increased because there was so much food and fuel going into you and your body was changing."

"I've gained five pounds though, and I've been eating less and working out."

"Have you been eating enough?"

"Probably not."

As a reminder, he went back to my lowest weight and looked at what I should weigh, compared to my height. He did the calculations and at that time, I was 85% of my ideal body weight. That was "critical", and is when health problems start coming up, like heart problems. That's when they look at hospitalization. It was a good reminder and scary to hear that I was once "critical," even though I knew it. But 85% sounded okay. Did I want to be 100%? Not really. I can't imagine what percent I was when I was overweight.

I tell him I'm not happy with where I'm at.

"You don't notice the good things. If someone paid you a compliment, you wouldn't see it. If guys were falling in love with you all over the place, you wouldn't know it."

"It's because they're not."

"You don't know that."

"Yes I do. I've been alone and lonely long enough to know that."

He switches gears. "How is your mood?"

"There's been a lot of crying at night. Sometimes I'll just stand in the kitchen and cry. I feel stuck, being home from L.A., but really, I'm afraid I'm always going to be like this."

"No, you won't. It will get better. Trust me. It will get better."

For some weird reason, I did trust him. I don't know why, but I feel like he knows what he's talking about.

Dr. Cagore, on the other hand, I'm not so sure about. She tells me today that I will never be in a relationship until I have a better body image. Well, I never had one. I guess I am doomed in that area.

The results of my bone scan are in, and despite the fact that I was just measured at a little over 5'8, and had always been 5'9, my results were…normal! My doctor was surprised too. I guess –2.25 is osteoporosis and –1.35 is osteopenia. I was .3, which is down there, but still considered normal. A healthy 30-year-old woman should be .10. Something to strive for, I guess.

I am sure that all that yogurt, milk, cottage cheese and calcium pills at the "'Frew" helped. He told me he'd like me to gain more and I said, "no."

"Well," he asked, "what weight would you like to be?"

"I'd be okay with 135," I told him. "But 130 would be good. I'd really like to be 125."

He scrunched his face.

"Okay. 130."

"I don't approve of that either," he says. "You're at a good weight now."

"But I'm not comfortable."

He pulls out my file and looks at my past weights. I explain that I don't want to get back to that point and once I start to gain, how do I know when it will stop?

"It will," he tells me. "You have to trust your body. The important thing is getting your life back. Your recovery could take a year or so, but you are a smart girl. It's hard to focus on your writing when you're focused on food, so hopefully we can stay on top of this and get rid of it."

Can you get "rid" of an eating disorder, I wonder?

Through the depths of it all, I had been told that an eating disorder is static in my head. At first, it consumes my head—it is all I can think of. As I begin recovery, the noise of the eating disorder diminishes, and quiets, and I begin to hear other things, noises of life, that I hadn't heard before. Eventually, it is merely static in the back of my head. Yes, static. Little blips that come up now and then that I have to remember are just merely that—static. I don't want them to become more than that. I remember how painful it was to have them explode, and I want them to remain quiet.

Hang In There… Wherever "There" Is

Some people say an eating disorder never goes away, and that is why they remain static in the back of your head. You either control them there, or, they can burst out at any moment.

My friend Charlotte says something different. In her 30's now, she tells me she is fully recovered and does not believe in the notion that those who have had an eating disorder cannot fully recover. She says that if she were not a singer, she would be a chef, and I believe her. She tells me she is a complete foodie. I know how she struggled, and now, what she has accomplished. She is an amazing singer-songwriter, and knowing the depths of eating disorders, I know she would never be able to do that with one. To me, she is an inspiration. And, she loves food! She is healthy, and knows her body well. She is everything I want to be one day. She has taught me so much, without realizing it. She suffered severely from an eating disorder, and helped me so much with mine. Now, recovered, she truly believes that recovery is possible, and she is a glowing example of this. She has inspired me in more ways than one. She has faith in those who have been hurt and suffering and believes there is a better life for those out there. She has given me hope and faith, which has not only given me hope in my recovery, but also prompted me to help those in return.

I had to have blood work done and on my way out, Dad called.
"Have you been eating your three meals a day?" he asks.
"No."
"I didn't think so. I don't want to do this on the phone, but you need to stay on that. Instead of meeting me at the baseball game, I'd rather you go home and get dinner."
"Okay, I will."
I would. I guess he noticed, or rather, cared.

135 lbs. I was trying to be good. My comfort level was coming back. Holly told me she was worried about me all weekend, but I told her I'm okay. I went out to dinner with Dad and had a grilled chicken salad. I almost ate the whole thing. I felt so gross.

Holly asked me about my bone scan and how I felt that it was normal. I tell her it's good, but maybe part of me still wants to be sick. She understood, and said she hears that a lot.

It is a weird feeling, I guess, wanting to be sick. I don't know if it's for the attention, or because I'm sick. I don't have anything to do with my life—even though I want to do things with my life. Or just as if I'm sick, it's that sort of pathetic nature, it's always…oh, I'm sick. I can get away with it. I truly don't know.

I was always the together one, everything was always expected of me—I'd always volunteer to do things, whether it was just drive Dan to practice or lead the March of Dimes. It got to be exhausting. Now I can just be sick and everyone can leave me alone—no more expectations.

I could tell these things to her completely because she listened and understood more than my psychologist. Then again, she was a nutritionist and we had to talk about food. She took a look at my food journal.

She loved how I wrote down the emotions I felt as I was eating. She even laughed at some, and so did I. She tells me she could tell I was a writer. Also, it gives her a better idea of not just the foods I ate, but how I felt when I ate them. That's a big part of this.

She saw a trend in the lack of lunches and the end result was…restricting. I tell her most of that is because I have so many appointments—her, my psychologist, psychiatrist, doctor and support group. It is like my life is one big treatment team. It's exhausting.

We talk about the guilt I have when I eat certain thing like candy and ice cream at night because I feel like I am binging. She tells me that maybe I had more than one serving but it was certainly not binging. I tell her I don't know when to stop. It's feast or famine. I was so used to overeating when I was overweight that I'm afraid to eat certain things now because I'll jump back into that trend and I don't want to be that heavy again. So I stick to foods with nutritional value. She tells me that's okay for now, but she'd like to see me open up to other foods and have them in moderation.

I had been told before that recovering from anorexia is much more difficult if you had been overweight before. Essentially, you have to start eating more, and that can be scary, when most of your life had been consumed by eating. So yes, I am scared. But also, if that's what it takes, I will do it. I need to get out of this disease.

The big issue was the fry situation. I went out to dinner with my Dad and he got a burger and fries, and I got a salad, though I would rather have had his meal. Those fries teased me. I wanted them so badly and he had offered some to me. I took one. I couldn't tell if it tasted good because it was forbidden, or if I truly liked it.

"Help yourself," he said.

I think he was glad to see me eating them. I tried another and then became terrified.

"No more," I said.

I knew then that I'd want the whole thing if I kept going.

"I ate too many. I shouldn't have had one," I told him.

I think he was upset. Not mad, but I think at first he was happy I tried them, but my being scared of them scared him.

If I started eating them I would want them all the time. I can't.

Holly explained to me that they are a social food and two fries are not binging. She knows this is hard and that I am struggling.

I don't want to hurt my Dad. But damn it! I want to eat fries too! There are so many things I want to eat. I am scared of what they will do to me. I feel now, more than ever, that this is going to be a long process.

Hang In There... Wherever "There" Is

I then went to see Dr. Cagore. We spoke a lot about my past and what I was doing now. I tell her how fatigued and exhausted I have been, and she tells me that I'm in recovery. I should be getting rest. My body needs to catch up with me. I have no focus or energy and always fear that I might fall back into the traps of anorexia.

"It's easy," she tells me. "You get back into the gym, then have your four baby carrots, then do that forty times, and there's your pattern and you can't get out of it."

I already know I'm eating the same foods, but she is right. You do one little thing. Then you do it again. You think it works so you continue—and pretty soon it's a pattern, and that pattern is called "anorexia."

I tell her how that had happened to me—just little things I had done—and I never thought I would be sitting in her office at this moment. Ever. Amazing how things work out.

It is clear that she spoke with Holly, as she brings up my minimal eating and my depression. I do want to talk about what I can do to look toward a more hopeful future. She is still hooked on the idea of my screen-writing, which is what I see as a definite failure, but she dwells on it, which makes me feel worse.

The good Doc also expresses her concern with my working out and not eating enough, but I think that there is no point in eating more if I am trying to lose weight. Of course, she doesn't know that I'm trying to lose weight. Oh, will this madness never end? If I stop working out, I would gain a ton of weight, or I couldn't eat, and so the eating disorder continues. I cannot lead a normal life and probably won't ever be able to.

When I come home at night, I go to make dinner and find that I am frozen. My plan was to make my regular salad, but then I see a piece of bread and think, maybe I would like a sandwich. I stare at my empty salad bowl for a minute and Dad comes in the kitchen, and just sighs. I decide to make the salad and grab some vegetables while Dad talks to me and again, I am stuck, just staring into the refrigerator. Then come the tears.

"What's the matter?"

"I had planned on having a salad, but then I thought I'd try a sandwich, but the bread scares me, even though I think it would taste good. I hate this. I wish it weren't so hard. Eating should not be this hard."

He gives me a hug. "I know. I saw you standing there. I hate to see you cry like this. I know it's hard, but either one is a good choice. What if you did half a sandwich and a salad?"

I nod, wiping tears and snot from my face. That voice of reason helped more than any therapist had. That meal is what I make and I felt okay with it. I hate putting so much thought into meals.

We talk after dinner and I tell him about my fears that I will start to overindulge again.

"You don't want to end up where you just were either."

"I know. I don't. Recovery is such a long process. It was hard living with the eating disorder and it's hard living like this. I still have food on my mind all the time, and deciding what to eat becomes such a project."

"I can't imagine how tough it is, but I still worry. I can already see you falling back into old patterns, eating-wise."

"I'm not comfortable with my weight though."

"You still need to gain 20 pounds."

"What? You're crazy. No, I don't. Then I'd be overweight. They are going to keep me in this weight range, but don't want me to go too far over because that would trigger the eating disorder."

"Well, you can't tell me you weighed what you did when you were at Renfrew."

"No. I lost weight, but not a lot. I'm close to the weight I maintained there. I had gained about 7 lbs. when I got home and was at day treatment. But my treatment team is keeping track."

"I just worry."

"Me too."

I was looking a little anorexic today. Part of me liked it, part of me was scared. I can fit back into my 00's, but they are tight and my flab hangs out. My face looks gaunt, but I am also very tired. So tired. I just ate a little frozen yogurt though. Fat.

People seek me out to know the amount of calories in things. It's brutal, but they do it. "How many calories in this coffee drink?" Do they think they can ask me because I know, which I do? I don't tell them, because a) it would get me focusing on the calories, and b) I tell them they shouldn't worry about the calories, which is true. Easier said than done, I suppose. I think people sometimes forget I'm in recovery, or even had an eating disorder. One of the worst things to do to someone recovering from an eating disorder, someone who used to count calories endlessly, who read calorie websites for a hobby, is to ask them about calories. I used to sit there at my computer and spend hours just going through a website reading the amount of calories in things—in general food, in packaged foods, in fast food—and think, "well that's okay, maybe I can allow myself to eat that item this week." I would think about it and know that it wasn't a great amount of calories, and then completely focus on getting that item. One diet cookie would have been too many calories for me, never mind a cracker. I'd never allow myself to actually get it and eat it. No way. Too many calories. I was afraid of an item with thirty calories at the time. My dreams of frozen yogurt would have to hold off.

Now I notice how often people say, "I'm starving," just when they want lunch, but they really have no idea. It's not that I ever felt "starving." I never felt that hungry. I certainly wanted certain foods, but would refrain. But I never felt starving, even though I truly was. I was literally starving. Strange to think of it that way. My body was starving. My mind was starving. I was starving, and I didn't even know it. It had become a lifestyle for me. Now I know if my stomach grumbles, it means I need food. Nourishment. It doesn't mean that I'm starving, because I've been there, and I know that's not the right way to live. It's not living.

I think back to the pro-eating disorder sites I used to go on, which I still visit occasionally, because there is one area for recovery. I know how visiting those sites spurred the disease, but I know how they were comforting at times too. From encouraging me with weight loss then, they are now helping with recovery. My eyes are more open now to the reality of these websites. I see what they, young girls and boys, are saying, and I ache for them. I want to tell them no, to stop, and I wonder if anyone is looking out for them. I read how they have to strategically plan out their eating, or non-eating, in front of their family and friends, and how they can secretly burn more calories. What foods, they ask others, are easier to purge than others? They say what health problems they are having and ask if they are "normal" or not because of what they are doing to their body, and others will reassure them that yes, they went through that also, and it is all part of this "thing." This "thing" they do. It is very hard for them to admit they have eating disorders. It was hard for me too. They wish each other luck with their goal weights, and provide pictures of thin women as "thinspiration," as well as inspirational quotes. They post their weights and progress, and when they "slip up." They talk about how they fear the restricting, the purging, the exercise, will control them forever. And I worry the same for them. I worry the same for myself.

These girls are in pain. This is where they go to seek solace. The disease, which started as a diet, is now torturing them, and they don't know where else to turn. They can't tell anyone, because that means they would have to stop. But they can't stop. They haven't reached their goal weight yet. And that was how I felt. There were times when I wanted to tell my doctor, and I thought he knew, but I wasn't ready. Just five more pounds, I thought. So instead of turning to him, I turned to my friends online, and they congratulated me, and some even asked for advice on weight loss when I hit my goal weight. But that wasn't good enough, of course, so I set it lower. It is sick. I was shocked when someone asked me for advice, and I could not tell her to do what I did, so I told her to just eat healthily and exercise, and never take it to an extreme, because it's a horrible way to live. And I knew that for a fact, because I was living it. But somewhere out there right now, is another girl claiming her weight loss victory, and a perhaps younger, more influential girl, asking her advice, and this time, she might get it. And so the vicious cycle continues. In a disease where there is an isolation too hard to bear alone, there is a community where secrets of sickness bring solace, and pain is shared and triumphs of the illness are glorified. So you're not just losing alone, the group is losing together, and friends are made in the depths of disease.

I talk to a girl from Renfrew and tell her I've been struggling. She tells me, "You can do this Nicole. I've seen you kick ass before." It's encouraging and mind-boggling how other people can see it in me. Why can't I?

All these girls thought that I was so confident, the epitome of recovery. I am so weak. I'm sliding like crazy. Or rather, it's slippery. I want to be thin still. I want to be tiny. I don't want to be "ideal" or "average." I want to be little. Yet, I want to be healthy and "normal" again, rid of all the demons. I'm on a roller coaster that won't let me off.

As I think of Renfrew, I realize that there are nights after dinner when I could use an MST—Meal Support Therapy, but I guess this isn't Renfrew any more. I have so much post-meal anxiety. Usually, everyone clears the table, like normal folks, and I am left alone. I guess I need to "sit with it," like they said at the "'Frew."

I know that it's just food to them and most people and I wish it were to me, but it's not. It's like poison. I don't think they realize how difficult each bite is for me. They think, "Oh, she's eating. Good." They don't know what's going on in my head with each forkful, and that's the hell of it.

I wonder what food will be like again when it is just food, if I ever get to that point. I can't imagine ever taking a bite and not worrying about it. Or not having to go to the gym to burn off, say, 1000 calories. I feel as if my life will always be consumed by some hellish focus on food and weight and I will never be content with it, so I will never be comfortable with myself. And if I'm not content with myself, surely I cannot present myself in a positive way to others. Who would want to be around me anyway? I can't stand to be around myself. This has got to get better.

I was finally brave enough to try on clothes, shorts and pants—the most dreaded because they tell the truth. I fit into a size 0. I guess I have lost a little weight. Dr. Cagore tells me that now that my weight is at the lower end where there is really no margin of error. It makes them nervous, but me happy. It makes me feel comfortable with myself again, with my weight and how I look. My hips are okay but my stomach still looks bloated. I am working out and yes, eat the minimal amount, but I do have ice cream every night. I wonder if this will be a continual pattern again. If I keep this up, will I keep losing weight? If I stop, will I gain? I don't know how to maintain, which would be the best for me. Even though Holly tells me the meal plan will help me maintain, I can't trust it. I can't trust anything. I don't see it working. Since I've been restricting, my metabolism is probably off again. It seems like I've screwed myself up so much, I won't ever be able to eat normally. I'll always need to workout at the gym to justify eating. I hate that. I hate that I have to think so much about food and eating and weight and my body. I wish I could be happy and that myself and someone else could appreciate my body. No judgements.

Dr. Cagore makes a strange admission, which I already knew, that I know more about foods and nutritional vales than most people. It's true. I am quite an expert. After months of obsessing about calories online, I know the contents of every food—calories, carbohydrates, fats…it's draining.

She goes on again about how she thinks they let me out of the inpatient and day program too early, and while I was very pro-active at Renfrew and came across as a very together person, it is inside where people don't realize I have a really hard time. Like making a decision between a sandwich or salad, and I don't always let that show. She says I am a very together person, so once we've got this food thing out of the way, I'll be able to go very far. Nice to hear that she notices a bit of my attitude and potential.

She is concerned about me following my meal plan and wants to talk to Holly about setting up a solid one for me to follow through with, so that I won't have to think about the food so much and can get all my nutrients. It's not to make me gain weight, but to teach me I can eat different things and maintain weight. She tells me that the bloating and oedema has settled so my weight really needs to be watched.

I go to see Holly and she asks me what foods I like.

"None."

"What are your trigger foods?"

"Everything."

I'm a mess.

"Do you hear yourself?" she asks. "I'm afraid you aren't going to want to eat anything any more."

Truth is, I don't. It's such a chore. Why do we always have to be putting food in our mouths? I still think it would be easier if there were a little pill we could take that would give us all the nutrients we needed. But that's why I'm here, because I tried to fit my life into a pill.

Dr. Cagore is pissing me off. So much so that when I came home after our appointment, I was crying and couldn't eat dinner. Dad tells me to switch therapists.

I go to see her and she asks all robotically, "How are you?"

I ask if she talked to Holly about the meal plan and the exchange system, like Renfrew had, and how it bothers me.

She asks me to tell her why.

"I don't like the exchanges because I'm always worried if I got my starches or proteins in."

"I'm not familiar with exchanges. It's more a list of foods for you to eat because right now, you're not doing it on your own. We need to take control away from you, Nicole. It's hard because you like being in control—like all anorexics."

Anger. "Like all anorexics?" Is that all she sees when she looks at me? I am a person, you know? There is so much more to me than an eating disorder.

"I know what I need to eat, and I was eating that before, so it's just a matter of doing it."

She shakes her head obnoxiously. "But you're not."

I haven't been eating as I should, but I am eating. I hate how she keeps calling me anorexic and talks down to me like she knows me so well. She's the model of therapists I hate.

I tell her how I'm afraid I'll be eating the same five things forever. She says it won't be that way. It's the disease, and in time what I like will expand.

I have to fight it. How much I fight will show how much I want to recover. She tells me to give up control and trust them. I have worked hard to get where I am, which isn't even the greatest place.

The thing about our sessions is it's usually her talking at me. No conversation. I sit there, listen, and become more depressed. She makes me feel worse about myself. Also, she always wants to talk about eating. Yes, eating disorders revolve around eating, but are so much deeper than that. I have Holly for the nutritional aspect. We haven't talked about any of the aspects that drive the eating disorder, so I suffer in silence. I feel as if I am regressing.

I tell her this, and we open up to it.

We talk about my days and what I do, that it's mostly writing. She tells me I don't have a real structured job and should get one.

She asks about my (non-existent) social life. That emptiness does give me time to think about food and the eating disorder. I tell her about my friends, Erin and Danielle in Boston and how I am reopening the lines of communication with them. She had never even known the story about them, so I tell her. She thinks it's good to talk to them, but then criticizes my choice of friends.

I tell her how I long for a good friendship.

"Your choose self-absorbed friends, that way, you don't have to open up."

Hmm…maybe it's worked out that way, but I don't believe I have "chosen" it. I make friends with certain people I meet, it just happens. I don't go around saying, "Hey, are you self-absorbed? Let's be buddies!" She is totally the kind of therapist I've always made fun of. At least when I go to the support group, I have more energy, can chat, and the therapist tells us, "It's okay to feel what you feel." Dr. Cagore makes me feel guilty about everything and I sit there awkwardly the whole time, afraid to have a personality, probably because she has the personality of battery acid.

I shouldn't be crying when I come home from her appointments, as Dad tells me. I come home and don't even want to eat. I have some cereal, apple sauce and water melon, then go downstairs and cry. Dad hugs me and tells me if she's making me feel worse, then maybe it's time to find someone new. I tell him how I'm aware I still have issues with food, but that's all she wants to cover, and eating disorders aren't about the food really, there are so many other issues and we aren't covering any of them. She treats me like a kid and talks down to me. We haven't worked through any issues, and she thinks I was let out of treatment too soon.

Dad says, "First of all, that day treatment wasn't helping at all. Second, if she's not helping you, maybe it's time to look somewhere else. There's no need to come home crying and feeling worse afterwards."

"I know, I didn't even want to eat. How is that therapeutic?"

I decide to see how it goes on Monday, and if it still doesn't seem right, then I am going to find someone else. Therapy is supposed to help, not hurt. I have hurt too much. I don't need this.

Dad got pizza for dinner. I made a salad and he asks me if I want to try some pizza. Me? Pizza? I make excuses at first. You know, I don't know if I like that kind, too much sauce, bread, but finally, he convinced me. I do think he is really worried about my eating. I ask him if I could cut a piece in half or something. They were small to begin with.

"Go ahead. I'm all set."

So I cut off a piece and eat it. It was okay. Nothing spectacular. I couldn't get into it. At the top was a lot of crust. I just didn't dig it. He asks how I like it and I say, "a little too much bread for me, but okay."

Later, I thank him for getting me to try it, and he said there was more in there if I want some later or tomorrow. I tell him I'm not so sure. It was a start. It's hard because I don't enjoy the things I used to like. I am so thankful for my Dad, for his encouragement and motivation in my recovery. I so need it. He is great.

Easter. It was good. Dan came home. But there is something planned. A cake. A belated birthday cake. An ice cream bunny-shaped cake. After we had dinner, no one had dessert. They knew I got the cake and it was special to me. It is April and my birthday was in November. It was kind of a big deal to finally have my birthday cake. I felt settled enough with myself to have cake. I wanted my family to be there for that. So we all had the cake. It was good and not so scary. We were all glad, and it is progress.

Later, they ask about Dr. Cagore and if I will stay with her. They tell me I owe her nothing and I need to do what is best for me and my recovery. They suggest I see her and see how the next session goes, and if she is still negative to tell her she is not helping my treatment and I'd rather see someone else. Sounds good, and it's nice to have their support. I hope I am brave enough.

Dr. Cagore's session.

"Do you want to be the better anorexic?"

Oh, here it goes.

We were talking about how I still pick up on other people's eating issues.

"No," I tell her. "It just bothers me when I am doing my best and I see people restrict."

"So it's a competition for you?"

"No, not at all."

"You're jealous they are eating less?"

"No, it's just difficult to see. I want to be eating."

Then it was a staring contest—neither one of us had something to say. Quite productive.

"Oh, and by the way, don't get those magazines at the grocery store checkout line because they always have stories of anorexia in them."

"Okay." I've lived it, seen it in others, I could handle a story. I guess she doesn't want it to trigger me.

She tells me why it's slippery and I eat like a dieter. Hey, I'm eating more than I was. She was mad because I had a sandwich with no mayo. She told me that was dieting. I can't win.

"If someone saw you," she says, "they'd wonder why you eat like you do. They don't know your history. You're like one of those people who say they can eat anything and not gain weight."

I disagree. I tell her about the weight I gained during day treatment. She says I was on a lot of calories, but it still wasn't as much as Renfrew.

She makes my point—I can't eat anything I want. I have to be careful.

She says it is fear from when I was overweight, which is true. That's why I feel so compelled to watch my weight now. This "normal eating" thing will never be part of my life, and what I am doing now is still not a fun way to live.

I try to tell Dr. Cagore how bad my depression has been—the crying episodes—and she seems stunned.

"Why didn't you tell me about this?"

"I did. I told you I was having a tough time being back from LA and feeling stuck and there are times when I endlessly cry at night."

"Nope, you just talked about it casually. There's a big difference between breakthrough crying and uncontrollable crying where you can't stop. I wish you had told me earlier."

"I did."

"Well, you like to control people and people relinquish control to you."

Anger rising.

"I don't agree. These feelings have been around for a long time and quite notable. The hysterical crying may be more recent."

"Maybe your medication will help and we can forge on from there."

Instead of almost scolding me, she should have been there for me to see how I was. I tell her I had addressed these feelings, but she doesn't always want to go into details with them or goes off onto other things.

I think I upset her.

"You can always interrupt me and tell me that's not what you meant."

"I feel sometimes you talk and I just sit here."

"That's because you're not contributing. You're not open."

Okay. I'm pissed off. I'm done.

"You never asked about my past, and when I bring it up, you seem surprised."

"You need to learn to be comfortable with yourself, so you can open up to another person."

Well, maybe, but not her. It was time to break up.

"I don't think this is working out," I tell her.

"Hmm...why not?"

"It's been three months and I don't think a lot of progress has been made."

"That's because you don't put a lot into it. It may take you years to open up."

I don't have years, lady.

"It has been a long time since someone has wanted to leave," she tells me, which surprises me, "but it happens. You need to do what is best for you and your recovery. It's very mature and responsible of you to come in and say it to me. Some people just never show up again."

She went on to describe her way of therapy, but I knew I was done. Released. Free at last!

***

Holly had a voicemail from Dr. Cagore saying we were no longer working together so not to provide any information to her, as that would not be ethical. She also says, "Nicole is not as fragile as people think. There's a real strength to her."

I guess those are good parting words.

Holly said she knows a wonderful therapist she works with who she thinks would get along great with me. HOPE!

I write to Jason, tell him about the therapist disaster, being afraid to take the initiative to get better, some bad things I have done, and thank him for recommending a show on addictions and how it helped. Always inspirational, he writes, "Get better! Eat. Don't be stubborn. You are going to do permanent damage to your body. You have a long life ahead of you and you are way too young to deal with chronic health conditions. It's not about being told what to do, it's about people caring for your well being."

I think he should be my therapist.

I talk to Melissa from Renfrew. She is having a tough time and is back to binging and purging. She says it just feels "normal" for her. I tell her I can relate, since I have restricted a bit and am working out and have been taking diuretics.

"Does anyone know?" she asks.

"My parents know I don't eat a lot and I work out. They're concerned. My therapists still calls me anorexic."

"My Mom doesn't know, and she's gone all week."

We have a long conversation about how tough it is and she doesn't think she'll fall back into it. I tell her I knew before I went into Renfrew that when I got out I'd want to lose the weight. It's hard and a struggle, but I tell her that I know what a fighter she is and that life will be so much better without the eating disorder. I am worried about her being alone this week, but she said she's going to try and keep herself on track. I send her a card for motivation and to let her know that I'm here for her. That we were admitted to Renfrew together and will work towards recovery together. She said she's relapsing and I say, "No, it's just a lapse." That can be turned around.

I have been crying every day on the way home from the gym. I keep thinking of LA—flashbacks, memories, even random things like being on the beach or going to the Farmer's Market. Just thinking about how much I miss it, and then how much harder it will be when I go back to get my stuff.

I also still think about Renfrew and how surreal it seems that I was actually there. I think back to the first weekend where I was crying on the phone to Mom and Dad about the huge meals (which I still don't think I could eat now), about being on locked bathroom because of the shared suite, and about 5:30 weights and vitals. Seven weeks of treatment and look where I am. Still a nightmare.

I know it's a lot of work and a long road of recovery, but still, I am here. I'm amazed at how much a "normal" thing, eating, can ruin your life.

Ding dong…wedding dresses.

My time to be fitted. Ugh.

They took my measurements. 35 ½ for hips. Recently they were 34 ¼. At my lowest they were 32. So shameful.

The sample dress is a 12. She put me down to an 8, then a 6. These are not normal sizes, but particular wedding dress sizes. I snuck a look at the other bridesmaid sizes, and I have the smallest waist. How obsessed is that? I hope I can stay this size, or lose a little. Which means, really, beating myself up with workouts, restricting, all that crap. Hello, anorexia!

Hang In There… Wherever "There" Is

I have been trying to work harder though. After all, I, like others, am amazed that I am alive. Thinking back to all of the things that I did to myself, how I was living, actually "living," while doing those awful things, is beyond me. The body is resilient, I know, but I have to thank mine for putting up with the things that I have done to it. I know now that you have to love and respect your body, and truly take care of it. Perhaps I am stronger because I survived it, or tried to, or at least struggled through the worst of it—the deep well of anorexia, and now, trying to find hope through recovery. I am still struggling with the realization that it happened, or is happening, and that I can actually pull through all of this. I can and I will.

I realize if not now, for myself, then maybe I can help others. I know the struggle and pain that comes with eating disorders, and no one should have to go through this. If I can be an advocate for others, then perhaps in a way I will be helping myself. After a little research, I found that the Eating Disorder Coalition in Washington, D.C. was holding an Eating Disorder Lobby Day to fight for equal rights for those with mental illnesses, and presenting a new bill for eating disorder health equality. There was no hesitation. I register and am soon on a train to D.C.

Chapter 31
Post Renfrew: 3 Months—May
Lobby Day

Holly was glad I was going but nervous about the food situation—to eat or not to eat, it was up to me. I knew it would be easy to completely slide off track, but I had to think of where I was going and what my mission was, and I had to make an effort. Besides, if I go to an Eating Disorder Lobby Day and don't eat or use my symptoms, I'd be going against all we were fighting for and then would be a prime example of a victim. But I'm not, I'm a survivor.

First day in D.C. I got to my hotel, settled in, and then made my up to the capital for training. I was early, and not hungry, but I knew what was right. I stopped in a café and got a sandwich, though if anyone saw me, they'd wonder what the hell I was doing by pulling off pieces of bread. Baby steps. I had a yogurt too.

I head over to the meeting and meet the Executive Director of the Eating Disorder Coalition and then I take my seat, happy with my decision to attend. Next to me is a young guy, college-aged, and it's nice to see guys there. Of course, not nice in the way that they are suffering, but nice that they are showing up to break the stigma that eating disorders just affects young females. I suppose, in a way, I am doing that too.

We receive all the information on what lobbying is and that we will be meeting with staff and presenting two bills—the Mental Healthy Parity Bill and the FREED ACT, which is the Federal Response to Eliminating Eating Disorders. By presenting these bills, we will incorporate our own stories. They tell us to be powerful, yet remind us that we only have a few minutes. I am the only one from Connecticut, so I am paired with a few women from Ohio, who are so nice—two sisters and one girl, who is the daughter of one of them.

One woman, Andrea, is now 50 and had anorexia when she was 12, got down to 62 pounds and almost died. Her sister, Leslie, after being so affected by it with her sister, never wanted to go through something like that again, but then her daughter became anorexic. They almost went broke paying for treatment because their insurance wouldn't cover it. For Andrea, she wants to send the message that recovery is possible if you receive the right care. In the '70's, insurance was different and she got treatment, but now, she suffers great health effects. Twice a year, she has to have her oesophagus expanded due to other issues she had with bulimia.

I tell them about my eating disorder and experiences in the ER and they can't believe it. They think I have a powerful message about the medical field and health professionals needing to be educated. I agree, and it gives me even more courage and the desire to advocate for those in need. No one should be treated like that—whether you have an eating disorder, headache or a broken arm. If this were a physical illness and I had been in the hospital with a broken leg, they'd put a cast on it. This is a mental illness and you can't put a cast on it. Just because others can't see it, doesn't mean that I'm not hurting. Doctors are trained to take care of the ill, no matter what that illness is. Why didn't they take care of me?

After all this eating disorder talk, the Ohio gals ask if I want to go out for frozen yogurt and then tell me they will give me a ride back to the hotel, which is sweet. We go to Georgetown and they say it is the best frozen yogurt place ever. I was scared at first but I did it. Fat free peppermint frozen yogurt, and damn, it was good. We sit outside and talk about serious things and joke around. It was nice to have cliqued with a group because I was a little worried. I was nervous about eating with them, but they were so kind and knew that I was early on in my recovery.

Andrea says to me, "You are very brave for coming down here alone, especially so early on in your recovery." I was surprised. I didn't think I was brave, rather, just passionate about this cause. Apparently, I am the "youngest" recovery-wise. A lot of people here have been in recovery for 7 or more years. However, there is one lady who is so in the grips of anorexia, it's sad. She says that she's been to treatments and nothing has worked, she just feels as if she has gone backwards, but she hopes she can help reach younger people by sharing her experiences. Now that, in my eyes, is true bravery.

There is another couple I met earlier who had a daughter that suffered with anorexia and bulimia for years. They never thought it was that serious, until she died this past November. It was so sad to hear them talk about it. They are here for her and to bring awareness and help others.

It is so amazing to hear the stories in the room and people calling themselves "survivors." I hadn't truly considered myself one yet, but amongst these "friends," I do. I am a little nervous about the talking at lobby day, but I know it's a good thing and it will be a good experience. If I don't talk, who will?

The day exhausts me, just the walking alone, but it is all worth it. Our group talks and figures my platform will be proper medical care. We all present the bills, then each tell a bit of our own stories. I surprise myself by talking so much, and the staff were so attentive. They feel bad that I went through so much and had bad experiences with the medical field. They too tell me I am very brave to be there so soon after being an inpatient and in the midst of recovery.

I couldn't believe that I was so comfortable talking about this subject when there was a point that I was afraid of it. I really wanted to get the message out there—that people are dying and with proper medical care, they can be saved. I was lucky, but not everyone is. I really hope that we made an impact. It was a good experience and I am glad that I came out to speak. I know that I am still suffering but I think that my experiences can awaken other people to the dangers of eating disorders.

I talk to Dad later and he tells me, "I wish you didn't have to go through what you did, but it's good that you're tied to a cause to support and can really make a difference." I hope so.

D.C. was so liberating and gave me this purpose, and now I am back to a "normal," or sub-normal life. It's given me a drive to continue with advocacy work. I also feel like I am making more progress. It's been a year since I purged—now there's an accomplishment. I tell Holly that, and then mention my depression and she tells me it's a good thing. If I think back, the last time I was having these crying fits and felt this depressed was when I wasting away in LA. I was unsure of what to do with my writing, I was homesick, with no friends, and so I turned to the eating disorder. It made me numb. Numb to depression.

Now that the eating disorder is slipping away and I feel emotions again, these feelings that I didn't want to feel—of uncertainty, loneliness— are creeping back, hence the depression. Now I have to face it. I cannot turn to the eating disorder. I am able to face what is bothering me, figure it out and overcome it. That is the way to move on with my life. Not hiding behind the gym and food, but finding what I fear and conquering it. It's not going to be easy, but everything I've been going through has been pretty damn hard, so how is this different? Oh, it's for the better.

Chapter 32
Post Renfrew—4 Months
Summer of Recovery

I had an article published in the Hartford Courant on Eating Disorders. This advocacy thing has brought me to a whole new level. Not only do I want to help others, but also I feel stronger myself. Others deserve better treatment. I want to treat myself better. I guess I "outed" myself by writing this, but I don't care. I am not ashamed of my eating disorder. Yes, it was devastating because it was difficult, but whatever stigma people have about it, I'm not a part of that. I suffered, survived and am ready to overcome.

The biggest challenge ahead of me right now is returning to Los Angeles. I have to go back to Sam's to get my stuff. I am going for nine days to pack up and ship out my things and hopefully do some of the stuff that I neglected to do while I had my eating disorder—like go to Zuma Beach more or see some of the sights. Even all that touristy crap that annoyed me so much.

I have so much anxiety and am very nervous. I wake up at night thinking about what exit to take off the freeway. I think about the last time I was there and how sick I was. Hard to believe it was about seven months ago. I imagine myself walking to the gym or to the bank just to burn some extra calories, even when I felt so sick and weak. I can see myself sitting on my bed, making the call to my parents that I had been in the hospital yet again and I knew why I had been sick—because I had an eating disorder, anorexia, and I hated it. All I wanted to do was lose some weight, I told them, as tears ran down my face, but then I couldn't stop.

This is why I'm nervous to go back. I am not quite sure what to expect. I don't know what emotions will come flooding back to me. It will be hard to be back, I am sure, because I will in the same place and it will feel like the same time and emotions, even though I have changed so much and can recognize the things I did then as harmful. I am wondering about Sam, and if she will be looking over my shoulder food-wise, or the questions she will ask about therapy. I'm worried about what I will eat and how I will "perform" in front of her. Also, I can't go to the gym—what if I gain weight? This shouldn't be so damn hard. It shouldn't be this worrisome.

My big fear is that as I see all these happy people strolling through LA, I will be reminded of why I went there, what I went to do, and how I failed. How I spent valuable time and energy on an eating disorder instead. If I had still been there, pursing my goals, and healthy with no eating disorder—where would I be? Well, probably fat, alone and depressed. I still can't win.

I know I need some sense of closure because I feel as if I've just been wandering around since I left. In recovery, but still thinking of LA. I need to go back and settle things, visit places, go to some favourite stores, see sights, catch a movie and, most importantly, remember what I did accomplish there and how many people would not have been brave enough to go out there. Maybe my timing was off. Or screen-writing wasn't right for me. I was led to LA with the notion that something could just happen, and it was a lot harder and with more pressure than I could handle. Whatever the case, I think the message is clear now. I can't work on the things I want to until I am healthy, or getting there, and have moved on a bit. A large part of me is still in LA, hanging on to that dream. I need to go back and close that door for a while so that I can focus on my life and goals in Connecticut right now. Whether I end up back there or somewhere else in the future, I do not know. I will never be able to move on if I stay stuck like this in the past. I need to free myself of this depression and this longing for a place that I thought I knew and loved. I never knew it, thought I wish I had. I need to realize it wasn't meant to be for me at the time or right now. I need to be here, and when you leave something, it needs a proper "goodbye." So I need to go say farewell to LA for now. I'm nervous and stressed, but I hope I enjoy some of it.

Before I set off for my trip, I meet with my new therapist, Comer Rudd-Gates. She's amazing. I feel so much more comfortable with her. She's so nice and friendly and "gets" me. She actually communicates with me. I tell her my whole story and she is shocked by all of my encounters with doctors and the hospital and tells me that I should be a resource for educating medical professionals about eating disorders. It made me want to do more advocacy work. She reassured me about LA, told me how far I have come and that the person I truly am will never change with location. It was refreshing and she was so positive. I can't believe I stayed with Dr. Cagore for so long. Comer has already opened me up to a new way of life.

Holly is afraid I will lose weight in LA because I am nervous that I can't work out. We put together a meal plan for there (that I will also tell Sam I have) and some snacks to bring. She too said to focus on the positives of this trip and go to the places I used to like. Enjoy the time there, don't stress about it. And to contact her if I need to. They were both so supportive that I feel I have my true treatment team finally in place.

Right before my trip, I tell Dad how I am stressed about LA, and he tells me not to let it get to me and that I am not a failure.

"You did a lot out there and it won't do you any good to live in the past. Everyone makes mistakes or looks back and wishes they could change things, but you have to move on," he says. "I know it's probably hard, but look at this as a vacation. Do some enjoyable things out there." Dad…my voice of reason.

It's strange going back to LA right now when this time last year I was visiting home. Amazing, the difference a year makes.

Odd, to get on a plane to LA, knowing I am coming back in a week and a half. It was always, get on a plane in Hartford and say, "see you in six months." Definitely a different feeling this time, but still sad in a way. Dad tells me to eat, that's his biggest concern, and I tell him it's mine too, but I will.

After all the travelling and getting my rental car, I arrive at Sam's late in the evening. It is good to see her, and we make chit chat and then take the dog for a walk. Then the conversation sets in. She asks me about therapy and being an inpatient, and gives me her opinions about how they relate to drug and alcohol programs.

"I wanted to believe that you could get better here and just eat more, but I realize that people just telling you to eat isn't how it works unfortunately."

"No," I tell her, "it's still a long road ahead."

"Must be hard."

She talks about some of her weight issues and metabolism and I just listen. She asks me how many calories I am eating. I tell her at Renfrew it was 1800. She says that's not enough.

I saw Bally's, the gym, and it was okay. I'm trying not to focus on it, but it's so close to her house. It was this area that got to me more, even though the problem began earlier. I am hoping to start packing and getting everything out soon, so then I can venture out and truly enjoy things.

Where did I get all this crap? My suitcases are full and I have three bags of garbage. I went to Staples to get boxes to ship things in. It's amazing how you accumulate stuff.

The packing and shipping takes two days. Then what? I am homesick. How? I was L.A.-sick when I was home! Dad told me to treat this as a vacation, so I did some retail therapy. At least I don't see the credit card bill now. I did get myself a Lotus necklace, because the lotus rises out of the mud and is a beautiful flower, so it's a good image for people overcoming things. Something positive to take away with me, at least. Oh, and of course I got my L.A. haircut too.

When I get back to Sam's, I am bored. I realize there isn't that much you can do in a day. The next morning, bored again, I have a breakdown. She is at work and I am by myself with nothing to do. So isolating and reminiscent of how it used to be for me in L.A.—alone, crying, feeling helpless—except then I had the gym to turn to and that occupied about four hours of my day.

Now, I go out for a little bit and then I am stuck here, crying while I make dinner, whispering, "I want to go home." Maybe that is the answer. This is not the place for me. I hate that "out of place" feeling. Alone and disconnected. Almost rejected. Like I never fitted. I was always just a visitor who overstayed her welcome, so they hurt me. Or I hurt myself.

I'm hurting now. I need to talk to someone. I call Mom. We chit-chat, and then I tell her how I feel.

"I wish there was something I could do for you. I hate being so far away."

"It's okay," I tell her, but when she says it, it reminds me of what she would say when I called her struggling with the eating disorder. "I'll be fine," I continue, "I've been through worse."

"Yes," she assures me, "you've been through a lot."

Why did I come here? Will I ever find my place?

Dad calls.

"What's the matter? You're not having a good time out there?"

I explain the situation and the isolation factor, except how before, at least I had the gym.

"Now do you see why you can't be back there? You'd go back to your old routine in no time with your workouts."

"I know, but it's different being here now because I'm stuck and don't even have the desire to do things. I don't even know what to do."

"You were miserable at home the last six months and I don't think you were ready to go back to L.A."

"I was scared to come back but I had to. It was something I needed to do, and I couldn't let it go on much longer."

He could tell I was upset. "Why don't you just check the flights and take the next one home and I'll pick you up whenever?"

"I thought about that, but there are things I want to do and I need to be braver."

"Who says this will be the last time you are out there? Who knows where you'll be in two years?"

"There are things I want to do before I leave this time. I may not know what yet, but if I come home, I will feel like I failed again. I won't do that to myself."

"You sound just like you did when you were out there before. It's like going back in time."

Back in time…is that better than being stuck? I'm certainly not moving forward.

That night, when Sam came home, she wanted to discover more about my eating disorder and treatment, then popped the most absurd question: "So why do they think you had the eating disorder?"

Was she kidding? I had lived with her and we had gone over this. I thought she knew the story. I didn't want to talk about it, yet I went over it again, but my story did not please her.

"It's a cry for help, though. You were slowly killing yourself. How is the gym now?"

"Okay, but I do still work out."

She asks if my inpatient team skill keeps up with me, and I tell her about my treatment team now.

Shocked, she says, "You have a psychiatrist *and* a therapist?"

I had to tell her about the medication, anxiety and depression, and that they are good to talk to.

"Why the medication? Be careful what medication you take. Why are you depressed? Is it personal or because of how the world is?"

Oh my gosh!

"They say depression increases as the eating disorder slips away and you move forward in your recovery. I'm fighting the depression and trying to work out my issues."

Then came her big revelation. "Maybe this had to do with men, and maybe I'm wrong but you seem to be avoiding that area. Some people lose weight as a defense mechanism. You said you never dated that much in college."

So much for this being a vacation.

"I would like to have a relationship with someone, but I have never been that comfortable with my body."

"A lot of overweight people have boyfriends."

"Well, I'm picky," I laughed. "I don't think, no matter what size, I will ever be comfortable with my body."

"It's in your head. You need more self-confidence. You're cute, you are a pretty girl. Do you realize that?"

"No."

"You could easily have a boyfriend."

It's not that easy. I know I wouldn't want just anyone. I've always had someone built up in my somewhat crazy head, who would really love me, and whom I would love, and it would just be amazing. I'm afraid that I'm never going to find that.

"Of course," she goes on, "you may have had the eating disorder because of a past life issue."

Of course! Problem solved!

We sat outside at a cute restaurant in Venice. It was nice to eat a normal meal with Sam and not feel completely insecure. Then we walked over the footbridges at the Venice Canals and talked.

"You do seem to be doing better," she tells me, even though she knows I am not 100%. "When you were here last, it was really hard to watch."

It was strange to hear her say that. I didn't know how much it affected her. I just figured it was all annoying. I apologize, tell her I know it was hard, and on me too. I did not want to be doing what I was but couldn't stop. I hated living like that, it was torture, and needed her to know I didn't want to put that pressure on her and never want to go back.

"That's good, Nicole. Always keep that in mind. Be good to yourself. Do things that take your mind off it."

I went to Zuma Beach in Malibu, putting my feet in the Pacific Ocean for what might be the last time. The water was cold, and pounded against my feet, yet while a child might squeal, it made me feel life. It brought me back to why I came to L.A., why I left, and why I had returned. The beauty of California, I knew, would stick with me for years to come. The memories, the triumphs and tragedies, would stick with me as well, but it is now part of who I am and how I will grow to who I become.

I wondered, if everyone goes through a personal struggle to "learn" something about themselves, was this mine? Was I off the hook? A stupid notion, as this was the worst thing that I'd ever had to go through. But sometimes the worst things that happen to you are somehow for the best. Not that the eating disorder was good for me, but I have learned a lot about myself, and life, and that I cherish it and my family.

I threw out my old gym sneakers and my broken-in measuring tape. I cut off a piece of the shoelace and tape—memories. More so, warning signs. To remember where I was, the things I did, and how far I have come. Getting rid of those things was getting rid of a part of my past that I no longer need. Liberating.

I leave tomorrow night. My time in LA is coming to a real close...for now? I don't know. I have no clue what I want. This makes it official. All my things will be gone from here, so "I" will be gone from here. For a while, part of me remained. Now, I am saying goodbye to a city I once called home and I don't know how I feel about it. What did I even do while I was here besides make a mess of myself? I tried to enjoy myself I guess, treat myself, make myself happy this week or so, instead of stressed, worried or sad. But the one thing that I didn't really reflect on was the thing that brought me out here in the first place—screen-writing. The time was consumed with talking about my anorexia or what's reminiscent of it, and I realize that did overwhelm my stay here. It took over the true purpose so I couldn't focus on the screen-writing. I know I have to have a clear mind if I want to do it but the questions is, do I want to do it? Then, do I have what it takes to do it? And ultimately, when I try something again, will I just fall back into the arms of the eating disorder?

I realize now that I lived three different lives in L.A. First there was the new, fresh and exciting one in West Hollywood. That first summer, when it was just the screenwriting class, beach, shopping, concerts, a few friends and going out. I was meeting interesting people and it was fun. I decided to stay even through people were moving, but I had to move too—across town.

The second "me" was on to Hollywood. A little lonelier, but I felt a bit of encouragement in my writing. My teacher liked my script idea and I got an article in the LA Times. An Agent even wanted to look at my book proposal. As time moved on, so did I. As all things in Hollywood must fade, I did as well. The writing did not go so well. I became isolated. I got a gym membership, and that is where I spent all my time. I was lonely, sad and depressed. Homesick. Broke. I cried a lot. I didn't know what to do. A lot different from the girl who first came to L.A.

Hang In There... Wherever "There" Is

The slow decline...

Third was when I truly needed help. I knew I couldn't do it on my own, and Sam invited me to live with her. I had decided to stay in L.A. after the writing course so I could pursue screen-writing. I was now really on my own. There was nothing truly holding me here, just my own will and desire to be successful. Instead of focusing on writing, I used that will and desire to lose weight, and soon my eating disorder overcame me. For a girl who at first loved the constant sunshine, I came to despise L.A. I only went out to go to the gym or the Farmer's Market to get fruit. The rest of the time I spent crying, waiting, and for what, I'm not sure. To be happy, or for someone to save me? To notice? To leave L.A. and go home? Is that what I really wanted? Is that what I want now? I guess it doesn't matter, because I am leaving, and who knows when I will return?

"You look like you lost ten pounds out there," my Dad tells me at dinner.

He also just saw me give a piece of my burger to the dogs.

"Have you eaten any of that, or are you just feeding it to them?"

He tells me every time he looks, I am feeding my food to them, but I think he just looked that once and is worried. I can understand why he is worried, but he shouldn't be. I did eat in L.A., I didn't work out, but I did lose a little weight. I know I'll gain it back now that I am home. Holly thought I would lose weight, a couple of pounds, and I tell him that.

"You lost more than a couple of pounds."

"There's no way I lost a pound a day."

"I can see it in your face. When I picked you up at the airport, I was shocked."

"I was tired, and stressed. It was a long and exhausting trip."

"I had been worried about your eating habits before you left, now I'm more worried."

I know how scary this whole thing is for him, and for me as well. It is frustrating when they think they know what's going on with my body or my "habits" and they don't.

The issue of coming back from Los Angeles was tough. Before, my things were out there, so part of me was too. Now, all of me is here and I still feel stuck and lost. I've been grieving over wasted time, missed opportunities, lost dreams, hopes and accomplishments. I've been crying over a city that I entered with hope and left in despair. That city will never cry over me.

Chapter 33—Post Renfrew: 5 Months
Mending A Broken Heart

The girl I was last summer is a stranger. That is a good thing, yet I have this desire to know who she is. The poor thing, what was she thinking? What was she doing to herself? She needed help, wanted it, but was too scared to ask.

That girl has changed, many times, and transformed, I suppose, into me. Now, I am moving forward, with difficulty, but trying. I think that all these things were happening before and I was so numb to it that I couldn't really process it. I want to remember and take it all in so I know I got out of it. I want to go over it and the disease, without dwelling on it too much, but to know how it got me here. I want to comprehend it. I never paid attention to myself at that time, nor was I aware of what I was doing to myself, and now I want to be able to recognize the pain and devastation in myself, so I can understand it better and stop it if I notice signs of it again. Basically, I want a life. I want to live.

I just did an interview with Matt Nathanson—one of my favorite singer-songwriters and a guy I have known for a while because I booked him in college and have interviewed him a lot. It took us two days to actually do the interview because we spent so much time catching up. He wanted to know about my treatment and how I was doing, and congratulated me for my hard work. He's so in tune with everything, having been through his own stuff. He told me, "Some people are never awake and it's important to get to a place where it's dark and shitty so that you can experience the depths and colours of life. It builds character and allows you to navigate life."

He's like my Guru.

"It's a long process," he went on, "to go through that. Being a human being is hard. But it's fun too. Sometimes you just want to be fixed, but it's not that easy."

Does he know me or what?

He continues: "To be alive is to be dynamic. Think about where you were a year ago and where you are now. What you understand about yourself and human beings, that's just fucking great. You understand things on a deeper level because you're figuring it out, unpacking things, and it does make life more enjoyable because you are alive and awake. You understand it, and that's kicking ass."

I don't know if it's karma or what, but sometimes when I'm feeling down, it's like the people who have the most wisdom just appear, and my thought processes change. Matt did that for me.

So does Jason. He has been travelling for work but he checks in to see how I am. He keeps on telling me to take those protein shakes. And tells me to "Hang in there." I tell him that I am feeling good, but a lot of people that I was in treatment with are going back to treatment now, which is sad.

"That is scary. You do not want to go back. I saw a segment on T.V. the other night about it. It's so sad. Your life is way too precious for it to be beholden to a disease like that."

I am amazed at how much he cares, but perhaps it is because I am not used to people caring so much. Either way, I am grateful now for so many people who do care in my life. They are helping me in ways they have no idea of.

**

I have already had a damaged and weak heart, so how can I trust my strained heart with another person who might damage it more? I need to try and keep it safe. No one knew what it had been through, so it couldn't take any more pain. It, and I, are vulnerable. Which is strange—we used to be so tough.

So there came the area of dating. How do you date after, or during, an eating disorder? I was never much of a dater, always being overweight and insecure with my body. Sure, I had crushes, but I shied away from boys and men, because I did not feel comfortable with myself. Who, anyway, would ever like me?

After some coaxing from Sam and some other friends, I decided to try eHarmony. I don't know why, but it seemed easier then stepping into the scary world of bars and restaurants. Besides, really, how does an anorexic meet someone?

To my surprise, I did meet someone online. His name was Eric, and he was from my town. A Correctional Office and an Artist. We emailed a lot and had much in common. I told him of my past and he was okay with it, as he used to do bodybuilding and took it too far, but is okay now. He is sweet, creative, kind, ambitious and understanding. How does he exist? How did I find him?

We talk on the phone and make plans to get together for our first date, which in reality, is my true first date, as I never really dated much before then. Our marathon date went twelve hours. We met at a book store in the pouring rain. He puts his hand out to shake and I give him a hug. I can't help it. Must be my nature. He tells me he's nervous, which is cute. Surprisingly, I'm not nervous at all. We go to Borders and get coffee and a treat. Me, yeah, a lemon bar. My favourite. He paid, even though I took out money in an honest way. Not the fake way some girls do. I wasn't nervous to eat in front of him, which was a good thing. I surprised myself, and I think him too. We talked, asked questions, and he told me he was still nervous, which shocked me. I really don't think of myself as someone who would make another person nervous. I'm a nerd when it comes to this stuff.

After we finished, he suggested a movie, or renting a movie and going to his friend's house where he was house-sitting. I braved the latter idea. We got there and well into the movie he finally grabbed my hand. My head was on his shoulder. It was nice to be with someone like that. To feel protected. I've craved that for so long that to finally have someone just to snuggle with was nice. We talked a little and he told me how beautiful I was. That he thought I was beautiful in my picture, but when he saw me get out of my car he was shocked. He couldn't believe that I wasn't taken or married. Which was really sweet, but I was like, you're crazy, I'm amazed you want to hang out with me. It was cute of him to say but of course I couldn't believe it. It was nice to have someone appreciate me because I've never had a guy treat me like that, so it was a big turnaround for me.

After the movie, he asked if I wanted pizza. I was squeamish. He asked if I was sure and if I would be okay with eating that, and I said, "yes."

I found out moments later that he knew me better than I did.

I went into the bathroom and when I came out, he said, "how about Subway?'' What a relief.

We went there but then saw an Ice Cream place, which is my weakness.

"Do you want one?" he asked.

I said, "of course." We got our ice cream first, ate it, and then saved the subs for later. You know, dessert first.

We went back to the house and watched some T.V. Cuddling on the couch, I had never felt so comfortable. Both with myself or another person. Then he kissed me.

Knock.

There was a knock at the door.

The people he was house sitting for came back early.

Just my luck. It was hysterical.

We chatted with them for a bit and then decide to go back to his house to eat our subs. He shows me his artwork and it was incredible. We spend the rest of the night talking and soon I go home. I couldn't eat the entire sub and he understands. I am surprised that someone understands. He doesn't push me and knows my limits. I think it's somewhat of a miracle that I met him. We say goodbye and figure we will make plans for another day.

Eric and I do get together again, and again. I cannot tell if we are dating or if he is my support. I went to Burger King with him, for the first time in so long. Nervous at first, but I embraced it. I just got a wrap, and fries (which I didn't finish), but I knew it was a breakthrough in my recovery. We do end up getting that pizza one day, and more ice cream. We have ice cream one day at his house too. Again, he never pushes me and wants me to be comfortable. From hanging out at his house, to walks on the boardwalk, to simply talking, he is like a friend I never had. Yet, all good things must come to an end.

I realize, though dating someone is what I crave, it is not something I am completely ready for, and it is not fair to him. I still have so many insecurities, and he should not be worried about me all the time. He is such a kind person, he should be focusing on his own endeavors, instead of worrying whether I will eat my sandwich or not. He was so caring, and I could not do that to him. I was still in recovery, and with all my appointments, it was my main focus. While I wanted to be with someone so badly, I knew I couldn't be too invested in. There was too much going on in my life. The amazing thing was that he understood and knew I needed to take care of myself first. More than that, we continued to be friends. It was about trust, and how many people had I been able to trust before? I was grateful for the relationship I had formed with Eric, and knew that it wouldn't end there. Maybe I jumped in too soon to the dating thing, but regardless, it changed me. It helped me. I did learn to trust and be happy with someone else. Someone who understood me. And that could never be taken away.

Holly was concerned about my weight because she saw it drop. What she didn't know was that I was wearing two pairs of leggings underneath my jeans and drinking water before our appointment when I got weighed. I was down to 124 pounds. I knew if my weight were lower, she would be more concerned, and I didn't want to be forced into more treatment. I could maintain a better weight, I knew, but I liked being thin again.

I had just been struggling. I want recovery, and I will achieve it. I do not want relapse. Recovery is hard, but it's harder to fake recovery. I know I am working towards recovery, but it's hard to be honest about the real weight loss because they think I would need a higher form of treatment and I don't want that. But the next week, I went up, and she was happy to read my food journal. The Burger King made her ecstatic. Thank you, Eric. I love it that my nutritionist is supporting me eating Burger King. She told me I looked in better spirits whereas I used to just look tired, and she can usually tell whether someone is doing OK or not when they walk in the door.

"I never realized I looked so bad," I tell her. Did I?

She was also happy to learn that I reconnected with my friend from Boston, Erin, who I separated myself from after our confrontation with the eating disorder.

"I've worked hard and been frustrated, but I don't think I'm relapsing."

"I didn't mean you were, but your weight kept dropping, so we should look at relapse prevention to keep you on track."

"Okay. I want to stay on track."

I received a letter from Renfrew that I wrote myself. When I got the card in the mail, I was surprised to see something addressed in my own handwriting, but then I remembered. While we were there, we wrote a note to ourselves that would be sent months after discharge. In it, we were to write where we wanted to be in recovery. I could not remember what I wrote, so I peeled open the envelope, and read:

February 8, 2007

Hi Nicole... it's Nicole,

I'm writing this letter sitting on the couch next to Jen and Meg with our Fraggle Rock stuffed animals. They just turned Fraggle Rock off for this group. I'm supposed to be writing about what I will need to hear months after discharge because they will be sending these to us. Honestly, I've recently been feeling rather hopeless in my recovery. I had a span of feeling positive last week and now am just thinking, well, I'm already planning out what meals I can skip when I'm home and how much exercise I can do... so does that mean I plan to revert back to the eating disorder? I want to lose weight but I don't want to torture myself any more. I fell like, what is the point? Is there a future for me? That is why I extended my stay a week.

But since this is called the "better letter," I'm supposed to be giving myself positive affirmations I guess for when I do feel hopeless— which is often. One girl, Tara, left today, and she told me to recognize my talents. That's hard for me to do, since I see them as quick glimpses of hope and then large falls of defeat. But then I realized here that a lot of people would dream of being published in the LA Times, and maybe that's not as far as I wanted to go, but it was definitely a huge accomplishment.

Speaking of writing, how is that going? Are you working on anything big? I hope so.

I know that moving home is going to be a tough transition for you, but please be patient with Mom and Dad as they are going to be patient with you. It's gonna be hard and you will be sad leaving LA, especially not being so independent any more, but remember, you're sick Nicole. You can't do this alone. I know it's hard for you to admit to. Also, you will mess up. But there's a fine line between messing up because you're struggling and emotional, or because you're trying to hurt yourself. Take care of yourself, Nicole. People tell you that you have a lot to offer and so many people care about you. I hear it but I don't believe it. Maybe I should.

I want to be happy. I hope I am.

I want to know what the root of this problem is, and I know that working through it will make me sad, but at least you won't be keeping those demons in any longer, and can hopefully live a better and happier life because of it.

Again, take care of yourself. People tell you that you are worth it. I hope by now, you have realized it.

Love,

Nicole (and Boober, my Fraggle friend)

Hang In There... Wherever "There" Is

Wow, amazing that what I needed to hear, I told myself.

Chapter 34
Post Renfrew: 6 Months
Forming a Beautiful Life

It has been six months since I was discharged from Renfrew. Sometimes it seems like I was there only yesterday. Sometimes, like forever ago, and sometimes, like it was all an illusion and I never went. I still find it hard to believe that I was an inpatient to treat my anorexia, or more so, that I had anorexia. It's very surreal. Everything I went through there, from the meals to the therapy—it's so odd to think I had that experience. Of course, with time, I became accustomed to it, but it still seems bizarre. Yet here I am, six months later, still struggling but fighting the good fight. More than just being discharged six months ago, I realize that I have been in outpatient treatment for six months. Unbelievable. Now that is a lot of hard work. I think I can give myself credit for that. Mainly, I am drained from appointments and reflection and working on food. It's like a full-time job.

I told Holly about this, and that I am not sure I was where I wanted to be or what I have accomplished.

"Are you kidding?" she asks me. "You have come so far with your progress and taking risks, and the way you think. You went back to LA—that was huge! You were very sick a lot at first and now you're not. That is a sign of improvement."

I guess it is a positive change. I have tried risk foods, even though I still work out. I still have that fear instilled in me that this is going to be a terrible cycle and I'm going to have to live with this forever.

***

I purged. Not a normal purge, but I did it. I had a bite to eat and I felt so sick that I purged. Then I had a drink of water and felt sick and I purged. Something is not right. I am not doing this on purpose.

The sickness got worse. I became nauseous after everything I ate. Sometimes, I'd feel sick, like I would throw up, but I didn't. It was after everything I ate or drank. I tried to do anything that would settle my stomach but it didn't matter. I couldn't even drink water. I went to my doctor and they ran blood work and an ultrasound of my gall bladder, both of which were fine. From there, they recommended me to a Gastro Intestinal Specialist.

I saw the Doctor's Physician's Assistant first and he threw out things like ulcers and gall bladder problems. He also said that some of the laxative abuse and restriction from my eating disorder might be causing this, because the stomach had no food to churn up. I gave him my history and that is when his ignorance hit me.

"How come you had your eating disorder at this point? Don't most people develop it at thirteen?"

I was boiling.

"You know," he continued. "Their body image issues. Does your therapist know why you got it?"

I was beyond pissed off.

I responded calmly. "I was going though a rough time being in LA by myself, and I was homesick. I didn't have any friends and went to the gym for comfort. I started to diet and then the restriction just continued and I couldn't control it. But eating disorders can affect anyone. Males and females at any age. Most women I was in treatment with were in their 20's and 30's, and some in their 60's."

"Right," he so knowingly tells me. "But it usually starts when you're 13."

I wanted to smack the bastard, but I didn't. How dumb are people? This is why medical "professionals" need to be educated.

I finally saw the real doctor, who also thought it was an ulcer, but wanted to do an upper GI Endoscopy to make sure. Turns out, they were all wrong.

They did the procedure and told me I didn't have cancer. Wow, a relief, as I never even thought of that as a problem.   I have gastritis, a reddening and inflammation of the stomach lining, which can cause pain, but there could be more. It also comes, they say, with eating disorders. How, after six months of recovery, could I be having these setbacks? I had been doing so well.

She gave me some medicine to help ease my stomach, but it didn't help. The pain got worse, and after the endoscopy, I had sharp pain in my stomach and abdomen.

I went back to my GI Doctor, who wore Sally Jessie Raphael glasses, but first I had to see her PA again. This time, a female.

"I can't understand why you would be having pain from an Endoscopy. You have gastritis and your biopsy was normal."

She became fixated on my eating disorder, asking me a ton of questions and if I had been stressed lately.

"No more than usual," I tell her.

She had me lie back and pressed on my stomach, which of course hurt.

"Flex your muscles," she told me, and then pressed down again. "See, I can press harder now. You were just timid before. That was why it hurt."

She cured me!

Sally Jessie came in the room and I hoped for some answers. Tough luck, Nicole.

"I don't know what this pain could be. We did the ultrasound and endoscopy and there is no way what I did then could cause pain like this. Nicole, do you have someone to talk to? Your therapist?"

I sat up.

"Sometimes anxiety can cause nausea; not that your stomach pain isn't real, but if you're worried or stressed about something, it can bring about this pain."

Anger rising, my hands clenched the table.

"Perhaps something is bothering you in your eating disorder treatment," Sally said. "That could be the cause of all of this." She nodded at her PA, who seemed to agree.

I got so heated, yet was holding back tears.

For so long during my illness, I let doctors push me around, saying they thought they knew what was wrong with me when they didn't. Shouting out "anxiety" when they didn't care or know the cause. Well, everyone has wanted me to be more assertive. This was my time.

"Look," I tell Sally and her grinning PA, "this is not anxiety. I wouldn't be here unless I had real physical pain. I have a therapist, nutritionist and a psychiatrist who all know what's going on and are concerned, but I am the most frustrated."

Sally just stared, but before she could interrupt, I kept going. "I want to get back on track with my recovery and meal plan, which is hard to do when I feel so sick when I eat. I want to eat. I'm offended that you would say something like, 'it's just anxiety,' when I came to you to help me. My therapist, who you know, and I were just talking about how medical professionals misdiagnose or disregard those with eating disorders and ignore their physical symptoms because of the mental illness."

"I wasn't trying to offend you," Sally said, looking a little shocked. "Maybe I could talk to Comer about what's going on."

"Why would you do that? And wouldn't you need a release?"

"No. I don't think so." Yes, yes you do.

"I don't think you need to talk to her. I think you need to talk to me. She knows it's not anxiety and it's physical pain. This has been going on way too long. And another thing. She told me about a case where a girl was recovering for a while from an eating disorder, then had stomach problems and had to have part of her stomach removed. I'm not the first person who had an eating disorder that has stomach issues."

"Yes, that is what I meant. Maybe this is related to your eating disorder and I could talk to Comer to see what she knows about these things."

Aren't you the Gastroenterologist?

"I just don't want to try anything too aggressive on you. Clearly, the medicines we tried are not working. Let's get some x-rays of your abdomen to see if your intestines are distended."

Amazing how she changed her mind so fast.

I am glad I stuck up for myself, and in a way I felt like I stuck up for the girl of the past that was too afraid to stand up against the doctor's who put her down. Who she couldn't ask for help.

What I couldn't believe is that yet again, I was sick with a physical pain and the doctor wanted to brush it off as anxiety. Such a simple diagnosis for a crazy like me. I spoke up because I thought I deserved a real answer and the doctor needed to know she was out of line.

It's a good thing I did, because my feistiness got results. The x-ray showed my intestines to be completely distended, which is one of the reasons for my abdominal pain, but not the actual stomach pain. She finally set me up to have a gastric emptying test, but only after she talked to Comer, who informed her that Holly, my nutritionist, had two clients with Gastroparesis.

Why are there so many avenues, and dead-ends, on the path to get treatment? A "normal" person would not have to go through this. If she didn't know that I had a history of an eating disorder, then she probably would not have blamed it on anxiety. Instead she would have kept looking for the problem until she could treat it. Isn't that what doctors should do?

Yet here I am, still with a stigma placed upon me, trying to recover in a prejudiced world that apparently looks down upon those suffering and recovering. Well, I look down on them.

Holly is trying to help me with a meal plan. The weird part is I'm okay with soft, warm foods or cold foods. She says, "Hey, whatever you can keep down!"

It's different and she knows that. It's aggravating that I hit a mark in my recovery with 6 months, and then I get sick. It's as if this illness now doesn't want me to eat. It's a cruel joke. In my recovery, of course it would be my luck to get a sickness where I'd get nauseous every time I eat. Even my body wants me to starve now. Payback.

"How do you really like not eating, Nicole?" says my body.

"I don't, Body. Let me eat."

I tell Holly, "I just want to eat!" She was excited to hear that, but, wow, when would I ever have said that? She tried to help me but it seemed as if there was no help for me. I felt like it was my fault for all the torture I did to myself.

"You didn't ask to be sick like this," she tells me, "just like you didn't ask for the eating disorder. The important thing is to figure out how to get through it."

I had my Gastric Emptying test. Big fun. I had to eat radioactive eggs, and I've always hated eggs.

"I've never seen anyone look in so much pain while they ate," the nurse told me.

Little did she know.

"Now, if you're going to get sick, yell, so we can close the doors. We'll need to shut down because we can't have the radioactive material everywhere."

That's reassuring. I can put the radioactive material in my body, but if I puke, watch out! Comforting.

I manage to get most of the eggs down, then lay on the bed, while a screen is put over my stomach. It takes images of how long it takes for the eggs to move out of my stomach into my intestines. It emptied okay, but the final verdict is: Gastroparesis, which literally means paralysis of the stomach. The nerves in my stomach are so damaged from restricting, diuretics, laxatives, and diet pills, that when I eat, the food just sits in my stomach. The nerves are supposed to make the muscle contract and then the food move into the intestine. My food just sits there, taunting me. Making me nauseous and full, so I can't eat more than a bite and feel so sick. At least I have a real diagnosis now. Unfortunately, there is no cure. Sally put me on some non-FDA approved medication that I must take twenty minutes before each meal. That will charge up my stomach like a battery and get things moving.

"It may be chronic, it may not be. Only time will tell."

Wonderful.

Still sad to know that this was my own doing and the effects of my eating disorder may last forever.

Instead of sulking on the negatives of my eating disorder, or being pissed off at doctors that maintain the stigma of what an eating disorder is, I decided to get out there and make a difference. First, since I was still angered over my E.R. experience from L.A., I wrote to the head of the Emergency Department about my awful experience and about eating disorders. Of course, he wrote back and said he viewed my file and everything seems to have been done correctly. He did apologize though if I felt like I did not receive the proper treatment. Of course I didn't, I almost died. However, I wanted to reach the public and educate them about eating disorders—all of them. Those suffering, doctors, parents, loved ones, and students. I spoke with Comer, who already had her own non-profit, and she thought it was a great idea. I founded my non-profit under hers and decided to name it "Beautiful Lives," for many reasons. First, because when I was in treatment, there were so many beautiful girls and women, inside and out, who didn't realize what beautiful lives they had. I want people to realize that. I need to realize that. Second, my friend Charlotte, the singer, has a song called "Beautiful Life," and I drew from that as well. I asked for her permission to use her song title as a spin on my non-profit and she was thrilled that she could be any sort of influence or inspiration. In it, she sings, "The sun may come up and go down again, but I'll still swear it's a beautiful life." No matter what happens in life, it is beautiful, and we must learn to love it. I even got a tattoo, designed by Charlotte, on my inner forearm that reads "beautiful life," so that I can always remember what I have, and what was almost taken away from me.

The goal for "Beautiful Lives" was to first attend Health Fairs, which we did, and of course we were met with positives and negatives. The negatives were aggravating. People walking by and saying, "I don't have an eating disorder, but I could use one." Even parents saying to their children, "You have an eating disorder. You eat too much." Some people are clueless.

Others were very interested. I had people come up to me and thank me for being there, because they too suffered. We shared stories. Others were from medical programmes and wanted more information. Some were from schools and asked if I could come and speak, which thrilled me. The more people I could reach, the better. I was excited at what possibilities "Beautiful Lives" held, and what my own beautiful life held in store for me.

I wrote up materials, worksheets for students and teachers, and put together a package with the mission statement on the front:

The mission of Beautiful Lives is to bring awareness and education to the people of Connecticut about the truth of eating disorders, while bringing together a community of those who have experienced an eating disorder (whether directly or through a family member or friend) and celebrating life and recovery. We celebrate life with other survivors and encourage those suffering to recognize that it is worth the fight. It is a beautiful life, and we are worth it.

Remember...
Eating Disorders are a Disease, not a Choice.
Recovery is possible.
You deserve a healthy and happy life.
You're not alone.
An eating disorder is not worth it, but you are.
You have a Beautiful Life—it's time to embrace it.

My beautiful life was just beginning.

Chapter 35
Post Renfrew: 7 Months
The Anniversary versus The Wedding

October was a strange month for me. I knew my death-scare anniversary was coming up, yet so was my sister's wedding, but did they have to happen at the same time? My sister was getting married on October 20, 2007, and October 19 was the year anniversary of the night I was in the E.R. and thought I was going to die. I had to be happy for her, but could I shake off the awful memories?

My friend Carol, who I had met through Comer, and who did some "Beautiful Lives" work with me, and had coincidentally done the Eating Disorder lobby day also, wrote me a note. She seemed to be the only one who understood how difficult the weekend would be.

"*Hi Nic,*" she wrote. "*I know this coming week is going to be really tough for you. A lot of things happening all at once—a funeral and a wedding. I say 'funeral' because maybe it's time to put to rest a bad time in your life. You're a survivor—you are the author of survival! In honour of your survival and your beautiful life, I'm sending happy thoughts and fun things your way.*"

She sent me all things to do with the autumn that I love, for example, pumpkin bread. Funny how us fellow anorexics send food to each other, but I do love my pumpkin bread. She was right though; I did need to put some things to rest.

Instead of looking back sadly at the weekend where I almost died, I instead looked at this one-year anniversary as a celebration of life. I lived. Now, I needed to take care of myself and enjoy life. Don't dwell on the past, it will only haunt you. No more, "what ifs?" Live for today, the "right now," because that's all you have, that's all you can do, and that's all you should focus on. I needed to celebrate my bravery for making it this far, the courage I've had to continue, the power to heal and the love of life that has been instilled in me. Live for today and embrace it with all I had.

That is what I told myself, but I was still anxious. I'm not sure if it was the anxiety of the past memory, or of my sister getting married. There was a mixed moment though, when I told Kelly, "I am so happy to be here for your wedding. Last year, when you were talking about it and making plans, I was so sick. I would cry, thinking, I'll never make it to my sister's wedding. I won't be alive. But I am. And I can't wait to see you get married."

She doesn't like the sappy stuff, but it was true. I feared not seeing my big sister get married because I would be dead. But the big day had come, and we are all here, but I'm scared as hell. Not for her, but because I might trip walking down the aisle.

The wedding day was gorgeous and so was she. It was so nice to see my parents and brother all dressed up too. I was not too self-conscious about how I looked in my dress. All that worrying for nothing.

Dan and I walked down the aisle together and we pulled it off smoothly, no giggling. Well, the occasional look and smile at each other, but no giggling, and most importantly, no tripping.

During the ceremony, I was a mix between laughter and crying. I couldn't believe that my big sister was getting married. I pushed all bad thoughts away of the year past and focused on her. This was her day and I embraced it. I embraced her. After the wedding, she would be moving to New Jersey, and in a way, it felt like I was being abandoned. Not at her fault. She was moving on with her life. But since we had established a better relationship, it had been so nice to have her around. I knew I would miss her. As she walked down the aisle, I already did.

Weddings come and go, but sisters stay the same. Yes, Kelly was in New Jersey now, but had already been home a few times. It was nice, and reassuring to know she wasn't that far away. She was only a phone call away.

Things got back to normal after her wedding. Kelly got married, she moved, she had a new life. Weren't we just five years old playing in the backyard? When did we grow up?

I know, I know, I have a hard time with change.

Eating disorder-wise, it has been a wild ride. My weight has fluctuated but I have tried some crazy-ass risk foods, like steak, turkey clubs, chicken nuggets and fries at McDonald's, and it's incredible to think that a year ago I wouldn't dream of touching these foods.

I decided to head down to Renfrew for one of their "Multi Family Group" Meetings, that we had used to have to attend weekly. The one where I met those women who were worried about their daughters. And where Meg set off the whoopee cushion. That was funny.

I met up with Amy, who I had been in treatment with. She looked wonderful. It was so good to see her and catch up, but also to be surrounded by a group who understands and who I can relate to. The room was filled with residents and parents and former residents, such as Amy and I. After some talking, we both speak up.

I tell the room, "I was here earlier this year. I was scared, probably like many of you. I hated what was going on with me but didn't know how to stop it. I give you so much credit for being here. It was the best decision I made, and I hope it is for you. There is life beyond an eating disorder, and beyond these walls. It's hard, but possible. And for the parents, I know it's hard to see. It was, and is, for mine. But know that your child is going through a difficult time. There's no blame, they are just suffering. They need your love."

I sat down and got applause. I was surprised, since there are so many mixed feeling between parents and patients, but I spoke of what I knew, and what I know will bring me further into recovery.

Chapter 36
Post Renfew: 9 Months
The Fear of Pasta!

So I decided to date again. It was time. I was due. Girls date, right? Maybe not this girl, but I needed to get over the fear of both dating and eating with other people. He came in the form of a nice guy, tall, with dirty blond hair, and worked at a college. His name? Mitch. Now that is a name a girl can swoon over.

We also met online and had marathon emails. He eventually popped the question: "Do you want to talk on the phone?"

I knew that was the next step, so I agreed, and we had a really nice conversation. Then the next step came: "So, do you want to go out to dinner some time?"

Be brave, Nicole.

"Definitely," I told him. I did want to meet him, and I would not let a stupid meal stand in my way. I had spent too much time letting food ruin my life.

"What do you like to eat," he asks from the opposite side of the phone line.

"Nothing." I said it completely serious.

Then there was silence.

"I'm kidding!" I yell back at him, and he just says, "Oh," and then my laughter and quick apologies prompt his laughter, and the situation was saved. I guess not everyone could take the eating or non-eating jokes as lightly as I could. Especially not a first date.

He knew about my eating disorder, and as a runner, had some experiences with friends who had anorexia, so was familiar with the disease. He didn't judge me, and if anything, wanted to accommodate me. That was the situation I found myself in, and it was one of those types of situations that was all too uncomfortable—even before all my eating issues. The, "what do you like to eat?" or "where do you want to go to dinner?" I was thrown both those questions from him.

"I like...normal food," I tell him.

"Okay," he said, with a slight chuckle. "So, I'm thinking, Indian food is out?"

"Yeah, I'm not doing that, sorry."

"Have you ever been to Pete's Pasta?" he asked.

Oh no, please, no pasta!

"No, I haven't."

"Then it's settled, we've gotta go there!" He was so excited that I couldn't say "no."

"It's good?" I asked. Please say no, please say no, please say no.

"It's the best. I love it there. I can't believe you've never been there. Is that...is that okay with you?"

No. But...take a risk Nicole.

"Yeah, that sounds great."

We made plans to meet and I found myself not so worried about the date, but worried about the meal. I hadn't had pasta since I was in treatment, which was nine months ago. I mean, I had tried a couple pieces of ziti, and some of my Mom's spaghetti, but I didn't have the taste for it any more. I had such a bad reaction to pasta when I was in treatment that I had lost all desire to eat it any more, and didn't know if it would shock my system like it had before.

Back in treatment, I would get a quick pulse and feel sick when I ate it. I figured it was due to the fact that I hadn't had it in a while and was a strange effect of the re-feeding process. The nurses, meanwhile, were worried that it had to do with how my body was metabolizing the starches and that it could be a blood sugar problem. Eventually, it stabilized. But my pasta fear didn't.

Good thing I had a nutrition appointment before the big date.

"This is fantastic!" Holly says. She was more excited about the date than me. "I love this guy. He sounds great. And pasta? Okay, let's think of some options…"

"Holly, it's a first date. That's worrisome enough. How can I do pasta too?"

"You have to give yourself credit for both things. This is good that you're going out and meeting people. The fact that you agreed to a restaurant with 'Pasta' in the title shows how far you have come. We just need to think of options beforehand so you won't be anxious when you see the menu."

I got anxious when she said the word "menu."

"Okay," she says, and takes out a sheet of paper. "Red sauce or white sauce."

"White."

"I think that's a good idea. Now what can you get in the pasta?"

"I do like chicken."

"Maybe chicken and broccoli?"

"That sounds good."

"Okay, so some sort of pasta in a white sauce with chicken and broccoli. You're all set."

"Oh really. That simple, huh? Why don't you go and eat it?" I say and she laughs.

"You'll be fine. And remember, it'll be a big dish, so you don't have to eat the whole thing. Don't focus on the food. Focus on him and the conversation. Just be comfortable. And if you panic, go into the ladies room and call me."

"I'm panicked. Can I call you now?"

I arrive at the restaurant and Mitch calls to tell me he's running a few minutes late. It's fine, because I go in and grab a table, which gives me a chance to peruse the menu. Let's see, there's pasta, pasta, more pasta, oh, a salad, and yeah, more pasta.

I will not geek out. I will not get a salad.

I notice a couple of dishes I could handle when I hear the door open. I look up and know it's him. He has a cute grin and I stand up to meet him.

"Sorry I'm late," he says.

"It's fine. I ate last week, so I'm good."

He looks at me, and then gets the joke.

"So what do you think of the place?"

"It's cute," I say, and it is. A very quaint restaurant that will allow for some nice first-date chatting.

"So, what do you recommend, since this is your favourite place?"

"Everything is good. They make the pasta fresh. You can't go wrong with anything on the menu."

Give me some direction, buddy.

"Well, for a girl who has never been here…"

"The Chicken Parmesan is good, that's probably what I'm getting, but…" and he points to my menu… "I'd be real impressed if you got this."

I check it out. Pasta, of course, white sauce, OK, chicken, yup, and, eww, mushrooms.

"I don't like mushrooms."

"Neither do I, but for some reason, I eat them here."

I put on my brave hat and when the waitress comes over, that is what I order.

"Wow," he says, "I am impressed."

"Hold that thought. I haven't eaten it yet."

I didn't need to call Holly that night, though she did want a full report in the morning.

I emailed her and told her what a nice guy Mitch was, that I ordered something a little different and even ate the mushrooms in it. I couldn't finish it, but the pasta was actually good. I can't believe I've been missing out on it all this time.

Mitch didn't know about my pasta fear, and I didn't tell him, especially since I had overcome it. For that night, at least. It wasn't as scary as I thought. Neither was getting back on the dating train. Mitch and I continued talking and he soon invited me over to his apartment—so he could make dinner for me.

"It's a surprise," he tells me.

"Okay, will I like it?"

"I think so."

The unknown made me slightly nervous, but he knew what I liked and I trusted him. No guy had ever made dinner for me before. We meet at his apartment and ta-da, it's chicken! Thank you, Mitch. But not just any chicken, because this boy can cook. It was chicken with mozzarella and tomatoes. And it was pretty damn good. I wasn't afraid to eat in front of him and he never pushed the topic at all. It was nice being in the company of someone who enjoyed food, which ultimately made me more relaxed about it.

I brought dessert and a movie, but we were both too full for dessert, so it was just the movie. As we cuddled on the couch, we shared our first kiss, and I realized I could get used to being in his arms. To having meals with him. To just being with him.

I quickly woke up from that reality when I realized how late it was, and that I had an early appointment with Holly.

"I should go," I tell him. "I don't want to. I like my treatment team, I like Holly, but I feel like I am always going to appointments."

He sat up and put his arm around me.

"But you need to do that right now. You need to go and see her. Just to get healthier. It's going to help you."

Where did I find him?

"He is so wonderful!" Holly says.

"I know. He was so supportive about me coming here, and he made me dinner and he's great."

"Have you had pasta again?"

"No, not yet, but I will. Dating him has opened me up to new food choices."

"He's a good influence. I like him."

"Me too."

From basketball games, to seeing his room mate's band play, to going out to dinner, Mitch and I dated for a little while longer. Then, I brought him to the airport to visit his family, picked him up when he returned, and then, we just faded out. I'm still not sure why. It was a bit sad at first, because I did enjoy his company and thought something might have happened there. Was it me? Was it because I was recovering from an eating disorder and people just don't want to deal with the issues that come with that? I never found out. The radio dial went from high velocity and slowly dimmed, until there was a dull static and then…nothing.

What I do know is that I learned a lot from Mitch. Not only did I enjoy our time together, but also he taught me what's it's like to let go and have fun. To have a meal and enjoy it. Not to worry. To have a conversation with someone where you aren't focused on food and what it's doing to you inside. I appreciated the meal that he cooked for me. I appreciated him. And though we went our separate ways, I will never forget how he brought pasta, and a little bit of confidence, back into my life.

Chapter 37
Post Renfrew: 10 Months
A Holiday Worth Remembering

This recovery thing isn't easy. Eating disorders are torture and want to hang on and it's much easier to let them in than to fight them. It takes a lot to be strong and push them out of you, and then close the gates so they can't get back in. It can take years and slips and relapses. It's exhausting work, but so was the eating disorder. At least recovery will lead to something better. Something better is what I am ready for.

December is strange. Last year at this time, I was trying to get all I could out of the holiday season because I knew what lay ahead was Renfrew. That soon, my eating disorder would be ripped away from me. That the only real piece I knew of myself would be taken away. I was a mess, miserable, and I am sure I made other people miserable as well. What an awful way of life that was.

This December, I know I am in a better place. I have gained weight and am becoming comfortable with that. I am healthier, eating, and have some sense of hope. There is a way out of this mess. I like to think that I am proof of that. There were so many times when I didn't think I'd live, never mind recover. Yet, here I am, still plugging along, and I am so grateful for that.

I can truly enjoy this holiday season. Go Christmas shopping without feeling as if I will pass out. Bake Christmas cookies and actually eat them, not fear them. Watch Christmas movies and laugh, not just sit there morose in my depression. It's not just a year later; it's a new life.

I did have some sense of anxiety going into Christmas day, and not just the meal, but also the social aspect. Of course, I spoke about it with Comer and Holly, and they helped me devise a plan. Eat what you can, and don't let other people's comments bother you.

I did eat what I could and enjoyed it.

The comments still came.

"How are you feeling?"

"What are you doing now?"

Then, the ones that used to really bother me, but not as much any more: "You look good" and "you look healthy." Those used to signal to my brain, "you look fat" or "you've gained weight."

Now I realize, sure, I have gained weight, but I'm healthy. I'm back in the low 130's. I needed to gain weight. Does it still bother me, the extra weight? Sure. But I am in a normal weight range and if I weren't, if I weighed less, my body would be deteriorating again, and I don't want that. No one does, or should.

As Comer says, "Your body is your temple," and it should be treated that way and be taken care of. I neglected it for so long. It is my home, in a way, and I forgot that. I forgot what home was, where it was and what I was searching for. A home, in so many senses. My body is my home, and my family is my home. Now, I have both back.

I spent some time talking to Popie, who I was so scared for me when I was in L.A. and he had his stroke. He is doing okay now, but still has difficulty with things. I asked him what was new, and he said not much. There was some silence and then he told me, "I didn't think it would last this long," meaning the effects of his stroke. It made me so sad. I love him and I can feel in a different way the pain he goes through. What he said is similar to eating disorder recovery. I wonder if it's ever going to get better. When I can live a life again. Why were we both burdened with an illness to begin with? My heart went out to him. I gave him a hug. I wished we could go back to old times. How much easier life would be then.

Spending time with my loved ones should not be something to be feared, nor should eating with them. Uncomfortable at first, I gained a bit of confidence and remembered what it was like all those years spending the holidays with them. Fearing food should not get in the way of spending time with those you love. I don't know if I could have said that a year ago. I'm finally realizing that what Comer and Holly say is true. I have come a long way. I may have further to go, but right now, I can be proud of where I am.

Chapter 38
Post Renfrew: 11 Months
Spreading a Beautiful Life

I sent a letter to my old middle school to see if they might be interested in a talk about eating disorders, and they were thrilled. It turns out that they do different health-related lessons for their eight graders and wanted me to come in on two separate days, for four sessions each day. A daunting thought at first, but I was ready. No more shame, no more fear. I stepped up to the plate and was ready to talk to these students about my experience, eating disorders in general, and to answer any questions they might have. And boy, did they have questions.

The experience as a whole was quite beautiful. The kids were so attentive as I told my story, and the teacher gasped a few times when I mentioned the treatment I received from doctors. We went over eating disorders, what they thought about them, and I explained the myths versus the truths. Many thought people have eating disorders just because they want to be thin, and I explained how it is a disease, not a choice. They tell me how shocked they are at how it took over my life, and they too can't believe I didn't have better medical care. Some were familiar with the topic as they had family members or friends who had struggled with the disease. I myself was shocked to find out how many students were skipping lunches in an effort to lose weight, so I made sure to tell them how important it was to eat all their meals. I even had lunch with them.

The questions were the part I think they enjoyed most. I got some serious ones, such as them asking about my exercise regime now and about treatment. When I told them how eating disorders affect all organs of the body, even the brain, and can cause lack of focus, concentration and memory loss, one student asked me: "Will you ever get your brain cells back?"

"Yes," I tell him, "my brain is functioning much better now."

They all wanted to know my weight, now and then, which I would not tell them, because I told them I don't focus on the numbers now.

"Do you eat McDonald's?" one kid asked.

"Yes I do."

"French fries."

"Of course."

"What about pizza?"

I laughed. The teacher tried to turn them back to more serious questions but I told her it was fine. "Yes, I eat pizza. But it took a while. I wouldn't at the early part of my recovery. My Dad helped me with that. First I had a bite. The next step was half a slice, and then eventually, I had an actual piece of pizza. I'm happy I did. It's good stuff. The thing is, you can eat anything. They say it's about moderation, but all food has nutrients, and that's what your body needs."

One girl was sheepishly raising her hand, so I called on her instead of the fast-food questioning boys.

"Do you ever think you want to go back to your eating disorder? Or that you might end up anorexic again?" She slid her hand back down.

"That's a good question, and a scary thought. No, I don't want to go back there. I never thought I would be there to begin with. Recovery is a long process, and tough, but I am happy to be here now. I hope that if I ever really find myself sliding back, I will know enough to catch myself and get into treatment if I need it. They say that eating disorders are like static in the back of your head. When I was sick, it filled my whole head. Now, it's just a little static, and the point is, to make that noise become more and more quiet. If it ever gets louder, that's the warning sign."

Another boy raised his hand.

"Are you single?"

The class laughed.

"I am."

"I'll give you my number after class."

"I think I'm too old for you."

He winked.

The teacher had the students fill out surveys and then gave them to me. They wrote comments and had to rank my talk 1-10. I got mostly tens and many of the students added multiples of 0's on the end of the ten. I couldn't believe I had reached them that way. Their comments were astounding and when reading them, I knew that if anything good came out of this disease, it was that I could give back to others.

Most of the comment sheets reiterated what I said during my talk: that eating disorders are a disease, you can die from them, it can hurt you physically and mentally, you need help from others to recover, and it can cause many other health problems. Also, that sometimes it's hard to know at first that you truly have an eating disorder.

Then, there were a couple comments that really caught my attention:

"I think you are doing a wonderful thing going around and talking to kids about your own problem. It's amazing what you have done."

"I think this was a good lesson. I have many friends that don't eat a lot, and I get worried."

"I think it was a great lesson and I'm glad you're all right. I learned that eating disorders are not good."

"Very good to see a real-life person talk about their story."

"I think that it will help and encourage any students that think they may have one."

"You can die from anorexia. I thought Nicole's story was amazing. Terrible and sad, but amazing."

"I loved the talk. It really made me think twice from my thoughts of almost cutting everything off."

And my personal favorite: *"Her doctors were stupid."*

That gave me a chuckle. Kids are smart.

To my surprise, a week later, I got a package from the students. There were two gift cards and a bundle of thank you letters. It brought me to tears, I was so touched. The students made the cards themselves and each wrote such beautiful messages. They thanked me for coming in, told me they liked my story and admired me for telling it. Some students themselves had eating issues, or family members who had them, and one student said he was now going to talk to that family member because of my talk. When I went in to speak, I thought, if I can just reach one person, I would have done my job. I did not think that I would have reached so many. Most of them also wished me well in my ongoing recovery.

Some of the cards that really struck me weren't the ones decorated with markers and flowers (though I appreciated them all), but the ones whose words spoke to me the most:

"Dear Nicole,

This might not be the fanciest letter you'll receive but I'd still like to write this to show my thanks. I learned a lot about eating disorders and what people go through. If I find someone I know who has one, I'll help him or her with the disease like your friends. Also, somehow if ever I catch an eating disorder, I can try to stop it myself. I learned a lot from you and I want to help anyone I can.

Sincerely,

"A"

I do like how he put "catch" an eating disorder. But what a sincere boy he was.

This girl put stars on it:

Dear Nicole,

Thank you very much for speaking to my class about eating disorders. I really enjoyed your lesson and learned a lot from it. Your story about the battle you fought with anorexia inspired me to stay healthy and respect my body. I hope you use this in your writing so it inspires teenagers as it did me. I also hope that you stay healthy and happy.

Sincerely,

"L"

This girl's note was both decorative and thoughtful:

Dear Nicole,

Thank you for coming to our class and teaching us the dangers of anorexia and other eating disorders. I think you did an awesome job and taught us a lot about it and your story was very interesting. I enjoyed it and I think the rest of my class did too. Your story might have saved someone's life if they were thinking of becoming anorexic or having a different eating disorder. It must have been a very hard time for you but you made it through and that's what inspired me, that you didn't give up! Once again, thank you for telling my class your story.

Sincerely,
"A"

Each note struck me in a different way, just as each student had, and though they said I taught them, they had encouraged me in my recovery. I knew I now had a mission. I would continue to visit other schools under "Beautiful Lives." They needed me just as much as I needed them.

Chapter 39
Post Renfrew: 1 Year
February 23, 2008
A Celebration of Recovery

"When you are a bear of very little brain, and think of things, you find sometimes that a thing which seemed very thingish inside you is quite different when it gets out into the open and has other people looking at it."
-The House at Pooh Corner, A.A. Milne

Today is my version of "New Year's." I'm starting afresh, with a new and brighter outlook on things. I have been discharged for a year now. A year ago today, I left the Renfrew Center for Eating Disorders, after seven weeks there, and prior to that a horrible battle with anorexia. I was on my way back to Connecticut, basically starting my recovery and quite unsure of what was in store for me.

Released from the depths of inpatient treatment, I was then thrown into outpatient treatment, and it has been that way for a year. Growing, processing, struggling, and fighting. Basically, recovering. My weight has gone up and down, but now it is back to that stable weight it was at Renfrew, maintaining between 133 and 135. The fluctuations still bother me, but I cope with it. It is, after all, just a number, and you can't judge your worth by the number on the scales.

It is hard to believe that it was a year ago that I was stepping out of those doors, releasing my security blanket, and going off into the world, full of fear. And of what? Here I am, and look how far I have come. Even if I didn't realize it at first, I have come a long way from those doors.

Last week I started crying as I put the bread on the table for dinner, not because I was afraid of eating it, but rather, because I knew I would eat it. What brought the tears was realizing that a year ago, I never would have been able to even look at the bread. I knew then that everyone who told me that I had accomplished a lot might be right.

A year is a long time. I guess time flies when you spend most of it between therapy and nutritionist visits and planning meals. Things much needed, but draining too. My ties to Renfrew are getting farther away, as they just sent me my last follow-up survey. I haven't taken it, as I don't want to disconnect. I clearly don't want to go back there, but there is something symbolic about ending that connection. The cord is getting shorter, and while that should be a good thing, it makes me want to hold on tighter. There are too many memories there—struggles yes, but certainly triumphs too. I learned how to eat again, to accept myself (still working on that one), and I learned more about myself. I gained a newfound will to live, and I can't turn my back on that. They gave me a gift, which I will cherish forever.

So how does one celebrate one year of recovery, or, recovery-in-progress? Looking back, I don't know what to call this past year. It has been a whirlwind. I was pretty sure that no one else would remember the date, and I wanted to take things into my own hands. Be assertive and decisive. I sent out little invitations to my parents, sister and brother-in-law, and my brother, to go out to dinner, my treat. To celebrate and recognize my one-year anniversary in recovery, and to thank them for all the support they have given. One of the things I kept saying when I was really struggling and in treatment was, "I want to be able to go out to dinner with my family again and be 'normal.'" After all, I was afraid to eat in front of them, my own family, and we had shared meals together for years. Even though my stomach hates me, and it has every right to, I am inviting it to the celebration as well. Because, as some wise girl once told me, "the food is going to make you healthy." And so will a night out with my family.

Luckily, despite some snowy weather and busy schedules, everyone made it home to celebrate. I was ready to celebrate, all of it. I know what I have been through—the hard work, the tears, the pain, the suffering, the triumphs, the roadblocks, the successes. The risks, the scares, the sacrifices, the fears, the hopes, the willingness to take the brave next step, even when I didn't know where that led. It was a day for me to look back, even though I had probably done too much of that. But this time, it was a good anniversary, finally. Not like all the sad ones. Today I had something to be proud of. Myself. I had never really been proud of myself.

Before we left for dinner, I had everyone sit down because I had got little gifts for each of them to show my appreciation for sticking by me. They sat, and I stood, and they must have been dreading a speech, but I spoke anyway.

"Since today is my one year of recovery, I want to thank you all for being there for me. Through all of it. I know it hasn't been easy and I appreciate your support and you celebrating this day with me."

Kelly clapped. I laughed. She doesn't like awkward situations.

"I guess that's the end of my speech." I handed bags to everyone and their cards, which I wrote a lot on. How could I thank them enough? As I watched them, I realized that I had spent all this time trying to teach them about eating disorders and what I was going through, but really, they were teaching me. I just didn't know the lessons I was picking up. I don't even know if they were aware they were teaching me.

Like love—the love of family. That they love you in good and bad and will be there for you no matter how old you are or how stubborn you get. They will amaze you with their love and you will be amazed by your capacity to love.

Compassion—Being sick with a disease that many look down on or cringe at is not something my parents did. They embraced me, cared for me and just wanted me to get better. They wanted to know why I felt the way I did about myself and were upset by it because all they saw was good.

Hang In There... Wherever "There" Is

Most importantly, the gift of family. I was such a lucky girl to have them. How could I have almost lost all of this?

After they read their cards and opened their gifts, they surprised me with cards and gifts also, and my parents gave me flowers. Dan wrote a thoughtful card where he told me he's always looked up to me and is so proud of me for fighting this battle, and that, "I love you to death and will always be proud of you and who you are. Remember that."

I may not know who I am, but I am learning. It's nice to know that whoever I am, in sickness and health, I am appreciated. I am loved. Through all my struggles, I have learned to appreciate and love things more. Like food!

And yes, dinner was great.

Epilogue
Hanging in There and Finding Closure
August 16, 2008

I remember my first night in LA. I checked five times to make sure the door to the apartment was locked, as well as my bedroom. I missed my family and didn't know what was in store for me. I *really* had no idea.

I remember the scripts I wrote and how I had no idea what Hollywood or that business was like. I had no idea what LA was like.

I remember extending my stay. I remember things getting harder. I remember things getting bad. I remember getting sick, but not knowing how it happened. I remember the ER. I remember being scared.

I can still almost hear every footstep that I left behind in LA— every step to the gym, to the farmer's market, on the stepper at the gym. Step, step, step, step.

So many steps I have made now though. It is August, 2008, and I am two years from the sad, scared girl who was battling an ugly disease that she didn't even know existed within her. I am so far from that girl, but I can still feel her pain.

I am back in LA, just visiting for a couple of weeks, and it is amazing to see it again with such different eyes. No anxiety, no fear, no sadness. I wanted to come back. The same old memories had been haunting me and I needed to absolve them. To come back with fresh eyes and see L.A. with a new point of view. A healthier one. To revisit the places that gave me these bad memories, walk in my old footsteps and release that pain I still hold within. Say it's okay, because it is. Or at least, it will be.

I used to say that I could still see that girl, me, walking down Hollywood Blvd. to the gym, crying as she ate her apple. Though it didn't seem like me any more, it was another person, and all I wanted to do was reach out to this girl and tell her that it was okay, she didn't need to do that. I felt like she still walked that mile to the gym, almost haunted that street, her presence still known.

The last time I was in LA was just to pack my things and I didn't go near Hollywood Blvd. I couldn't. This time, as strange as it sounds, I knew I had to—to rescue 'her'. So I did.

I drove to Hollywood Boulevard, grabbed a coffee, and walked down the stretch to the gym. There were no tears on this walk like there used to be. My head held high, I saw the gym clearly as I approached it. I crossed the street and just looked for a moment, then, I flicked it off. That was the last time it would see me, and suddenly, I had released the ghost of my past.

I walked back to my car and drove through the busy streets of L.A. Not so scary any more. I got thrown off when I saw my old doctor's office, and the memories there, but that was then and I am different.

Hang In There... Wherever "There" Is

I needed a new vision of Los Angeles. I couldn't be afraid of my past or the city. I came back from the depths of anorexia that brewed within me here, but that doesn't mean I have to fear the places that surrounded my illness. This time in L.A., I enjoyed myself. I looked out at the Pacific Ocean where I saw, for the first time, dolphins. I put my feet in the water. I wore a bikini and didn't care how I looked.

I visited with a brave face and heart, and though the memories here are painful, I am releasing them. I know now that I can put some things to rest. I can face myself and what I have gone through.

There was a point when I just wanted to forget my scary past of Los Angeles. Now, I have found my closure, and will always remember the good. I can go back to L.A. now and not be scared. I am no longer afraid of a lot of things. I have grown, mentally and physically, and am happy with who I am and the new life I have made for myself.

www.ingramcontent.com/pod-product-compliance
Lightning Source LLC
Chambersburg PA
CBHW022352280326
41935CB00007B/163